THE MILLION DOLLAR BACKFIELD

THE MILLION DOLLAR BACKFIELD

THE SAN FRANCISCO 49ERS IN THE 1950S

BY DAVE NEWHOUSE   FOREWORD BY BILL WALSH

FROG, LTD.
BERKELEY, CALIFORNIA

THE MILLION DOLLAR BACKFIELD

Published by Frog, Ltd.
Frog, Ltd. Books are distributed by
North Atlantic Books
P.O. Box 12327
Berkeley, California 94712

Book cover and interior designed by Carolina de Bartolo.
Printed in the United States of America.
Distributed to the book trade by Publishers Group West.

Library of Congress Cataloging-in-Publication Data
Newhouse, Dave, 1938-
The million dollar backfield : the San Francisco 49ers in the 1950s / by Dave Newhouse.
    p. cm.
Includes bibliographical references.
ISBN 1-58394-007-3 (alk. paper)
1. Running backs (Football)—United States—Biography. 2. San Francisco 49ers (Football team)—History. I. Title.

GV939.A1 N49 2000
796.332'64'0979461—dc21

00-032765
CIP

1 2 3 4 5 6 7 8 9 / 03 02 01 00

Y. A. Tittle, Joe Perry, Hugh McElhenny, John Henry Johnson—a million dollar's worth of thrills.

To Pete Costanza, who was my best friend and like a father to me.

— J. H. J.

To my mom and dad, Hugh and Pearl McElhenny, who were so supportive in everything I did as a youth, and who shaped my character.

— H.M.

To my mom, Laurah Perry, who was my rock, my pillar, my everything. To my wife, Donna, a steadying force. And to Tony Morabito for his honesty.

— J. P.

To my wife, Minnette, who's No. 1 in my heart, even though she thought she was No. 2 to football. To Odus Mitchell, my high school coach, who convinced me I could be somebody.

— Y. A. T.

To Al Newhouse, the father who planted the seeds of a son's journalism career by taking him to his first 49er game in 1948.

— D. N.

TABLE OF CONTENTS

Foreword by Bill Walsh — xi

Introduction — xv

Acknowledgements — xxiii

Joe Perry ★ The Jet — 1

Hugh McElhenny ★ The King — 47

Photos — 92

John Henry Johnson ★ Mister Meaner — 101

Y. A. Tittle ★ The Bald Eagle — 147

Index — 201

FOREWORD ⭐
BY BILL WALSH

When I attended high school in Hayward, right across the bay from San Francisco, I saw the Million Dollar Backfield play at Kezar Stadium. And I managed to get home safely. It was wild! As a kid, I was just in a state of shock over those 49ers fans.

But, gee, here were four players who could play in any generation, any era, and they would have been the greatest players on the field. There is no time span for their performances. There would have been other players from their era who would have been undersized in today's game. But not these four. They were such great players.

Hugh McElhenny was, along with Gale Sayers, one of the greatest open-field runners of all time. McElhenny could make people miss. He had excellent speed. He had natural inherent moves that are instinctive. And he had tremendous leg action like Roger Craig, whom I coached on the 49ers.

And McElhenny was one of the best utility backs I've ever seen. He was a great pass receiver. Injuries really cut short one of the greatest careers ever, but you'd expect that with the style of football he played.

What an exciting player to watch. Every time he carried the ball, everybody would stand up waiting for something to happen.

We actually went to the same high school, George Washington in Los Angeles, before I moved to Hayward. I was in the ninth grade when he was a senior. I didn't know him because he was the elite. He and his [future] wife were two of the most incredible looking people.

I was a quarterback on the "B" team, but I'd watch him every week. He was incredible. He averaged fourteen yards a carry.

When we'd go to all-black high schools like Jordan and Jefferson, he was the hero. He'd get off the bus and the kids would just crowd around him. And he'd win every race. He was a tremendous track man, with tremendous explosion and leg movement. He was the greatest athlete I had ever seen. No one could stop him in high school. I once saw him in a track meet in Los Angeles against some of the best hurdlers in the country. He was leading them all until he hit a hurdle near the end and fell. Here he was, though, out in front at, I believe, a record pace, and he was in high school. A teenager!

Running backs today are bigger, more powerful men. The game is played differently. Everybody is faster. But McElhenny was the king of changing directions so quickly and maintaining his speed. He didn't have to stop and start. He just kept going.

John Henry Johnson is one of the toughest, most physical, meanest football players of his time. He could play offense and defense. He was as tough and powerful a football player as you'll ever see. He could do everything. He wasn't pretty to watch, but he was fast, and so physical.

By today's standards, he would have been, along with Ronnie Lott, the greatest safety men ever to play football. That's how much of a hitter John Henry was. When he played offense, he was equally great. He fit in perfectly with the other guys. He could block, he could run. But he had such raw intensity that people couldn't believe it. He'd do the same thing today. He'd be the most physical, meanest, dominating player on the field.

I remember what a great all-around athlete he was at Pittsburg High School, which was about forty minutes away from Hayward on the same side of the bay. No one would go into Pittsburg. You might run into him! He was the toughest, meanest guy in the Bay Area.

When I was at San Jose State, we played against John Henry at Arizona State. And we beat them, because when John Henry played defensive back, we faked into the line, then threw over his head for the touchdown. But he was all over the field, making every play.

Joe Perry would be like Emmitt Smith, like the guys who play today. Joe was extremely fast. He actually had more speed than McElhenny. Joe could run probably 100 meters in about 10.4 seconds, maybe 10.3. He had a tremendous start, one of the fastest starting backs. He was Joe the Jet.

He had pure power and quickness. He could run for power, and he could go the distance. He was so explosive. He'd still be one of the greatest backs in the game if he played today.

Y. A. Tittle was one of the greatest competitors to ever play the game. He was an absolute natural forward passer. He had the natural instincts to play quarterback. He could take a terrible team and make them a winner, like he did with the New York Giants.

Y. A. wasn't necessarily a touch passer, but he was a super downfield passer. He was very, very accurate twenty yards and farther downfield. He could run, and he was one of your great quarterbacks from another era, when the quarterback called all the plays and ran the team.

Those quarterbacks decided who could beat whom, and they told guys what to do in the huddle. On the sideline, Y. A. would tell McElhenny, Gordy Soltau and Billy Wilson what to do on the next play. It was like, what do we do now, Y. A.? Well, we're going to beat so and so, and here's how we're going to do it. That's how Y. A. was.

Y. A. audibled at the line. He was in that great group of quarterbacks, like Sonny Jurgensen, who managed the game. Y. A. would almost draw the plays up and do it. That was an era when the quarterback was the central figure in the organization.

I remember as a kid, reading about Y. A. Tittle of Louisiana State University in the magazines. Then I watched him on movie newsreel highlights. Then, finally, on television. Much later, Y. A. and I played each other in tennis. He's a competitor. We had some battles in tennis. Great matches.

I've spent time with all four guys from the Million Dollar Backfield. They're all great guys. John Henry is just as mild and as great a guy as you'll ever see.

Where would they play today? That's a good question. Joe would start at running back no matter what. McElhenny and Johnson, I don't know how they'd use them, but it would be great to have them. By today's standards, Johnson probably would be the best defensive player in football. McElhenny would be dangerous running the ball or out in the flat, catching passes, where he could really use his moves and speed. Y. A. would have to get used to coaches calling the plays.

I'll tell you this, I'd take all four of them in a second. Who wouldn't? They're all Hall of Famers, and some of the greatest players ever.

— *Bill Walsh*
General Manager, San Francisco 49ers
October 1999

INTRODUCTION

Once upon a time, there were backfields in football. Real backfields, with real backs. These long-ago backfields didn't have such contrived names as flankers, I-backs, and H-backs. They were backfields formed out of the original T-formation concept of a quarterback, two halfbacks, and a fullback.

In real backfields, the halfbacks and fullback had varied responsibilities. Running, of course, but also blocking and receiving. And, additionally, punting, placekicking, some forward passing, and even defensive duties.

Call them old-timers, if you choose, but they weren't the one-dimensional backfield men, blocking backs, third-down backs, short-yardage backs, who make far more money for much less work today.

In other words, the game has become more specialized, which hasn't necessarily made the game more special. There is heavy emphasis nowadays on the passing game in the National Football League, to the point where the quarterback sometimes is the only back lined up behind the offensive line.

Everyone else, in that kind of formation, is spread out towards the sideline, looking to catch the ball. If these flanked players manage to throw an occasional block, it will help their negotiating power at contract time.

Somewhere, Bronko Nagurski is scratching his steel jaw in disbelief.

There are no great backfields anymore because, well, there are no backfields. If a flanker doesn't carry the football regularly, he can't be a back. Back of what? He is nothing more than a wide out. A split end who might be reluctant to go over the middle. True backs live for the middle of a football field, because that's where the collisions are.

That's football.

Thus football's real backfields are attached to a forgotten era–long before Indianapolis Colts quarterback Peyton Manning was born, and even before his father, Archie, began throwing passes for the New Orleans Saints in the early 1970s.

But over the course of eight decades of professional football, there are only a few backfields that are truly memorable.

As an example of full backfields that fell short of greatness, who filled out the Chicago Bears backfield with Nagurski and Red Grange in the early 1930s? Who was the fourth member of the Baltimore Colts' backfield with Johnny Unitas, Alan Ameche and Lenny Moore in the late 1950s?

Chicago's other forgotten NFL franchise, the Cardinals, now located in Arizona after a stopover in St. Louis, had a more formidable backfield than the Bears ever assembled with Paul Christman, Charley Trippi, Elmer Angsman, and Pat Harder in the late 1940s.

From this group, only Trippi is in the Pro Football Hall of Fame. From that Colts backfield, only Unitas's and Moore's busts can be found in Canton, Ohio. From that ancient Bears backfield, Grange and Nagurski are the only Hall of Famers.

There is only one backfield from which all four members have been inducted into the pro football hall. That would be the San Francisco 49ers' Million Dollar Backfield of quarterback Y. A. Tittle, halfbacks Hugh McElhenny and John Henry Johnson, and fullback Joe Perry.

This fabulous foursome played only three years together, 1954 through 1956, and experienced just one winning season under three different head coaches. Injuries also prevented the Million Dollar Backfield from playing as a unit for long stretches. But this is the greatest backfield of all time, bar none.

"I was lucky to be a part of it," said Bob St. Clair, the 49ers' Hall of Fame tackle who opened holes for the Million Dollar Backfield. "To break it up was a real disaster. I see the same thing every day with free agency and salary caps. With all the movement going in football, you take something out of the puzzle.

"When we broke up that backfield, we were in trouble because we didn't play great defense. And when you get people hurt [on defense], you don't have anything. We were only allowed thirty-three players in those days.

"But were Y. A., Joe, Hugh, and John Henry the greatest backfield? Oh, god. There was almost a song like that."

A song?

"There's no backfield like that backfield, like no backfield I know..." St. Clair improvised while trying to carry a tune.

Well, if the football business is, indeed, show business, then the 49ers' backfield of the mid-1950s was a showstopper, back when the 49ers were the only show in town. They were northern California's first major-league sports franchise, in 1946. The Giants arrived from New York in 1958, the Warriors from Philadelphia in 1962, the A's from Kansas City in 1968. The Oakland Raiders were homegrown in 1960. Likewise hockey's San Jose Sharks in 1991. The 49ers lead their neighbors in Bay Area-based national championships with five, though none with their celebrated backfield.

Nevertheless, there is no way to devalue the greatness of the Million Dollar Backfield, even though the combined salaries of Tittle, Perry, McElhenny, and Johnson fell considerably short of $100,000.

It was the clever 49ers public relations director, the late Dan McGuire, who came up with their catchy, though misleading nickname.

However, as the saying goes, they looked like a million dollars.

"If they had played [together] in New York," former 49ers executive Lou Spadia said, "they would have had a monument in Times Square."

That might have been the only way the Million Dollar Backfield would be remembered in this modern age of million-dollar backs. But as great as those four 49ers were, and they were all fantastic, they are unrecognized by a current generation of football fanatics who have no deep interest in NFL history.

Not only is it mentally challenging for these same fans to recall a real backfield, it's equally taxing for them to recall the names of great backs from decades ago.

The same can be said, unfortunately, of young sportswriters and sportscasters, who, unlike their middle-aged colleagues, didn't grow up reading about Pudge Heffelfinger, Fats Henry, Biggie Munn, Tank Younger, and other famous football names from another time.

Books about sports heroes, real and fictional, were more plentiful for hero-worshipping children a half-century ago, when radio, newspapers, magazines, and movie newsreels represented America's other main sources of information.

That was before the popularity of TV and computers shifted the focus from the past to the present. It's now Brett Favre, not Bart Starr. It's now Nintendo, not Nagurski.

That lack of history explains why numerous media organizations tripped over themselves in 1999 while trying to come up with the greatest sports teams and athletes of the twentieth century.

It was an impossible task, and also grossly unfair, because the selectors hadn't seen the fleet Fritz Pollard play in the newly formed NFL in the 1920s. Jim Thorpe, Ernie Nevers, Grange, Dutch Clark and Byron "Whizzer" White also were deemed too prehistoric for the selectors. The unparalleled reputations of these long-ago gridiron stars now were viewed as cobwebs in pro football's attic.

Thus when it came to real backfields with real backs, Tittle, McElhenny, Johnson, and Perry were overlooked by *ESPN* and every other media outlet.

Here is today's rationale: If a halfback played before the late, great Walter Payton, he has little chance of being recognized. And there are no fullbacks before Earl Campbell, unless his name is Jim Brown.

Such magnificent quarterbacks as Sammy Baugh, Otto Graham, and Sid Luckman might as well have been baseball players. Who saw their games?

If not for Paul Zimmerman of *Sports Illustrated*, the NFL's first forty years would have been lost, like a bedspread stitched by Betsy Ross, when century-ending honors were passed out. Fortunately, in the interest of credibility, Dr. Z started watching pro football in the 1940s, before the coming of the television age.

Zimmerman was kinder to the past than others in choosing an all-century team. He picked a receiver, Don Hutson, who started in the 1930s; a fullback, Marion Motley, who came along in the 1940s; and a quarterback, Johnny Unitas, and cornerback, Dick "Night Train" Lane, who starred in the 1950s. Jim Brown made the cut, naturally. And Vince Lombardi, who arrived in Green Bay in 1959, was Zimmerman's NFL coach of the century.

But imagine what *Sports Illustrated's* readers thought when they saw the name "McElhenny" listed as Zimmerman's third-down back: Wasn't Preston Pearson available?

McElhenny wasn't a third-down back by trade. He was an every-down player. Zimmerman simply wanted McElhenny on his all-time NFL team and awarded him that special designation.

Meanwhile, the Baby Boomers and grand-Baby Boomers, thinking of the only famous running backs they recognized, wondered aloud, "Hey, Dr. Z, where's Payton, Barry Sanders, Emmitt Smith, and Thurman Thomas?"

Such curiosity is justified in the cases of Payton and Sanders, two certified all-time greats. However, there are only so many spots available on an all-time team. And in defense of choosing McElhenny for his team, Zimmerman wrote, "The King could turn a short pass into a crazy-legged, broken-field adventure."

Without question. That's why McElhenny was The King, master of the change-of-direction play. When McElhenny grabbed the football at the end of a pass or at the start of a run, everyone followed his every movement, from linebackers to season-ticket holders. For nobody, not even McElhenny himself, knew what would occur when he improvised as only The King could.

It was easier to lasso the wind than to grab hold of McElhenny. He defied logic and gravity with his incredible moves. Of all the runners in the 1990s, only Sanders rivals McElhenny in the ability to make tacklers whiff helplessly.

"Mac was a big Barry Sanders, an impromptu runner," said Joe Schmidt, the Detroit Lions' Hall of Fame middle linebacker who played against McElhenny. "Mac's upper body was steady, but his legs were going this way and that way."

The three other components of the Million Dollar Backfield were special in their own right, and ranked among the greats at their positions. In fact, if they lined up against Dr. Z's team, you'd have to figure overtime.

Perry was the NFL's first player to rush for 1,000 yards in successive seasons, 1953 and 1954. And he did it when the league played a twelve-game schedule. Perry's gift was his blazing speed. He was a 9.5 track sprinter in the 100-yard dash before becoming maybe the fastest fullback ever. There hasn't ever been a faster fullback coming out of his stance. That's why Perry was known as The Jet.

"Perry had his own style of running," said Ernie Stautner, the Pittsburgh Steelers defensive tackle whose bust also is in Canton. "He would hit the hole, and he had great cutting ability. He was hard to keep up with or anticipate. He had it all."

NFL old-timers remember John Henry Johnson and immediately shudder. He was someone to avoid at all times, at all costs.

"He was a mean, nasty SOB," said Dick Nolan, former New York Giants defensive back. "I hit him a lot of times because I was plugging holes. It was like hitting a pipe. He had no fat, like he was made of steel rods.

"I remember him leading a running play one time. He made it look as if he was looking downfield. When Ed Hughes came up to make the tackle, John Henry threw an elbow and broke Ed's cheekbone. In those days, we were just getting into face masks, and John Henry did it to several guys that way."

Johnson wasn't just some bully, however. When he was thirty-five and playing in Pittsburgh, he became the oldest NFL player up until that time to rush for 1,000 yards. That happened in 1964, by which time the NFL was playing a fourteen-game schedule. And it wasn't uncommon, when the Steelers met the Cleveland Browns, for Johnson to outrush the legendary Jim Brown.

Tittle, like Perry, played in three decades in two pro leagues. Tittle was voted NFL Player of the Year four times, once with the 49ers and three times with the New York Giants. He threw seven touchdown passes in one game. He produced back-to-back seasons of thirty-three and thirty-six touchdown passes. The Bald Eagle soared higher than other great quarterbacks of his era.

And it wasn't only style. Tittle was the embodiment of toughness.

"He was tougher than whale shit," said Spadia. "He'd stand there obsessed with the idea of throwing the ball. He didn't care who was coming."

After Tittle was traded to New York in 1961, his game and reputation ascended to a higher level.

"To many Americans, Y. A. was a mythological figure," said his former Giants coach, Allie Sherman. "It was believed that Y. A. could throw the football whenever and to whomever he chose. He generated that type of confidence in himself and those around him."

The accomplishments of the Million Dollar Backfield have grown hazy over the passing years, even in the hallowed halls of Canton.

"I called the Pro Football Hall of Fame," said Perry, "and they didn't even know that they had the only complete backfield in the Hall of Fame. You can't tell me there was one person back there who knew, and I talked to two officials myself. And there never will be another backfield like us."

Not only in terms of a forgotten formation, but in forgotten legendary talent. They were four of a kind, four aces.

A Million Dollar pot.

ACKNOWLEDGEMENTS

Many voices, including those of legendary figures from professional football's rich history, are heard in this book, lending authenticity to the greatness of the Million Dollar Backfield.

But the book couldn't have been written without the total cooperation of the four men themselves, who gave willingly of their time in order that their stories could be told accurately and thoroughly.

To Hugh and Peggy McElhenny, John Henry and Leona Johnson, Joe and Donna Perry, Y. A. and Minnette Tittle. And to Dianne Tittle de Laet.

To those men who played with or against Million Dollar Backfield members, and who offered their observations: Johnny Unitas, Otto Graham, Ara Parseghian, Joe Schmidt, Ernie Stautner, Chuck Bednarik, Pat Summerall, John Baker, Bob St. Clair, Leo Nomellini, Gordy Soltau, R. C. Owens, Dick Nolan, Wayne Walker, John Brodie, Paul Wiggin, and Joe Rubay.

To Bill Walsh, who wrote the book's introduction. To Lou Spadia, who, like Walsh, witnessed the exploits of these four distinctive talents. To longtime journalists John Steadman and Paul Zimmerman, who shared memories and perspective on the dream foursome's timeless ability. To longtime photographer Morris Berman, who painted with his camera.

To Kirk Reynolds, Tom Hastings, and Chad Steele of the San Francisco 49ers' public relations staff, and Donn Sinn, the team's historian, for providing 49er game statistics from the 1950s through the early 1960s.

To Greg Aiello and Chris McCloskey of the National Football League, and Joe Horrigan of the Pro Football Hall of Fame for supplying valuable research material. To Jon Becker of ANG Newspapers, a helpful resource.

To radio stations KFRC in San Francisco and KPFA in Berkeley ("The Johnny Otis Show"), and to The Penguins, The Cleftones, Arlene Smith with The Chantels, Jimmy Beaumont and The Skyliners, The Moonglows, The Flamingos, The Cadillacs, Gene "Duke of Earl" Chandler, Fats Domino, and other rock legends who provided background music for long hours of writing.

To my wife, Patsy, for her love, her soul, and her gift of doo-wop classics. To my sons, Chad and Casey Newhouse, for their encouragement.

To Andrew Tertes, for typing the book's manuscript in a speedy, thorough, professional manner.

To Richard Grossinger of North Atlantic Books for accepting this project strictly on the author's enthusiasm. To Chris Pitts of North Atlantic, the project's editor, who was kind enough to extend the author additional writing time beyond the original deadline.

And, finally, to Bruce Jenkins, who generously went out of his way to alert North Atlantic about the author's idea about a book on the Million Dollar Backfield.

To all of the above, a million thanks.

— *Dave Newhouse*
Oakland, CA
June 2000

JOE PERRY ★
THE JET

California is looked at by forty-nine other states as a giant sandbox for kooks. And with some justification. California gave our country pet cemeteries, pet manicurists, and the Pet Rock, not to mention flower children, communal living, "Beverly Hills 90210" and Monica Lewinsky.

But California, for all its kookiness, is the most progressive of states. It can be argued, successfully, that the end of the Vietnam conflict began with student protests at the University of California in Berkeley. California is the first state with two women serving simultaneously in the United States Senate. California is the only state to send an actor to the governor's mansion, and then on to the Oval Office.

And the integration of sports has a strong California flavor. The man who broke Major League Baseball's color line in 1947, Jackie Robinson, was a Pasadena product and a UCLA alumnus. Baseball's first black manager, Frank Robinson, grew up in Oakland. So did Bill Russell, the National Basketball Association's first black coach and the first black in a big-league sport to coach a championship team.

The National Football League's modern-day integration began with UCLA products Kenny Washington and Woody Strode, both of whom played for the Los Angeles Rams in 1946.

The San Francisco 49ers' first black player, and the first piece in the franchise's famed Million Dollar Backfield, was Fletcher Joe Perry from the Watts section of Los Angeles.

Unlike Jackie Robinson, Perry refused to turn the other cheek to racist acts directed at him. And racism in football during the post-World War II period was more harmful physically than in baseball, which permitted beanballs, but not gang-tackling and gouging.

Trapped on the bottom of piles, hidden from public view, Perry's limbs were twisted, his crotch grabbed, and his eyes poked by white bigots who rebelled against having to play on the same field with a black man. Perry retaliated without hesitation, fighting back any way he could.

"It was no picnic," he recalled. "But my M.O. is, 'I won't take no shit.' Larry Brink of the Los Angeles Rams broke my jaw one time while I'm blocking on a punt. I'm spitting out teeth and Y. A. Tittle tells me, 'You're not going back in there.' I told Y. A., 'I'm going in there.' The next time Brink came in, he leaped over me to block the punt. I stepped back and kneed him as hard as I could in the groin. They carried him out. Years later, he told me, 'You sonovagun. You're the cause of my not having children.' I said, 'I tried to kill you.'"

There isn't one ounce of homicide in Perry's heart. But he had a mountain of revenge stored inside for racists who spewed their hatred. His modus operandi, then, was to hit back with the force of a mountain avalanche.

"I can never remember a season where I didn't hear a racial slur," Perry said. "Someone would say, 'Nigger, don't come through here again.' And I'd tell him, 'I'm coming through again, and you better bring your family.' Look at my nose. Ed Sprinkle of the Chicago Bears got me. If someone speared me, I'd find some way to jump into his face, even with my two feet. I could do that, and I have done that, because I'm athletic."

Perry had to be athletic to last sixteen years as a professional running back, from 1948 through 1963. Only Marcus Allen played as many seasons at running back, and without any of the bigotry that Perry had encountered.

"My favorite game watching Perry occurred between the 49ers and Buffalo Bills," said *Sports Illustrated* football writer Paul Zimmerman. "The Bills had a nose guard named Rocco Pirro. Perry got tackled on a play, and Pirro walked by and kicked him in the head. Perry was furious. I've never seen such fury. Frankie Albert, smart bastard that he was, gave Perry the ball five straight times. Perry was insane. He was going to get those yards no matter what."

Pirro felt Perry's wrath in the process. For Perry had sharp elbows, pistonlike legs, and those carefully placed cleats. He wasn't overly large for a fullback at six feet, 207 pounds. But he had huge thighs and calves, wide shoulders and bulging biceps. By combining his muscular physique with sprinter's speed, when Perry slammed into tacklers, it was with the force of a 240-pounder.

And if opponents taunted Perry because of his skin pigmentation, or worked him over in the pile with the same intent, he would come back and hit them as if he weighed 265 pounds. Anger added pounds.

"I didn't hear racial slurs from every team," he said. "But I heard them until I got respect. Then it was like, 'This guy can play. I can't intimidate him.' After that, we got along."

It might have been begrudging respect, but in the 1940s and 1950s, black athletes took respect any way it was meted out. Perry had to fight for that same respect on his own team, the 49ers. On a train trip from Milwaukee to Chicago, 49ers players were served by black waiters. Johnny Strzykalski, who played in the same backfield as Perry, had a disagreement with one waiter.

"One word led to another," Perry said, "and Strike called him a 'fuckin' nigger.' Then realizing what he had said, Strike turned to me and said, 'Joe, I'm sorry, I didn't mean you.' I said, 'Strike, you're not talking to me. If you were talking to me, it would be different.' Strike started crying. I think this woke up some things in him. We became closer after that. Why should I shut him out? I don't think he's a closet racist. I don't think so because he cried. He had hurt a friend. We never talked about it again. We took it as something that will never happen again. And it never did. To this day, I consider him a close friend."

Strzykalski, an original 49er in 1946, was the team's first standout running back. He rushed for 905 yards in 1947 and 915 yards in 1948 over fourteen-game seasons, and averaged an impressive six yards a carry. But he was no Joe Perry. Few backs, though, were Perry's equal. Perry joined the 49ers in 1948. He went through the normal rookie hazing of that time period, the normal hazing for a black man or white man.

"We stayed at Menlo College, south of San Francisco, during summer training camp," Perry said. "I caught a pie in the face from Strike in the dining hall. A few days later, the team was given the night off. I got dressed up to go out. As I stepped out of my room, someone dropped a bucket of water on me. When I got back to my room that night, I pulled back the sheets and there was a garden snake. I figured the players on the team either were hazing me or they liked me. Then I found out they really liked me."

No 49er supported Perry more than fullback Norm Standlee, whose job Perry sought. A big, swarthy man, Standlee played on Stanford's Rose Bowl champions of 1940. That year, the Indians, Stanford's nickname at the time, re-introduced the T-formation to college football under coach Clark Shaughnessy, who caused such confusion among opponents that Stanford went undefeated.

Standlee, Bruno Banducci, and Frankie Albert from that same Stanford team were original 49ers. The 49ers were formed in 1946 from a nucleus of college players who had attended San Francisco area schools and/or played on local wartime military teams such as St. Mary's Pre-Flight in Moraga.

Standlee, known as "Chief," hadn't a prejudiced bone in his 235-pound body. He was willing to teach the pro game to Perry in spite of the fact that they were in direct competition. Standlee was a team player, and a good and fair man, which Perry was about to learn when another black–white situation arose.

In 1948, when the 49ers played their third season in the All-America Football Conference, they met the gridiron version of the Brooklyn Dodgers at Ebbets Field, where Jackie Robinson played second base. Racism lurked that day, like many other days, for Perry. He took a hand-off from quarterback Albert and was buried by some white-skinned Dodgers. Buried and then abused underneath a mass of humanity.

"They had me down and were beating the crap out of me in full view of one official, who stood there watching," said Perry. "Norm Standlee came up to the official and said, 'Can't you see what they're doing?' The official said, 'They ain't hurting that nigger.' Norm grabbed that ref by the collar and punched the shit out of him. By that time, my teammates pulled those guys off me. When I got the chance, I got back at the Dodgers. I gave them both feet or a John Henry [a vicious forearm] alongside their heads. I wouldn't play dirty unless I had no choice."

No football movie has produced more tears than *Brian's Song*, a story about the special relationship between two Chicago Bears, a black man, Gale Sayers, and the dying Brian Piccolo, a white man. They were roommates in the 1960s, when such a living arrangement in sports was rare.

Yet two decades earlier on the 49ers, Perry roomed with a white halfback, Verl Lillywhite, on and off over a four-year period. And Perry needn't have been misled by the name Lillywhite. Perry's roomie was color blind.

"We had a lot of fun together," Perry said. "We played against each other in junior college. Verl was more like a brother to me."

How did Perry get along with his other 49ers teammates, all of whom were also lily white?

"We were like this," Perry replied, his fingers intertwined.

Perry paused in the office of his home in Chandler, Arizona, a Phoenix suburb built out of the desert sands. It was December 1999, and Perry was calling up memories from fifty years ago.

"Most of today's black football players don't realize the sacrifices made by blacks from my generation to get them where they are," he said. "Most of us worked one or two jobs to keep playing football. The money in football wasn't great, and we were in no position to demand anything.

"I can't answer what it was like for Jackie Robinson when he entered baseball. I can only speak for myself what it was like to be one of the first blacks to play football. Guys like [black Los Angeles Rams running backs] Tank Younger and Dan Towler were Johnny-come-latelies in that respect. They still were in college when I joined the 49ers."

However, racism wasn't restricted to the athletic arena when the twentieth century crossed the halfway point. There was the matter of road accommodations for black athletes. More often than not, Jim Crow would be standing behind the registration desk.

"I remember going to Pennsylvania with the 49ers," said Perry. "The team stayed at a country club. But I couldn't stay with them because I was black. Here it was Philadelphia, the Liberty Bell, peace and liberty for everybody regardless of race or color. Right? But is that liberty if you tell me I can't stay somewhere? Remember, I had gone to war for my country."

Perry stayed instead at the home of a white lady and her children, who were Perry's age, in their early twenties. This white family viewed life as a piano keyboard, with blacks and whites mixing. Perry exchanged Christmas cards with the family for years.

Finally, the time came when Perry wasn't going to take it any more. If he was giving his body to the 49ers while getting worked over by the bigots of the world, he demanded to sleep in the same hotel beds as his teammates. And ride in the same cabs.

"In Baltimore," he recalled, "I went to catch a cab. I go out there and the driver tells me, 'Go catch one of those nigger cabs.' Now we might have kinkier heads and bigger lips, but we're still human beings. I'm not a bitter person. I may forgive, but I don't forget."

Lou Spadia worked in the 49ers front office when Perry was signed. Spadia later moved up to general manager and team president after the 49ers founders, brothers Tony and Vic Morabito, both died. Spadia hasn't forgotten what Perry went through as the black sheep of the 49ers family.

"Joe went into the Lord Baltimore Hotel and a woman screamed," Spadia said. "Another time, he went to stay with a family, and he walked back to the hotel and told me, 'I'm not going to stay in that pigsty. I'm going home.' I looked at him and said, 'Oh, Joe...' He wound up staying with a black doctor.

"Joe and Jackie Robinson went through the same thing. In my thirty-five years with the 49ers, I received one gift from a player. A necktie from Joe Perry."

For all the racism Perry endured, he never drew a line between blacks and whites. When he was inducted into the Pro Football Hall of Fame in 1969, Josephine Morabito, Tony's widow and later team owner, was his presenter.

But Perry fought the white man's system and prevailed. The 49ers began booking him into the team's road hotels. Getting fed in the hotel dining rooms, though, was yet another civil rights battle to be fought and won.

"At the Lord Baltimore, I sat down to eat and they wouldn't serve me," he said. "Now there were black people working in the dining room, but black people couldn't eat there. If they were like me, then they had fought for their country. So I started turning over tables until I got my way."

Perry was brought a menu on the spot.

"Before the team arrived at the Bear Mountain Lodge in upstate New York," he continued, "I told Spadia, 'If there's going to be a problem with me staying there, tell me now.' He never told me. So the team arrived, and there was a problem. I had to put my foot down again, and then they showed me every courtesy. They probably had never seen a black person before."

Perry's separation from the team in terms of housing on trips during the early 1950s caught many of his white teammates off guard.

"Joe and I drove to practice together in Menlo Park or Redwood City, because we were the only 49ers who lived in San Francisco," said Bob St. Clair. "I can remember in 1953 going back to play Baltimore. Me being a know-it-all rookie, I asked Joe what night clubs was he going out to. He mentioned a couple, but he wasn't sure. And so I said, 'When we get to the hotel, I'll call you in your room.' He told me he wasn't staying at the hotel, but with a family. Then I said, 'You lucky bastard. We're staying at this stinking hotel, and you're a big shot who gets to stay in a private home.' I had no idea we were south of the Mason-Dixon line. We didn't know these things back then."

Any hotel owner, not to mention any restaurant maitre d' or taxi driver, should have been proud to have Perry in his company. Any football team, too. For Perry is a one-man rainbow coalition, a Jesse Jackson in shoulder pads.

Perry served in the military when blacks weren't welcomed in that make of uniform either. Yet in spite of all the indignities he encountered in the Navy, Perry remained pure-grade American. Red, white, and blue. Mother Goose and Fatha Hines. Apple pie and jazz.

"It makes me wonder, where did they get 'African-American?'" he wondered aloud. "I'm not African-American. I don't know a damn thing about Africa. If a black American moved to Africa, he wouldn't be called African-American. When I fought in a war, I fought for America. The blood ran red. Whose blood was it? White man, black man, there's no difference. Does it really matter what color you are? We're all Americans as far as I can see."

The bigots see it differently.

"When blacks started out in this country," said Perry, "we were called Negras. Then we were called Negros, then niggers, then colored. Then we were called black. Then Afro-Americans. And now it's

African-American. Why not American? Or black? I have no problem with you calling me black. But putting titles on things, like African-Americans, delays the process of healing the world. That's why I love that girl in there."

Donna Perry, Joe's third wife, is white and of Italian heritage. While her husband was being interviewed for this book, she could be heard chanting in the next room, practicing Buddhism.

"She thinks just like me," Perry said. "She doesn't have a prejudicial bone in her body. I get mad at people, but I hold no prejudices. I have a way of letting people know I can get along with anyone. But, like I said, I won't take shit. You can say what you want to me, but don't put your hands on me."

That's not just Perry talking. It is a combination of his mother and father talking through him. Perry's father taught him to fight for what's right. Perry's mother taught him to fight for the same thing, but to use restraint.

"My mom told me, 'You don't have to take anything from anybody. Just don't start something,'" Perry said.

Perry always listened to his mother, the most important person in his life. His mother's image is with him every day, on the medallion he wears around his neck. He hasn't removed that medallion since the day she died in 1969, except for a brief period when he loaned it to his sister. Perry also has his mother's name, Laurah, tattooed on his forearm along with the name of his first wife, Jewel. Their names are intertwined with two flowers, two hearts, and an arrow.

"You'll never believe why I got this tattoo," Perry said. "When I was in the Navy, I thought I would get blown away. So I had this tattoo done. I told someone, 'If I die, cut this tattoo off and send it to my mom.'"

Why not send it to Jewel?

"Because I loved my mother more," he said.

Perry was the only black among the 134 men in his platoon at the San Diego Naval Training Center. Since Perry was the only one of the 134 with a college background, he was named platoon leader. That title accorded him unlimited power during daytime training, but that same power was challenged nightly inside the barracks.

"There were guys in my platoon from Mississippi and Alabama," Perry said. "I'd overhear guys say, 'When my dad went coon hunting, he'd get him a nigger every time.' For thirteen weeks, I fought every night. But it was over in the morning. I don't have no grudges. When I caught cat fever, which is the fever you get before you get pneumonia, I woke up in the hospital and there were 133 guys there. That tells you what they think of you. Those guys decided a human being is a human being. You can learn to live together. It's what you got inside that counts. I think they came together at once, thinking, 'Hey, we might lose something we like.' As it turned out, they would have died for me."

That was fifty-five years ago, but the interaction of servicemen in wartime never dies until death itself. Perry attends Navy reunions whenever he can. Even the biggest racist from the Deep South, Perry said proudly, became his friend. At the last Navy reunion five years ago, the two of them, the black kid from Watts, the white boy from the South, were up there on the dais, laughing and joking together.

A refreshing quality about Perry is how easily he can change the minds of those who hate him because of his color into liking him because of his character. Perry's hard not to like. He's honest, sometimes skin-curdling honest. And he'll knock you down if he's provoked. But he has a good soul that, eventually, wins over everyone. Even racists.

There aren't too many battles in Perry's life, in fact, that he hasn't won. Need a yard for a first down, give the ball to Joe. Place a negative in front of him, on or off the playing field, he'll deal with it and triumph.

Perry says he won't take crap from someone, but he'll reach down and help that same person up after Perry has taught him a lesson in respect.

It is clear Perry hasn't fallen all that far from his family tree, which was planted long ago with a variety of seeds that grew into a strong oak.

Perry has Indian blood. One set of grandparents was black. His paternal grandmother was Cherokee. His paternal grandfather was black mixed with Cherokee and Blackfoot.

The married couple of Fletcher Lee and Laurah Perry produced Joe and an older sister, Louella. Joe was born January 22, 1927, in Stevens, Arkansas, near the Texas border. When Joe was a baby, his father suffered extensive burns over his body working in the mines. So Fletcher Lee moved his family to southern California, where he labored on a date farm before heading to Los Angeles to find work in a tin plant through the assistance of the Works Progress Administration, a federal program that was the brainchild of President Franklin Delano Roosevelt, who created jobs for those who had lost everything in the Depression.

"My dad was five seven, 170 pounds, but with shoulders as wide as mine," said Perry. "He was as strong as three bulls, and as mean as three pit bulls. He didn't take anything from anybody, black, white or green. My dad had a temper. You could see the Indian in him. He'd go on the warpath in a minute. I got my backbone from my dad. I got integrity from my dad. And I got my fairness with people from my dad."

Perry got his height from other branches on the family tree. He was six feet tall at age twelve, when he was challenged physically by other kids. But he held back because of his mother's cautionary voice and her sagelike wisdom.

"I could go to my mother and tell her anything," he said. "She would give me her solution."

Perry listened, though not always carefully. He didn't walk away from every fight. One day a kid teased him on a bridge. That skirmish ended when Perry fell off the bridge, breaking his left wrist. That should have been a problem since Perry was left-handed. But Perry trained himself to become right-handed. He had a strong mind to go with a strong body.

Perry's first encounter with racism of a broad scope occurred while he was attending David Starr Jordan High School. That encounter involved a Watts riot, but nothing like in the 1960s, when that area became an inferno.

In the early 1940s, when Perry was a teenager, a heavily used mode of mass transportation in Los Angeles was known as "Big Red," a streetcar that carried passengers to outlying communities such as Compton, Santa Ana, Long Beach, and San Pedro.

One day, when Big Red stopped in Watts, some white sailors got off and fondled a black girl in front of a group of black men, who then beat the sailors unmercifully. The next day, 200 white sailors got off the streetcar in Watts and laid into every black male they could find. Perry was safe in a movie theatre at the time, so his recollection of what took place was told to him later by those who were present.

"That's when it all started, the first riot," said Perry. "Blacks and whites fought with no policemen anywhere. And I don't blame them. The fighting went on for two, three weeks. Did I get into it? No way. My butt was home with mom. I wore the knickers back then. The other kids called me Little Lord Fauntleroy. Besides, color never bothered me. I never distinguished that way."

Perry thought with an academic mind. He was a good student, especially in mathematics. As a teenager, he planned to become an electrical engineer. His grades were good enough that he skipped two grades and was graduated from high school just shy of his sixteenth birthday.

"My mom wanted me to get it up here," he said, pointing to his head.

He had no indication at the time that athletics would replace academics in his life. The isosceles triangle was more important to him than becoming a triple threat in football. In fact, if there was an athlete in the Perry family, it wasn't Joe but his sister, Louella.

"She could fly," he said. "When I was ten or eleven, I couldn't outrun her. I couldn't even touch her."

When Joe reached the ninth grade, he became more involved in sports. He played softball, baseball, basketball and football. Every sport was acceptable with his mother, except football. She didn't want her son, the math student, going to class on crutches. So Perry tried to out-fox his mom. He forged her name in order to have the parental permission needed to play football. That deception didn't last long. Perry broke an ankle the first day of practice.

"I walked home afterwards," he said. "My mom asked me why I was limping. I made up some excuse, but the next morning the ankle was as big as a softball. But to show you what kind of person my mom was, she let me play. She figured if I wanted something that badly, why stop me."

It's hard not to love a mom like that. So Perry did attend classes on crutches, for a while anyway. He discovered at a young age that he was a quick healer. How else could he have lasted sixteen pro seasons? He rejoined football practice and became a varsity starter as a freshman. He dominated right away.

"They said I was mean," he recalled. "There was a defensive back named Pete. I can't remember his last name, but he was a senior. He came up to tackle me, and I leveled his head."

And Perry hadn't yet turned thirteen. Then he received a shocking baptism in the violent nature of football.

"Our first league game was against South Gate High, an all-white school," he said. "One of their players fumbled a kickoff, picked it up, and decided to come out of the end zone. Five guys hit him, broke his neck, and killed him. Now I gotta go home and tell mom."

Perry wasn't a triple threat, but a quadruple threat, since he ran, passed, punted, and placekicked. He was named third team all-city tailback in Los Angeles as a freshman. He never advanced to first team all-city in four years of varsity football. But while none of the white kids chosen ahead of him starred in college afterwards, Perry became an all-time great.

As a prep track man, Perry was timed at 9.7 seconds in the 100-yard dash and 21.9 seconds in the 220. He high-jumped 6 feet, 3 inches, broad-jumped 23 feet, 5 inches, and heaved the twelve-pound shot 55 feet.

He was also quite a baseball player, and an even better softball pitcher. And as his friends discovered on Saturday nights, Perry was a top bowler, too. He could knock down a linebacker or the ten pin. Outrun you or outpitch you. Perry is arguably the best all-around athlete in the Pro Football Hall of Fame.

"I wanted to go to UCLA in the worst way because of Kenny Washington and Woody Strode," he remembered. "I went to see the UCLA coach, Bert LaBrucherie, but he wouldn't talk to me. So I enrolled at Compton Junior College and scored twenty-two touchdowns in 1944. And here comes Bert LaBrucherie. I told him I wouldn't go to UCLA if it was the last school on earth. That's one of my beliefs: What goes around, comes around."

It was no time to think about football anyway. America was at war. Perry had turned seventeen and was about to be drafted. He joined the Navy instead, and served on an LST in the Pacific. When the war ended, he returned to San Francisco on the USS North to finish his military obligation.

His assignment was to decommission wartime ships that had moved to a watery retreat in Martinez, a town north of San Francisco famous only because Joe DiMaggio was born there. Those Navy vessels, known as the "Mothball Fleet," still sit there a half-century later, rusted memories of the United States' come-from-behind victory over Japan.

Perry was a coxswain in the Navy. His specific job at the Alameda Naval Air Station, directly across the bay from San Francisco, was to pull up anchor chains, when he wasn't playing sports. He was married by that time to Jewel Brown Perry. They had met at Compton JC. Jewel became pregnant after Perry returned from sea duty in the Pacific.

Becoming a first-time father nearly got Perry into serious trouble with the Navy. He wanted to be there for the birth, and so he asked for an extended weekend pass. The pass was denied. An irate Perry, in his take-no-shit mode, left the base without clearance. After his son, John, was born the following Friday, Perry returned to his base and received a deck courtmartial, ten days on bread and water. It was the most severe Navy punishment short of receiving a dishonorable discharge.

Alameda Naval Air Station won the All-Navy softball tournament with Perry as its star pitcher, and the only black on the team.

"We're playing softball in a Pacific tournament, we even played at Pearl Harbor, and a guy on watch tells me I can't go in some place with the rest of our team," Perry said. "The guy's a bigot, and he starts jostling his .45 pistol. A Navy captain who was traveling with us chewed his ass out."

Perry seems as proud of his pitching exploits as he is of his break-away runs in football.

"I learned how to throw all kinds of pitches," he said. "I can still throw a softball. That's something you never lose. A few years ago, my wife said she could hit me. So I gave her a chance. I whizzed some pitches by her. She looked at me and said, 'You could have killed me.' I said, 'Well...'"

Perry smiled. Even in his seventies, he still has control of his pitches. But once a competitor, always a competitor. Perry wouldn't even allow his own wife a loud foul. She hasn't picked up a bat against him since.

The Alameda NAS Hellcats also were quite a threat in football with Perry as their single-wing tailback. The Hellcats scheduled other local military teams, plus junior varsity squads from nearby universities such as Cal and Stanford. Well, not entirely JVs, as the Hellcats would learn.

"We played [coach] Pappy [Waldorf's team] at Cal, and we were kicking the crap out of them. I was running roughshod," Perry said. "Pappy was using his JVs, about thirty-three guys. When we came back from halftime, there were 100 Golden Bears out there. I think they won, 20–19. But we beat Stanford's JVs. I was the only black on the football team, too, but there was no distinction. We ate together, we slept together. We were hand in glove. They'd go to war for me. I'd go to war for them."

Assisting the Alameda team was 49ers tackle John Woudenberg, who recommended to team owner Tony Morabito that he take a look at Perry. When Morabito inquired what kind of runner Perry was, Woudenberg said, "Just give him the ball and point him in the right direction."

Intrigued, Morabito personally scouted Perry. It took two games for the 49ers boss to become convinced Perry was indeed special. In the first game, Perry carried four times and scored four touchdowns. His shortest run was fifty-five yards. In the second game, he played only the first six minutes and scored two touchdowns. Morabito needed no further convincing.

Before his professional career was launched, Perry ran in the Fresno Relays against USC's Mel Patton, who would set the world record in the 100-yard dash at 9.3 seconds. At Fresno, Patton was given first in a time of 9.4, while Perry crossed the finish line in a 9.5 clocking.

"And I had the tape in my hand. You figure it out," said Perry. "Mel was in the inside lane, I was on the outside. I don't think the judges saw me."

After three years in the Navy, Perry received scholarship offers from Washington, Oregon, USC, Nevada, and Columbia of the Ivy League. He still envisioned a college degree in engineering. But, now married and a father, he also had to make a living. So it came down to the G.I. Bill vs. pro football.

The 49ers wanted Perry, but so did the Los Angeles Rams, who offered him twice as much as San Francisco. Perry was swayed, though, by the "instant magnetism" between himself and Tony Morabito, who drove 450 miles from San Francisco to Los Angeles to negotiate personally with Perry.

"Tony had a lot of charisma," Perry said. "And he was another guy who didn't take shit from anybody. One time a San Francisco sportswriter wrote something Tony didn't like. Tony went after him with a letter opener. The whole time I played for Tony, I never knew what I made. I never signed a contract. I had that kind of trust in Tony, and he always took care of me."

"Tony loved Joe," said Spadia. "Joe was his favorite player."

The son of Italian immigrants, Morabito felt a sense of kinship with Perry, who was among the second wave of blacks to play professional football, and long after the first wave had crashed and receded.

From 1920, when the NFL was formed in an automobile showroom in Canton, Ohio, to 1933, only thirteen blacks played in the NFL. Then succumbing to the same kind of blanket racism practiced in baseball, the NFL signed no more blacks until 1946. The postwar period then did away with segregation in professional sports. The thinking was that if a man defended his country, he could defend his goal line, regardless of his skin color. George Preston Marshall of the racially sounding Washington Redskins became the last NFL owner to sign a black player in 1962.

But before the NFL was created by the likes of George "Papa Bear" Halas, professional football was a semi-pro game played on the sandlots. Players blocked and tackled for a few dollars. Occasionally they were paid off with IOUs, white and black players alike.

There were blacks playing a modified form of pro football at the turn of the century, although not that many. Charles Follis, known as "The Black Cyclone," became the first black pro football player, in 1904, for the Shelby (Ohio) Athletic Club, known as the Shelby Blues. Thus Follis represented pro football's first merging of black and Blue. Other black players were Charles "Doc" Baker, who suited up for the Akron Indians from 1907 to 1911; Henry McDonald, who played one year for the Rochester Jeffersons in 1911; and Gideon Smith, who played one game for a Canton team in 1915.

Fritz Pollard led Brown University of the Ivy League to the Rose Bowl before joining the Akron Pros in 1919. Pollard became the NFL's first black coach, in 1922, with the Milwaukee Badgers. He moved on to the Hammond Pros in 1923 and 1924, before playing again for Akron in 1925 and 1926. Pollard was a speed back, a smaller version of Joe Perry. Legendary sportswriter Grantland Rice placed Pollard in his all-time backfield with white players Jim Thorpe, Red Grange, and Ernie Nevers.

Paul Robeson, the famous actor and opera singer, was a lineman at Rutgers and one of the first black football players to be named an All-American. He then played professionally for Hammond, Akron, and Milwaukee of the NFL from 1920 to 1922. Rube Marshall, Harold Bradley, and T. Ray Kemp were other blacks to sign with early NFL teams. But the most famous black player from that era was Duke Slater, a tackle who played ten years in the league and was All-NFL in 1926, 1928, and 1929.

As America enters a new century, we can only imagine what race relations in sports were like nearly a hundred years ago. The movie *The Great White Hope* was based on America's quest to find a white man to take the heavyweight championship away from a black man, Jack Johnson. In real life, that was former champion Jim Jeffries, who was coaxed out of retirement, only to be thrashed by Johnson.

Pollard recalled this dialogue between himself and Thorpe, a Sac and Fox Indian, before they played an NFL game. "How are you doing, little black man?" Thorpe asked Pollard. "How are you doing, big black man?" Pollard responded.

Perry's mindset in the 1940s, when blacks re-appeared on the pro gridiron, was to stand up like a man at all times, in the image of his father. But don't initiate, only retaliate, as his mother instructed him.

"When you're much younger, you think you can handle it mentally," Perry said of racial epithets. "I never let it bother me. In that era, disputes weren't settled by guns, knives, and gangs."

Perry shook his head. Society has changed. And something else has changed with it, the country's backbone.

"Whatever happened to home life in this country, with a mother and a father?" he asked. "Where did the values go in life? Did the courts make it too easy on the kids? Nowadays, you can't touch a kid. My son, Michael, called the cops on my [second] wife, Barbara, for chastising him.

"Chastising!"

Unlike Jackie Robinson's experience with baseball's Brooklyn Dodgers, the white 49er players didn't threaten to boycott when Perry joined the team. Like Robinson, Perry proved he could play with, and even outplay, the white boys. In any kind of a sports setting, talent is the ultimate decider.

It's a story Tony Morabito loved to tell. The 49ers were playing the Buffalo Bills in 1948 at Kezar Stadium, situated on the outskirts of Golden Gate Park in San Francisco. Bills owner Jim Breuil had criticized Morabito privately for signing Perry. Showing how primitive, yet unpretentious, pro football was back then, the two owners sat together for the game. Breuil again chastised Morabito for hiring a black man over a white man.

"It makes it tough on all of us who don't sign a Negro," Breuil said to Morabito. "Besides, they're troublemakers. Why did you do it, Tony?"

Early in the first quarter, Perry entered the game. He took a pitchout from Albert and zipped around right end for fifty-eight yards and a touchdown. It was Perry's first carry in a league game. Morabito couldn't suppress a wide grin as he turned to Breuil.

"That's why, Jim," he said.

Perry wore a tackle's number, 74, and ran like a halfback. The AAFC's numbering system was different from the NFL's. AAFC centers wore numbers in the 20s, guards in the 30s, tackles in the 40s, ends in the 50s, quarterbacks in the 60s, fullbacks in the 70s, halfbacks in the 80s and 90s.

As a rookie, Perry acquired his defining nickname of The Jet. It was given him by Albert, who was the smallest player on the 49ers, yet who wore a guard's number, 63.

"We were practicing at Menlo College," Perry said. "Frankie called a quick trap. He took the snap, turned, and I was already by him. He said to someone, 'Perry is just like one of those big jets that come by here.'"

And The Jet had some kind of takeoff. As a rookie, Perry rushed for 562 yards and a career-high 7.3 yards per carry. He led all 49ers backs with eleven touchdowns, ten on the ground, while end Alyn Beals led the entire team with fourteen touchdowns.

Strzykalski, Standlee, Perry and Lillywhite combined to lead a punishing 49er rushing attack that set a pro football record with 3,663 yards. The 49ers averaged 261 yards on the ground, and 6.5 yards a carry while scoring 495 points. Their only two losses were to the undefeated Cleveland Browns, including a 31-28 decision that decided the Western Conference title. Perry scored twice in that game.

With such glittering numbers his rookie year, why was Perry played so sparingly on offense by coach Lawrence T. "Buck" Shaw?

"I guess Buck was entrenched with Norm at fullback, and Strike and Len Eshmont at halfback. Who did Buck want to take out?" Perry said diplomatically. "I could play all three positions. I guess it was a dilemma for Buck. None of the other backs could outrun me. None could catch the ball better than me. I couldn't block better than Norm, but I could block with him. I played more on defense. I'd go from cornerback to linebacker. I had no problem tackling, but I wasn't enamored by defense. The excitement for me was running over people."

Eshmont was a solid, though hardly dynamic, player. He is remembered today through the Len Eshmont Award, given annually to the 49er who best demonstrates Eshmont's inspirational qualities. Strzykalski was a tough, gritty back. Standlee was the bull of the backfield. Perry was the team's greyhound and its only breakaway threat.

Though Perry insists he wasn't upset by his limited use offensively in 1948, he asked a rhetorical question that did make sense.

"If I'm the only one in Canton," he said, "should I have played more?"

It wasn't racism, though, that kept Perry on the bench. The 49ers signed him at a time when most NFL teams had no black players. If any league in any sport was leading the charge to integrate rosters in the postwar period, it was the AAFC.

In 1948, Cleveland had three blacks: Marion Motley, Bill Willis, and Horace Gillom. The New York Yankees had Buddy Young. The 49ers had Perry and, later on, Bob Mike. Except for the Rams, the NFL had no other blacks.

Shaw was caught in a quandary. He felt a sense of loyalty to Standlee, Strzykalski, and Eshmont, since all three were original 49ers. But Shaw was no racist, and Perry wasn't a token black in San Francisco. The 49ers signed a second black that year in Mike, a defensive tackle from UCLA.

"When I got to San Francisco, they were thinking, 'Who's he going to room with?'" Perry said. "Well, Verl Lillywhite played at Modesto Junior College when I was at Compton JC. So not only had we played against each other, we liked each other. So we became roomies.

"When Bob Mike joined us, they roomed him with me for a while. It made sense, I guess, to them. We were the only two blacks on the team. But I threw him out. We didn't see eye-to-eye on some things. Color doesn't matter to me. Y. A. Tittle was my roommate for one week. He snored, really sawing logs. I don't snore. I got rid of him, too."

The 49ers cut Mike after two years. But it wasn't racially motivated.

"He was easily trapped," said Perry.

Ara Parseghian hasn't forgotten playing against Perry. Parseghian is most famous for rebuilding Notre Dame's tattered football legend after he became the Irish's coach in 1964. But in 1948, he was a halfback for the Cleveland Browns.

"Joe Perry was a heckuva football player," Parseghian, now seventy-seven, recalled. "I remember the preparation for both games with them, watching the films, and the concern our coaches Paul Brown and [assistant] Blanton Collier had about Perry."

Parseghian caught a touchdown pass from Otto Graham in Cleveland's 14-7 win over the 49ers in their first meeting in 1948. Then in early 1949, Parseghian's pro career ended after he suffered a hip injury similar to Bo Jackson's. Eighteen months later, after a fortuitous series of events, Parseghian, twenty-six, became the head coach at his alma mater, Miami of Ohio.

"Can you believe that?" said Parseghian, who since has had five surgeries on the damaged hip. "And I had once told my brothers, 'Anyone who coaches is nuts.' But it's like the golf bug, it bites you."

Parseghian also played against Tittle in 1948, when the latter was quarterbacking the Baltimore Colts.

"I remember Perry, but Tittle wasn't as well-publicized," said Parseghian. "He was good, but Perry was outstanding."

By 1949, Perry's burgeoning talent and blazing speed couldn't be held back any longer. Shaw shifted Standlee to defense, and Perry was given the Chief's fullback job without an ounce of rancor between them.

"Norm was a great guy," Perry said. "I think he moved to defense willingly. I say that because he'd always try to help anybody. Watching him, that rubbed off on me. From then on, I tried to help anyone on the team. And because of that [kind of attitude], the 49ers became family. If two guys got into a fight on the practice field, we'd throw them into the pool after practice. Hey, we had Italian owners. Tony believed in famiglia."

Perry jetted for 783 yards (6.8 average) and eight touchdowns in 1949. He won the AAFC rushing title and was voted All-AAFC in the league's fourth and final season. The 49ers' one AAFC highlight was a 56-28 victory over the dreaded Browns in 1949. That day, Perry rushed for 156 yards and two touchdowns in only the 49ers' second win over Cleveland in nine tries in the AAFC.

The last AAFC meeting between the two teams was for the 1949 league championship, in what was the 49ers' first shot at the title. The two teams had been grouped in the same division for three years before the AAFC consolidated prior to its farewell season. Although the 49ers had an impressive AAFC record of 39-15-2, they were no match for the mighty Browns, who were a sparkling 52-4-3. And so the Browns won that last championship, 21-7, in Cleveland.

"Definitely, they were stronger," Perry said of those Browns teams, coached by Paul Brown and featuring other future Hall of Famers in Graham, Lou Groza, Dante Lavelli, Motley, and Willis. "In that last championship game, I ran a couple of plays at quarterback. Sometimes I'd line up at center, with Frankie behind me in a quick-kick formation. Or I'd take the snap with Frankie playing behind me, and I'd run a sneak."

The 49ers were more clever than the Browns, but Cleveland wasn't fooled by trickery. Over the first ten years of the Browns' existence, spanning two leagues, they played in ten championship games, winning seven.

Trick or treat?

"Cleveland hurt us in both leagues," said Perry. "But we hurt ourselves more. We'd average thirty-five points and some teams would outscore us. You'd have to say that defense killed us. We didn't draft defensive players [in the 1950s]. We drafted for offense. Our drafting killed us."

The Browns' dominance over the 49ers in those days wasn't entirely player-motivated.

"You have to give Paul Brown 95 percent of the credit," said Graham. "He was well-organized. Before he got into football, the deal was that when the season was over, the assistant coaches went fishing and hunting for three, four months. Paul worked them year-round.

"Paul did more than any other coach to revolutionize pro football. He was the first coach to have playbooks. With blank pages. We had to fill in the plays ourselves. I was the quarterback, but I was expected to know every blocking pattern. Paul would test us on the team's plays.

Athletes who didn't do well on the test were gone the next day. It didn't matter who they were. I saw some really good players let go.

"The 49ers had good teams. Tittle had everything a good quarterback needed. He was smart, threw the ball well. I remember Perry catching a long pass against us and going the distance. McElhenny was a really good back, a great football player. Johnson was tough. And they were all nice guys. But to be good in football, you have to have a real team. Paul Brown wanted 100 percent out of us on every play. He didn't care if you were black, white, Catholic, Jewish, or Protestant as long as you gave 100 percent. And he wouldn't put up with social problems. The Browns really played for one another."

Brown also was the first coach to send in plays from the sideline, through the use of "messenger guards." Graham remembers an incident from the early '50s that showed the Browns were a loose team, too.

"George Ratterman was a character," said Graham. "He was in the game for me at quarterback when a rookie guard brings in a play. George told the rookie, 'I don't like that play, go back and get another one.' So the rookie turned and went back to the sideline. The guys were laughing so hard, they had to call a time out."

The 49ers were a fun bunch, too, with the mirthful Albert at quarterback. But the Browns took the humor out of the game for San Francisco. In 1950, when the NFL took in the 49ers and Browns as orphans from the defunct AAFC, Perry and Jewel divorced.

"We were both too young to know what love was," said Perry. "Jewel then remarried, and has grown kids from that marriage. We're still friendly. Jewel and Donna get along great."

In 1951, Perry was the Bo Jackson of his time, though only for a short while. Perry decided to give professional baseball a shot. He signed with the Oakland Oaks, a Triple-A minor league team in the Pacific Coast League. He went to spring training with the Oaks as a shortstop and centerfielder.

"With my speed, I could play both positions," he said. "I had a pretty good arm. My shoulders weren't messed up from football yet. I played in four [spring] games and batted a legitimate .333. I was hitting the ball well. Then I think it was [coach] Cookie Lavagetto who said to me, 'You've been away a long while, we'd like to ship you to'…it was some [lower-division] team in the Northwest. I said, 'You mean I'm going to trade an airplane for a bus league? I can't do that.' So I decided to concentrate strictly on football."

Single again, Perry was an immediate hit on the social scene as available ladies threw themselves at the handsome fullback with the winning smile. And they didn't have to throw themselves too far.

"I was out there winging it," said Perry, "and I finally met someone I liked."

Her name was Barbara Maxwell. They married in 1953 and produced a daughter, Karen. Joe and Barbara Perry moved into the San Francisco social scene, hobnobbing with such black entertainers as Nat "King" Cole, Lionel Hampton, Count Basie, and Duke Ellington at a nightclub called the Plantation.

"Then we'd go to Jimbo's Bop City in the Fillmore District after hours to listen to jazz," Perry remembered. "Billie Holliday performed there. So did Art Tatum and Stan Getz. It's a good thing I didn't drink. It would have ruined my career."

Perry played with broken ribs, a busted cheekbone, broken nose, and broken fingers. The little finger on his left hand still points sideways. Perry even tore the cartilage in his left knee without missing a game.

"Mac [Hugh McElhenny] would say, 'How do you do that?'" Perry said. "In Baltimore, at the end of my career, I tore the medial collateral ligament in my right knee. I opened up the season three weeks later. The doctor said, 'How did you do that?' I told him what I told Mac: 'I heal fast.'"

Bert Gustafson, a fitness expert, deserves credit for Perry's superb conditioning. Gustafson ran the Marine Memorial gymnasium in San Francisco. And he devised a special program for the 49ers' marquee fullback.

"Bert asked me, 'What do you need most in your profession? Your legs,'" Perry said. "Three times a week during the season after I got off from practice, plus five days a week in the offseason, I focused on my legs. Bert got me up to 2,000 pounds on leg lifts, using ten repetitions. Then afterwards, he'd have me swim to relax the muscles."

No running back, certainly no running back with speed, ever had a better-looking pair of legs than Perry. Muscles knotted on his legs like walnuts stored in a squirrel's cheeks. Perry's upper torso was sculpted even without benefit of weight training. Why add more chrome to a Cadillac?

"I had natural body strength," he said. "The most I ever bench-pressed with my arms was 350 pounds. But I really had strong legs. And what people failed to see when I ran was, although I had quick feet, my feet were always moving here and there. I had moves. You just didn't see them. McElhenny had flow. I had quick movement, quick feet. I made people miss me."

That aspect of Perry's game wasn't evident at first, not even by him. He'd break into the open, pick out the first tackler in sight, then try to plow over him. Perry had a halfback's speed, but a fullback's mentality.

"He was fast and he was tough," said Chuck Bednarik of the Philadelphia Eagles, the NFL's last sixty-minute man and a Hall of Famer. "He didn't quite run over people like Jimmy Brown, but he could run over people."

Sometimes, Perry's motivation for running over tacklers was retaliation for what had happened on a previous play or in a previous game. In 1950, the 49ers played the Chicago Bears for the very first time. Perry ran a sweep, the whistle blew, the play stopped. Except George Connor, the Bears' Hall of Fame lineman, then hit Perry from the blind side, cracking his ribs. An irate Perry threw off his helmet and chased Connor around the field. But he couldn't catch the big Bear with his ribs hurting and Connor's teammates blocking his path. After the game, Perry waited for Connor in the tunnel between the two locker rooms. But Chicago team officials wisely escorted Connor to safety in another direction.

It would be two years before Perry wreaked revenge on Connor, and then Perry sacrificed a touchdown to make his point. He hit a trap play inside, and there was only Connor blocking his path to the end zone. Perry only had to outfeint Connor, and it was an easy six points. Instead, Perry leveled him in a forceful collision. Perry staggered ahead for another six yards before another Bear dragged him down. But Perry had gotten even, and he would have no further difficulty with Connor.

Fullback or halfback, was any back faster than the young Joe Perry?

"Maybe Buddy Young," Perry replied. "We were supposed to have a match race over forty, fifty yards, but it didn't come off."

Young was an NCAA sprint champion at Illinois. He stood five-six, but weighed 190 pounds. "He looked like a rubber ball running," said one opponent.

"Where my speed helped me the most," said Perry, "was knowing where my help was coming from. If you're running a sweep, the safety's got an angle on you. But if I could sense a blocker coming across, I could use my speed to angle the safety into the blocker. My favorite play wasn't the wide pitch, which most people think. I really liked the 30-F or 31-F trap, because I'd have five yards before you blinked an eye."

Was Perry simply too fast for defenders, who were mostly white fifty years ago?

"I wasn't really that fast when, 90 percent of the time, my plays were run through the middle of the line, where the safeties are going to get you," he said. "On one trap against Chicago, I ran over both safeties on a fifty-yard run. But after five, six years in the NFL, the players got faster in general. Blacks or whites, it didn't matter. Some guys can run, some can't. Jack Christiansen could fly. Yale Lary could move."

Christiansen and Yary, two white Detroit defensive backs, are in the Pro Football Hall of Fame with Perry. These three had some great battles. The 49ers split with the Lions in 1950, but the 49ers won only two more games to finish their first NFL season a disappointing 3-9.

Philadelphia coach Earle "Greasy" Neale wasn't especially kind after the Eagles waxed the 49ers, 28-10.

"Frankie Albert is a wonderful faker, but he's not the passer some of the other boys are," said Neale. "And you've got to have big men in there to handle what they throw at you in this league."

Neale knocked the 49ers' offense and defense in the same paragraph. He wasn't the team's only critic. After the 49ers lost their first NFL game, 31-14, to the Washington Redskins, *San Francisco Chronicle* sports editor Bill Leiser sat at his typewriter and wrote what amounted to an obituary.

"Frankly, they did not look capable of beating any team in the National Football League," Leiser typed.

It would be a season of hard knocks for the 49ers. Perry amassed 647 rushing yards (5.2) that fall, fifth best in the NFL. He had five touchdowns on the ground and another on a reception. He rushed for 142 yards against Baltimore and 105 yards on nine carries against Green Bay, including a seventy-yard touchdown burst. Perry ranged from seven to eighteen carries a game as the 49ers were throwing the ball more often.

"The offensive complexion changed," Perry recalled. "We went to short passes."

Without much success. Albert had thrown an astonishing fifty-six touchdown passes his last two years in the AAFC, but only fourteen scoring strikes compared to twenty-three interceptions in his NFL debut.

"Frank was short, and the linemen kept getting bigger. He couldn't see over them. He was like [Jeff] Garcia," Perry said of the current 49ers quarterback. "And Frank couldn't throw a pass fifty yards, which Y. A. could."

San Francisco drafted Tittle in 1951 from the original Baltimore Colts franchise, which folded after a brief NFL run. The 49ers had assembled their receiving corps of the future in Gordy Soltau and rookie Billy Wilson.

"Not many people know this," Soltau said, "but The Jet was The King before Mac came. Albert named both of them The King. When Mac came on the scene, we had two Kings. Albert first called Mac The Little King."

The Little King was the name of a comic page character of the time. McElhenny would grow in stature, along with his nickname, midway through his rookie year. But Perry did carry himself with an air of royalty.

"Joe kind of practiced when he wanted to practice," said Soltau. "He had a personality all his own. He worked like a demon in practice, taking every carry fifty yards. But it would be Wednesday or Thursday before he'd practice. Joe did have bad knees, but nobody ever said anything to him. Buck Shaw left him alone. So Albert named Joe The King."

Perry was fifth once more in NFL rushing in 1951 with 677 yards (5.0). He had 115 yards against the Rams, with a fifty-eight-yard touchdown run, and 126 yards against Detroit on 22 carries. In no other game did he have more than sixteen attempts. Showing versatility, he threw a thirty-one-yard touchdown pass to Wilson that led to a 21–17 win over Detroit in their second meeting. The 49ers won their last three games to end up 7–4–1.

"About that time," Perry said, "they got into Buck's sushi about not winning enough."

And Shaw didn't even eat sushi.

The following year, 1952, signified change. Standlee was stricken with polio and forced to give up football. Strzykalski retired after seeing the light, a sensational rookie named McElhenny.

Perry rushed for 725 yards (4.6) that season, No. 3 in the NFL. Having McElhenny there lessened the pressure of being the only featured back, but Perry was twenty-five and entering his prime. He scored eight touchdowns. His best rushing outputs were eighty and eighty-six yards against Detroit, and 109 yards against Green Bay. He carried the ball twenty times twice as the team's workhorse.

Perry's worst game that season came against the New York Giants at the Polo Grounds. He rushed five times for only six yards, but had a valid excuse: a broken toe.

"The toe was black and blue," Soltau recalled. "We're getting dressed before the game. Joe's just sitting there in his street clothes. When Albert asked him if he's getting dressed, Joe said, 'I can't play.' Frankie said, 'Joe, we're playing New York. We need you.' Joe then got quite a few shots of Novocain and went out there and played on sheer ability."

Perry was named honorable mention All-NFL for the third straight year in 1952, a depressing season for the 49ers. After winning their first five games, they limped home 7-5. Pressure was mounting on Shaw, who had only one losing season in seven years as 49ers coach, but hadn't yet produced a championship. And all because he lacked a championship defense.

In 1953, Perry emerged as a superstar, a term that hadn't yet been invented, but certainly was applicable in his case. He began the season with a 145-yard output against Philadelphia. Before the schedule was halfway done, he rushed for 113 yards against the Bears. One week later, he amassed 148 yards against Detroit on a career-high twenty-six carries.

That was Perry's high-water mark of the season for attempts, but the yards kept on coming, 153 against Green Bay on sixteen carries, 108 against Baltimore on seventeen tries. There were plenty of big runs, forty yards against the Eagles, fifty and thirty-one yards against the Rams, forty-seven against the Packers, forty against the Colts, a fifty-one-yard touchdown romp through the Bears' safeties.

When it was all over, Perry had led the league with 1,018 yards rushing (5.3) and ten scores, while adding three touchdown catches, including a sixty-yarder from Tittle against the Rams. Delighted with Perry's year, Tony Morabito gave the fullback a bonus check of $5,090, $5 for every rushing yard. Perry was named first-team All-NFL.

The 49ers finished 9-3, building optimism for 1954 when John Henry Johnson joined Perry, McElhenny, and Tittle in a backfield for all time. But the 49ers slipped to 7-4-1 that year as injuries played a factor. Tittle broke his hand. McElhenny separated a shoulder and missed half the season.

Perry was even more productive in 1954. He led the NFL for the second straight year with 1,049 rushing yards (6.1) and ten touchdowns. He never carried the ball more than twenty-three times, but he had rushing outputs of 137, 124, 122, 119, 100 and eighty-six yards, plus long runs of fifty-eight, fifty-six and fifty-one yards (twice).

"Because Joe was lightning out of his stance," said St. Clair, "one of the toughest blocks I had to make was a trap play. That's where I sneaked through to block the middle linebacker. If I didn't get there quick, I mean really fly, Joe would run over me. People don't realize how fast he was, or how tough he was. When he'd get going, he didn't care who was in his way. He'd hit whoever was in front of him."

Perry had another hidden talent. At the start of the 1954 season, he was the 49ers placekicker. He kicked five points after touchdown in the opener, a 41-7 victory over Washington. The next week, he added another PAT and a fourteen-yard field goal in a 24-24 tie against the Rams. Soltau kicked two PATs in that Rams game after having been sidelined six weeks because of a fractured shoulder received in an exhibition against the Giants. The week after his return, Soltau was re-established as the 49ers placekicker. Perry wasn't ever asked to kick again.

"I could kick the ball over the end zone on kickoffs almost every time," he said. "Because I had a strong leg, the coaches wanted me to kick. I did it for a while, but I told them I was too tired from running the ball to also have to kick. They finally listened to me."

Fed up with winning records but no titles, Morabito fired Shaw after the 1954 season. Shaw would prove in time that it wasn't his fault, but the franchise's. He would win an NFL title with the Philadelphia Eagles in 1960 before promptly retiring. It wasn't until twenty-seven years after Shaw's dismissal in 1954 that the 49ers won their first league championship.

Perry's second thousand-yard season was even more remarkable than the first, given the fact that his backfield company included three other eventual Hall of Famers, plus a productive aerial game. Wilson led the NFL that year with sixty receptions.

"Y. A. and I loved him for this, tried to equally divide the football," said Perry. "After a game, it would be a variation of two carries among the three backs."

Perry wouldn't ever carry the football more than he did in 1953 and 1954, even though he averaged only 16.0 and 14.5 carries those two seasons.

"I really have no idea why I didn't carry the ball more," he said. "The more you carry the ball, the more you want it. I could have had better years if I had been featured more. Comparing careers, Jim Brown carried the ball 400 times more than I did. If I had as many carries as Brown, how many more yards would I have had?"

Entering the 2000 season, Perry ranked thirteenth all-time with 9,723 rushing yards, including his AAFC and NFL statistics. However, it should be noted, he has the fewest carries (1,929) of any running back in the top twenty. And Perry's career average of 5.0 yards per carry puts him in a second-place tie with Barry Sanders behind Jim Brown (5.2).

"I wasn't competing with Brown," Perry said. "I was only worried about Joe Perry. But if McElhenny, John Henry [Johnson] and I had played behind those big [300-pound] asses in Dallas that Emmitt Smith runs behind, you'd have no idea what we would have done. We ran behind guys who weighed 220, 230."

If not for McElhenny's season-ending injury, the three 49ers backs might have finished 1-2-3 in NFL rushing, though it's not certain in what order. That would have been a league first, three backs from one team. As it turned out, Johnson was second to Perry with 681 yards rushing, while adding nine touchdowns.

"John Henry was...John Henry," said Perry. "Knees, elbows, slashing, cutting—a wild, runaway bull. He'd throw his big [knee] brace into you. He was mean carrying the ball. It all accomplished the same thing. Mac was ballerina movement. Y. A. was tough. He wanted to win."

The 49ers' direction turned south, and sour, under Shaw's successor, Norman "Red" Strader. He enforced discipline on the players, where as Shaw had coached with all the authority of a kindly uncle.

On a Sunday, August 28, 1955, Tony Morabito honored greatness. He held Joe Perry Day at Kezar Stadium before the 49ers met their old nemesis, the Cleveland Browns, in a preseason game. Special days for athletes, when they are honored before the home fans, occur only occasionally. But for black athletes when Perry played in the 1950s, special days were nonexistent. Perry was the first black pro football player to be saluted in such a fashion.

"I was a favorite son," he said. "They named some street after me in San Francisco, I think near Kezar Stadium. It was a great day on Joe Perry Day. I got TV sets and a lot of stuff for the house. People said I got a car because there was a Pontiac sitting on the field. But I worked for Boas Pontiac, which put the car out there.

"I had just bought a home in the Excelsior district, so the TV sets and furniture were needed. I could have had a house in St. Francis Woods, a beautiful and exclusive area in San Francisco, without any problem. I would have been the first black to move in there. They already had welcomed me with open arms. But I didn't want to be isolated, out on an island by myself. So we moved to the Excelsior, where there was a mixture of people.

"I had done that once before, you know, being the first black to move into an area. That was in Palo Alto when I was living by myself, so I was never home. But as I've said to you, I never look at color. I just thought Joe Perry Day was one of the great honors of my life. What made it even greater was my mom got to witness it. She was really proud. I can still see her beaming."

Perry's popularity wasn't ever greater than during the mid–1950s. He was given his own radio show, five days a week, 4 to 6 p.m., on station KLX in Oakland. He spun records and interviewed famous celebrities such as singer Dinah Washington.

"She said, 'What are you doing?'" Perry recalled. "I said, 'I'm playing football.' She said, 'You don't have to do that.' She seduced me on the air, so I put a record on. She was going with [defensive back Dick] 'Night Train' Lane at the time, but she wanted to marry me. I could have had any woman I wanted. But that wasn't what I wanted. I wanted to better this."

He tapped his skull.

"I still wanted to be an engineer," he said. "I loved math. I loved working out equations."

Perry didn't become an engineer, but he worked out the necessary angles with females. He fathered five children, two out of wedlock.

If not for football, Perry might have been the Tiger Woods of bowling. Perry maintained a 190 average on the lanes. He had so many interests, and a wonderful presence. He dressed well, he had a million-dollar smile, and he drove a new car. He could discuss Duke Ellington or decimals with ease. No wonder the ladies found him irresistible, including all three of his wives.

"Did Joe tell you about how he had to dress?" Donna asked a houseguest.

"No."

"Whenever you saw me in public," Perry said, "I wore a coat and tie."

"Even in the hot summer?" the guest wondered. "Whose idea was that?"

"Just me," Joe replied.

"It was because Joe was black," said Donna, looking at her husband. "Tony [Morabito] wanted him to look nice at all times."

"He wanted me to set an image," Joe agreed. "He had two daughters. I was the son he never had. I still wear a tie even today."

"And it's not done down here," Donna said of the Arizona social scene.

"I only do it on special occasions," Joe pointed out.

Morabito's plan in 1955 was for Strader to bring San Francisco its anticipated first professional sports championship. That plan backfired like an antique car with a faulty exhaust system. Although the 49ers beat a strong Detroit team twice, their record that autumn under Strader was 4–8. Forty-Niner fans had high hopes, too, which explains why the team set a single-season attendance record in 1955.

Perry missed only his second game in eight years. A sprained knee sidelined him against Baltimore in the season finale. He rushed for 701 yards (4.5) in '55, but had only one 100-yard game, 149 against Detroit. His longest run was forty-two yards. He had a career-low two touchdowns rushing. San Francisco lost five consecutive games at one point that season. The constant frustration of frequent highs and lows in the 1950s made Perry rethink his decision from 1954 when he rejected a lucrative Canadian Football League offer from the British Columbia Lions to remain a 49er.

"Obviously, Canada recognized me as an excellent football player," he said. "But, in the end, there was no way I was going to leave Tony. When he asked me about Canada, I told him about it. He looked at me and said, 'I'll see you later.' As long as Tony was breathing, I wasn't going to leave him."

A perplexed Morabito then dumped Strader for the people's choice, Albert, who was an immensely popular figure in the San Francisco Bay Area, and one of the greatest ball-handling magicians ever to play quarterback.

"Frankie was fun to play for," said Perry. "He told me that if I didn't take him out with me after games, he'd fine me."

And there was nothing finer than to be a 49er, in Perry's mind.

"I always felt I was a 49er," he said. "Even after playing in Baltimore, I went into the Pro Football Hall of Fame as a 49er, not a Colt."

The 49ers made slight progress in 1956, Albert's debut as a head coach. The players relaxed under his casual, carefree style. Maybe they relaxed too much as the 49ers lost six of their first seven games. Then, facing a less-demanding schedule down the stretch, they produced four wins and a tie to wind up 5-6-1, thereby saving Albert's job.

Perry rushed for 520 yards, his lowest output as a pro, although he once again averaged 4.5 per carry. He didn't have a single hundred-yard game. His best effort was eighty-nine yards against the Packers. His longest run was thirty-nine yards. Nearing his thirtieth birthday, he felt he hadn't slowed down, but rather that McElhenny was the story in 1956 with a career-best 916 yards. John Henry Johnson left after that season, his third with the 49ers. He headed off to Detroit in a trade.

In 1957, although the neglected 49ers defense surrendered nearly twenty-five points a game, the offense was up to the task most Sundays. But during a five-game win streak, tragedy struck on October 27. Tony Morabito died of a heart attack during a game against the Chicago Bears. The 49er players were told of his death at halftime, when they trailed, 17-7.

"Just about halftime, we saw the medics going up to the press box," Perry remembered. "We knew it was Tony because he had had heart problems. It ran in the family. I hadn't played much that day. I told Frankie at halftime I wanted to go in because of Tony."

Perry didn't have a great game, statistically, with four rushes for eleven yards. No other 49er had glittering numbers that day, but the team, through grit and will, held the Bears scoreless in the second half and clawed back to win, 21-17.

"I was playing in the game and crying at the same time," Perry said. "From the time we first met, Tony and I were like father and son, and it was like losing my father."

Perry wasn't the only 49er in tears. Leo "The Lion" Nomellini, a professional wrestler in the offseason, bawled like a baby while man-handling Chicago's running game at the same time.

Vic Morabito, Tony's younger brother, assumed control of the team. The 49ers won their next game over Detroit, 35-31, then lost three straight in November. They emerged from that brief tailspin with three consecutive victories to finish in an 8-4 dead heat with the Lions for the Western Conference title. A tiebreaker game was set up, and it would be played in San Francisco. The 49ers were pumped up thinking about home-field advantage and their first-ever championship. And they built a 27-7 lead early in the third quarter before the unthinkable happened. The Lions roared back for a 31-27 win that drained the life out of the 49ers organization for the next thirteen years, or until a Dick Nolan-coached team finally made it to the playoffs.

Perry's numbers decreased further in 1957 as the 49ers unveiled something called the Alley-Oop pass. Perry rushed for only 454 yards, though averaging a sparkling 4.7 yards per carry. This proved his legs still were good. After a snail-like start, he came on with eighty-four yards against the New York Giants and 130 yards against Green Bay.

"Joe was the toughest running back you'd ever want to see," said 49er teammate R.C. Owens. "He didn't back off from anybody."

Perry's longest run in 1957 matched his number. Thirty-four yards. In the conference decider, he carried thirteen times for fifty-two yards (4.0), with a long run of twelve yards. Another fullback, Detroit's Tom Tracy, stole the show that day.

Albert lasted one more season as head coach, a 6-6 comedown in 1958 that led to his unforced resignation. The 49ers offense was again effective, but the defense gave up a franchise-record 324 points, or 27.0 per game. And Albert's only defense once fans began insulting his wife at the supermarket was to get out.

Perry led the team in rushing for the first time in three years with 758 yards, including a blast from the past, a seventy-three-yard touchdown run during a career-high 174-yard effort against Detroit on just thirteen carries (13.4 average). So the bloom wasn't yet off the rose. Entering the 2000 season, Perry's day against the Lions remains the seventh-best rushing day in 49er history. Perry finished third in NFL rushing in 1958 behind Jim Brown (1,527) and Baltimore's Alan Ameche (791). Perry's 6.1 yards per carry topped all league rushers. And in a 56-7 blowout loss to the Rams, Perry had the 49ers only touchdown on a sixty-four-yard pass from Tittle.

"Joe was the most durable person I've ever been around," said former 49er quarterback John Brodie. "He was always ready to play. And he was so fast into the hole that, if Joe wanted to, no quarterback could have gotten the ball to him."

Perry was Jesse Owens as a fullback.

Brodie didn't become Perry's teammate until 1957. One year later, at thirty-one, The Jet still felt he had the same after-burners. Unbeknownst to him, new 49er coach Howard "Red" Hickey felt just the opposite. Perry already had grown old in Hickey's eyes, and Perry's days as a featured back in San Francisco were over. Hickey was ready to anoint a younger J. D. Smith as the 49ers' ground-game savior. Smith had spent three seasons as Perry's apprentice, even filling in on defense while awaiting his turn on offense. And when the time came, in 1959, Smith exploded for 1,036 rushing yards and ten touchdowns.

Perry wasn't exactly chopped liver himself that year, rushing for 602 yards. Smith averaged 5.0 yards per carry to Perry's 4.4 yards. When the season began, they were used evenly. In the opener against Philadelphia, Perry had seventeen carries for seventy-six yards, Smith seventeen for seventy-five. The next week against the Rams, Perry had nineteen attempts for eighty-two yards, Smith nineteen for 103. Two weeks later, they unloaded on Detroit together, Perry fourteen carries for 147 yards, Smith twenty-three for 152. Perry followed up with a pair of seventy-nine-yard rushing efforts against the Bears and Lions. Then Hickey stopped playing him.

At thirty-two, Perry might as well have been using a walker as far as Hickey was concerned. He was plotting how to ease Perry and other aging 49ers out of the organization.

"Playing for Red Hickey was the worst time of my career," said Perry. "I told Vic Morabito to get me out of there or I'd kill his coach if he said two words to me. At a team meeting, Hickey called us 'pussies.' I got up and left. He said, 'Perry, where are you going? I'm not done yet.' I said, 'Those things you're saying to the players, you're not talking to me.' And I walked out.

"I wasn't the only one who hated him. He was trying to create his own image, like Joe Thomas would do with the 49ers in the 1970s, when he was hated by everyone just as much as Hickey."

Perry knew what Hickey was thinking without his saying it.

"He was cleaning house with all us older guys." Perry said. "The newspapers wrote, 'Poor Joe Perry, he's training J. D. Smith to take his job.' And I said, 'Surrrre I am.'"

Perry lasted one more year in San Francisco, 1960, when Hickey treated him with all the respect of a third-string free agent. Perry rushed for ninety-five yards. For the season! He carried thirty-six times, two weeks' work ordinarily, for a 2.6 average. He wasn't hurt, and he didn't feel all that old, but his name already had been placed in the team's alumni file.

Smith was the main man. But Perry needed a chance to play, somewhere. To his chagrin, Perry discovered he wasn't hot property around the NFL. He was traded, finally, to Baltimore before the 1961 season in a transaction that cost the Colts nothing because the deal was crafted on a "performance specification basis." This meant the Colts didn't have to give up an undisclosed draft pick to the 49ers unless Perry achieved certain agreed-upon statistics.

Whatever those statistics were, he didn't reach them. That's not to say he didn't have a productive year. He rushed for 675 yards (4.0) and caught a career-high thirty-four passes, Running and catching, Perry came within three yards of a thousand-yard season.

"He still had something left," said John Steadman, the *Baltimore Sun* columnist who has covered three pro football franchises in

Baltimore, including two different Colts teams, since 1949. "His heart was in San Francisco, but he had some great games for the Colts. When I think of Joe Perry, I think of someone who hit the hole like lightning, an undersized fullback who could change directions, was exciting to watch, and who could vault for yardage. Just a tremendous athlete."

At thirty-four, Perry showed Hickey, firsthand, that he was more racehorse than plowhorse. Facing the 49ers for the first time, he rushed for twenty-nine yards (4.1) and caught four passes for forty-eight yards as the Colts won, 20-17. Johnny Unitas was the Colts quarterback.

"Joe's the kind of guy you'd love to play your whole career with," said Unitas. "He always scratched and clawed for every yard. He was amazing on the screen pass, like McElhenny. Every time Joe carried the ball in practice, he'd go the whole field. He spurred Lenny Moore to do the same thing. Lenny used to go four, five yards and turn around. Joe embarrassed him into running all the way to the end zone. Joe was older when we got him, but he did well with us. He was a good blocker. We had good players, and we ran screens and draw plays that helped him."

Perry was taught by Strzykalski as a 49er rookie that every carry must be taken the distance. "It was the 49er way," Perry said.

Perry enjoyed playing for Colts coach Weeb Ewbank. The Jet's second season in Baltimore, 1962, though, marked the beginning of the end. He rushed for 359 yards (3.8) and caught passes for 194 yards. Fifty-six of those yards came against the 49ers in two games. Ewbank felt he had younger backs capable of the same production.

Perry still was amazing in one sense. He tore knee ligaments in a preseason game against Washington on August 17, after which the Colts asked waivers on him. There were no takers. Remarkably, Perry healed fast enough to open the season, still property of the Colts. At that juncture, he was pro football's all-time career rusher, though not for much longer. Jim Brown was about to come barreling past.

Would Ewbank bring back Perry for a third year? It became a moot point when Ewbanks was fired and replaced by a thirty-three-year-old, jut-jawed assistant coach from Detroit, Don Shula, a former Colts defensive back.

"I didn't care for the man," Perry said of Shula. "When I met him, he kept his eyes on the ground. He couldn't look at me. So I didn't have any use for the man."

Maybe Shula couldn't look Perry in the eye because he was younger than Perry, and also about to release him, which occurred during the summer of 1963. Their parting wasn't any more harmonious than their first meeting.

"When he called me in to cut me," Perry said, "I told him, 'OK.' I turned to leave, and he said, 'Wait a minute. Don't you want to talk?' I looked at him and said, 'Nope. I'm being cut. What's there to talk about?'

"All I knew was they were keeping a fullback from Wyoming, Jerry Hill. I could run backwards and beat him in the forty-yard dash."

Perry was thirty-six. Who would want him? Two teams, it turned out.

Vic Morabito called Perry and asked him to come home and retire as a 49er. The only problem for Perry, Hickey still was the coach. Pittsburgh owner Art Rooney also phoned Perry with an offer to come join the Steelers and team up again with John Henry Johnson.

"The biggest mistake I made in football was not going to Pittsburgh," said Perry. "I wasn't ever out of shape, and I still could run."

Perry's loyalty to the Morabito family was too powerful a pull, though. He returned to San Francisco. Vic Morabito assured him there would be no problems with Hickey, who had no choice but to keep him. Morabito had a plan. Perry would rejoin the 49ers on an inactive basis, then be activated for three games in order to qualify for the NFL pension plan. But any potential hassle with Hickey ended after the third game when he resigned under pressure. Forty-Niners assistant

Jack Christiansen, Detroit's great defensive back, replaced Hickey, but the 49ers continued to stumble.

Perry ended his career with a 4.1 rushing average on a team that finished 2-12. He had twenty-four carries for ninety-eight yards during his swan song; a season's productivity that would have been a day's work in his prime.

Perry's final game was against Vince Lombardi's formidable Green Bay Packers. The Jet had some fuel left, rushing ten times for forty-seven yards (4.7), and getting off a sixteen-yard run. Perry threw an incompletion on his last pass attempt. He wasn't called upon to kick. The 49ers lost, 21-17.

Twenty-seven years later, Pat Summerall, *FOX-TV's* No. 1 NFL play-by-play man, was asked how Perry would fare in today's game.

"He was so quick off the ball, so quick into the secondary, that I'd have him at tailback," Summerall said. "He'd be like the guy in Green Bay, Dorsey Levens."

After his playing days, Perry worked full-time for a wine distributor. He returned to the 49ers in 1968 as a special teams coach. But he didn't see eye-to-eye with Nolan, the head coach. Perry was re-assigned as a scout.

Twenty years after Perry had begun his professional career, Jim Crow still was around to confront him, this time working in a car rental agency.

"At the New Orleans airport, I rented a car to drive to Shreveport to scout a game," said Perry. "I had my wallet out, searching for my credit card, when the rental guy said, 'Here, boy, I'll find it.'"

Joe Perry was not a man to call a boy, especially when he interpreted the rental person to be talking down to him in a racist manner.

"If you touch my wallet, I'll break your neck," Perry told him flatly. "My wife doesn't go through my wallet. Who do you think you are?"

About that time, a security guard showed up. He put his hand on his pistol. Perry wasn't frightened. Not in the least.

When you've been on the bottom of a pile with hands reaching for your face and groin, when you've had your teeth knocked out, when your ribs have been broken after the play was over, actions that all might have been racially motivated, what is there to be scared about?

Perry looked the guard directly in the face.

"I told him, 'I'll break your neck before you get that thing out,'" Perry said. "He took me for my word."

Perry severed working ties with the 49ers in 1974. He continued to sell wine until San Francisco's climate began to chill his arthritic bones. So he moved to balmy Arizona, where he now lives in retirement at seventy-three.

Young man, older man, Perry still has the same M.O. when he feels victimized. The 49ers list him as their all-time rusher, but only with 7,344 yards, excluding his three AAFC seasons, when the NFL recognizes his career rushing total of 9,723 yards. That's a difference of 2,379 yards, and the slight annoyed Perry to the point that he wrote the 49ers in January 2000 to register his complaint.

"If years prior to the NFL are not to be included in club records," he said, "then why are records held by the American Football League included in NFL statistics? And why are the achievements of former 49ers who played prior to 1950 omitted?

"Some people have stated that those years 'don't count.' Don't count? To whom? Are you telling me Anthony J. Morabito didn't exist? Are you saying 1946-1947-1948-1949 never transpired? Or are you saying in the AAFC, we didn't play pro football? Perhaps only football was played in the American and National Football League? The Pro Football Hall of Fame includes records and statistics from year one in football. Why cannot a professional football team today do the same, at least for consistency's sake? What is, is. I leave you with these puzzling thoughts. If anyone is able to draw a reasonable conclusion, I would be very happy to hear your comments."

Still athletic for his years, Perry works out every day he can at a health club. And he's as mentally sharp about the game of football as ever.

His favorite running back of recent vintage?

"Barry Sanders," he said. "It's his elusiveness, his speed, and his power when he needs it. He runs with his head. Most runners today run with their feet. They just run. Running with your head, you see where you're going. Running with your feet, you're running straight ahead. Open your eyes. That's why you have them. You see [49ers back Charlie] Garner run with his eyes."

Perry grabbed the remote control. He switched on the 49ers-Carolina Panthers game about to start in Charlotte, North Carolina, in December 1999. Perry assigned himself the role of unpaid commentator in his own living room, although he was about to out-think, and out-anticipate, the announcers in the television booth at Ericsson Stadium.

"See there, watch Garner, how he uses his eyes...first down," said Perry, making the first-down call before Garner darted by the yard-marker.

"Now they're going to throw to [Jerry] Rice," Perry predicted.

Garcia dropped back and lofted a forty-eight-yard touchdown pass to Rice.

The houseguest studied Perry with amazement.

"And see what he did?" said Perry, motioning to the TV screen. "[Rice] threw the ball away. No dancing, which is stupid. What does it gain? What does it get you? I remember when I played. I scored and just put the ball down or threw it to an official. Then I got the hell off the field. All that dancing or gyrations, what are you trying to prove, that I'm a better dancer than you? A better clown? I never understood spiking the ball. When did dancing and spiking become part of football?"

The dancing, probably with Billy "White Shoes" Johnson. The spiking, definitely with Elmo Wright.

"They could get rid of that in a minute by fining them," Perry said.

The houseguest asked Perry what if he were twenty-five again, would he dance and gyrate like the others after scoring a touchdown?

"With my upbringing, no," he said. "Maybe I'm old-fashioned, but I never talked trash back then. I'd say, 'nice hit.' Or I'd reach down and pick up an opponent."

He shifted his attention back to the 49ers-Panthers game.

"[Carolina coach George] Seifert is going to eat them alive," Perry said of the 49ers, Seifert's former team before he resigned in 1996 with the highest winning percentage in NFL coaching history. "He got a raw deal."

It's third-and-15, 49ers with the ball.

"They can't run," Perry said. "They're going to throw to Terrell Owens."

Garcia hits Owens for a first down.

Perry is uncanny.

The 49ers face another third-down situation, six yards shy.

"They're going to throw to...Jerry," Perry hesitated.

Garcia throws instead to fullback Fred Beasley, who just gets the required yardage before he is upended.

Perry is human, after all.

"Look at [Beasley] fall," Perry said with disgust.

Two plays later, it's yet another third-down call, three yards from the marker.

"[Garcia] will never make it unless he throws the ball," said Perry.

First down pass to tight end Greg Clark.

The 49ers continue to move in small increments. It's third and one.

"Don't call [a play to] Beasley," Perry ordered the 49ers from his sofa.

Beasley blasted through a hole and didn't stop running until he crossed the goal line forty-four yards away.

The old fullback smirked. Can't get 'em all right.

"I'm glad you didn't dance in the end zone, sucker," Perry said to Beasley, who was 2,500 miles away.

The 49ers looked as pathetic as the last 49er team Perry played on in 1963. The Panthers began to put points and yards between themselves and San Francisco. Perry was accurate in his prediction. The 49ers were getting eaten up. Perry lost interest in this game. He turned to make a point to his guest about relationships.

"All my good friends in football were Southerners," he said. "You wouldn't figure it, would you? Bobby Layne, we were great friends. The first time we met, we were magnetized. Ray Collins, Y. A. Tittle, Jim Cason...all good friends. Chips Norris from my military football team is a good friend. There also was this guy named Steamboat, another Navy guy. He was from Las Vegas and he didn't like black guys. You could tell by the way he talked. He didn't use slurs around me, but I knew he felt that way."

Perry clicked off the 49ers–Panthers game. He had seen enough.

"I got along with everyone there, even Steamboat eventually," he said. "I get along with people in general. I've had people change their opinions of me all my life. If we can get beyond the differences of color and look inside a person to just see what's inside him, what a person is made of, if he's a real person or a phony, then we can really tell about people."

Joe Perry can tell.

"I kind of feel people out as individuals," he said. "That's how I am about all people. There's a meaning about everything you say and do to me. If a person can't look me in the eye when talking to me, I don't want anything to do with him. I'm not a bitter person. I'm nice, but I'm not naive. If you're straight with me, I'm straight with you."

Nobody is straighter.

"It has nothing to do with color," Perry said. "If one guy's got kinky hair, one guy's got straight hair, what difference does it make, if we all get along in this world? We're all in this together. The sooner we realize that, the better off we're going to be as Americans."

HUGH McELHENNY
THE KING

Progress doesn't always mean things have gotten better.

American automobiles are built more flimsily now than a half-century ago, when you got more candy for a nickel than you get today for sixty-five cents.

Marriages were more stable a half-century ago. So was family life. But *Happy Days* has lapsed into drugs, violence, and hate crimes. Richie and The Fonz would be in rehab together in today's society.

Values were so different fifty years ago. Likewise music. The ballad singer is gone, except for Tony Bennett, who is in his seventies. Kids prefer rap, which isn't music because it can't be danced to, not cheek to cheek.

Fresh-squeezed lemonade has disappeared from drugstores, and that's because the drugstore soda fountain is all but extinct, like the California condor. Anyway, it all fits, because what once was fresh now is processed.

So if this is, indeed, progress, where's the improvement?

The world of sport isn't necessarily all that progressive either, in ability or attitude. Athletes today view themselves as actors in front of the camera, dancing, flaunting, taunting. Sportsmanship has regressed, not progressed. Tact has given way to tattoos. Sports heroes now wear earrings in the heat of battle.

It has been drummed into us that athletes nowadays are bigger, faster, stronger, though not necessarily better. Study running backs in the National Football League. They've become clones of one another, motoring straight ahead. Big backs, small backs, they have no concept of the cutback run or how to reverse directions, drop a shoulder, give the limp leg to avoid tacklers. Only Charlie Garner and Barry Sanders of recent vintage have kept alive a lost art, the broken-field run of a half-century ago.

Back when The King was the absolute master in the open field.

The King. Hugh McElhenny.

"Mac was the most riveting player I ever saw," said John Brodie, a onetime teammate of McElhenny's and a seventeen-year NFL quarterback. "He was always Jack Armstrong as far as I'm concerned."

Push the VCR into the slot. After a slight pause, the broken-field magic of McElhenny appears on flickering black-and-white film. It was 1952 when McElhenny first freed himself from a variety of inescapable NFL situations, immediately becoming the undisputed Houdini of halfbacks.

Now here he is again, in highlight form, wearing the uniform of the San Francisco 49ers. He catches a swing pass behind the line of scrimmage and is immediately closed off by four Los Angeles Rams. No sweat. He jukes one Ram, shrugs free from a second, straightarms a third, jumps over a fourth, and takes off down the sideline. He bursts through two more Rams before he is shoved out of bounds, exhausted, seventy-one yards later at the 9-yard line, setting up a game-winning 49er field goal.

The scene shifts, and now it's an aging McElhenny with white horns on his helmet, playing for the expansion Minnesota Vikings against his old team, the 49ers. Quarterback Fran Tarkenton drops back from the 49ers' 32 as if to pass. But it's the Statue of Liberty play, another relic from the past. McElhenny wheels from his halfback spot, takes the ball from Tarkenton and avoids a hand swipe from tackle Leo Nomellini. McElhenny sweeps left, where he is pinned. He makes one of his indescribable cuts and begins weaving back to his right through a path of flailing arms. He gets to the end zone standing up, having run by nine 49ers, seven of whom actually laid flesh on him.

McElhenny was nearly thirty-three at the time, and hearing distant taps being played on his spectacular NFL career.

"It was the greatest run I ever saw," Norm Van Brocklin, McElhenny's coach in Minnesota, would say years later. "Whenever I think something's impossible, I put that film on the projector and watch it again."

Similar flattery has tagged other McElhenny runs. The VCR tape moves ahead. Six Chicago Bears trap The King on the sideline. Six! There is no escape route. No sweat. McElhenny twists his body into a variety of contortions. Improvising upon instinct, he eludes all six and turns what was almost an impossible predicament into yet another long gainer.

The highlight film continues. McElhenny is a 49er again, catching a pass downfield. He is knocked down and his helmet flies off. This is the early 1950s, when pro football rules specified a runner must be held down to be considered tackled. On this particular play, McElhenny's thick hair is uncovered. He resembles a helmetless player from the early 1900s. He jumps to his feet and, like a wild mustang with his mane blowing in the wind, sprints by a helpless defender for a touchdown.

Now it's a vignette of the young McElhenny, a rookie in 1952. The Bears punt to him near the goal line. He starts upfield, and his body reacts as if it's filled with jumping beans. He feints, he cuts, he jukes. Bears tacklers grope for him, but fail to touch him as his hips, knees, and legs play a samba on their best intentions He goes all the way, ninety-four yards.

The VCR offers further testimonials to his talent. A reversal of directions as he squirms, twists, lowers his shoulder to avoid a tackle. A dipsy-do as he gives a defender a leg to tackle, then cleverly pulls it away at the last second. A McElhenny straightarm, an ever-present weapon, shoots out to ward off a tackler as the highlight tape runs its course.

The film's critique so far? Here is a King among paupers.

"The closest thing I've seen to Mac, bobbing and weaving, was Barry Sanders," said 49ers' Hall of Fame tackle Bob St. Clair. "But Sanders ran straight ahead. He didn't zig-zag from one side of the field to the other like Mac. The 49er linemen learned to keep running because of that, because Mac would run sixty-five yards to make a thirty-yard gain. Other than Sanders, there is no one even close to Mac in the open field. Everyone else is a good back, with good moves. But Mac is No. 1."

Some pre-'59ers, those pro football players who played before 1959 and finally were rewarded with a pension plan by a once-reluctant NFL Players Association, must have had hip replacement surgery from trying to tackle the elusive McElhenny a half-century ago.

"It's all time and place, but I thought he was the most exciting runner I had ever seen," said former Cleveland Browns defensive end Paul Wiggin. "Then came Gale Sayers and others. McElhenny was a dancer. He was something. He was the man. He was on top of the world in the [San Francisco] Bay Area when I was attending Stanford. I saw him in a bowling alley once, and I was awed. There he was, The King."

Those who wore "I Like Ike" buttons in the 1950s and believed in hearth and home were mesmerized by The King's broken-field artistry. They also regarded him in a class by himself. But even his staunchest admirers still haven't figured out how he wiggled out of danger so frequently. With a football under his arm, McElhenny was harder to locate than Salman Rushdie. Ask those NFL greats who chased after McElhenny.

"Holy smokes! You didn't know where he was going," said Chuck Bednarik. "You had to reach for him, and he could cut on a dime."

Bednarik and McElhenny met every two, three years because the Philadelphia Eagles and 49ers were in different divisions. But that was enough exposure for Bednarik to rank McElhenny as the best open-field runner in history.

"I don't know anyone better in my era," said Bednarik, "and I don't see anyone as good today."

Ernie Stautner, the onetime Pittsburgh Steelers defensive lineman, later was a longtime line coach in Dallas. So he has seen many a talented Cowboys running back, including Calvin Hill, Duane Thomas, Tony Dorsett, and Emmitt Smith.

"McElhenny had great eyesight, great moves," said Stautner. "He was a special type of back who knew when to cut and when not to cut. It's tough to describe, believe me. Athletes are better now. The size of the game and the speed have changed. McElhenny wasn't the fastest guy, but he'd hit the hole. When it comes to running backs, everyone has their own style. It doesn't matter what the era is, if you've got it, you've got it."

And McElhenny had it, though his speed—he once was an outstanding hurdler—often gets overlooked because of his unpredictable moves.

"Hugh was a magnificent football player," said Joe Schmidt, the Detroit Lions linebacker. "He could run and make it look easy. He was loose, and had great acceleration and grace. You had to gang-tackle the guy right away. Once he broke the first tackle, you were in trouble."

McElhenny, seventy-one, is as fit in appearance as any senior-citizen Pro Football Hall of Fame enshrinee has a right to look. In 1999, he attempted with considerable difficulty to verbalize those same cuts and feints of his which used to leave others defenseless and speechless.

"I don't think a runner can tell you what happened," he said. "I don't know how I got into the end zone. The only time you think is getting the ball [from the quarterback] and running to a point. Then your legs take over."

McElhenny had big legs for a speed back. The uneducated fan wouldn't have guessed by looking at his powerfully built six-foot-one, 210-pound frame that he had been the California state high school champion in the high hurdles, low hurdles, and long jump. He also shared the national prep record in the high hurdles, and he set a state record in the lows.

McElhenny had the strength of a horse, the flight of a deer, the carriage of a peacock, and the instincts of a fox in an open field.

"I don't think you can explain it," The King said. "It's a gift. You don't teach a kid to be an open-field runner. I don't remember dodging people, but it's like something is coming down your back, and then you cut away. I really could sense someone on my butt."

McElhenny had a sixth sense mixed with something akin to peripheral vision. When a tackler approached from behind, and McElhenny needed to make the necessary move to get away, he made it instinctively. He ran with his eyes and his mind's eye. Thus he was able to see things without really seeing them. He only had to sense hands reaching for him, and before they could grab his uniform, he was gone.

"He knew where all the exits were," said Brodie. "And he had the most incredible balance of anyone I've seen."

However, it was in a crowd, circled by wagons, where McElhenny was different from all other runners of recent vintage except for Walter Payton, another true master of escape.

"The [seventy-one-yard] run against the Rams, that was hysteria," McElhenny said. "You just struggle. You don't want to get caught. It's fighting and scratching, like getting in a dogfight. It's kind of like reckless abandon.

"I used to say that I ran scared. What I meant by that was I had this fear of getting tackled. The embarrassment of getting caught. I just knew in my mind that I should move left or move right. But you don't think about it."

Not consciously. The great broken-field runner merely reacts, running from here to there and back again, all the time waiting for that one opening that will guide him through a maze of humans and possibly into the end zone.

"They used to say, 'McElhenny will run fifty yards to get ten,'" said The King, who was also known as Hurryin' Hugh.

But it's safe to say that no back was better than McElhenny in going sideways to create space straight ahead.

In thirteen NFL seasons between 1952 and 1964, he rushed for 5,281 yards and caught passes for another 3,247 yards. That's 8,528 total yards from scrimmage, although he likely ran another 4,000 yards to get those 8,528.

"I wasn't a very smart guy in school," McElhenny said. "But when you put the Xs and Os together, I didn't have to put them in my play-book. I seemed to know what everyone was supposed to do on a play. On a sweep right, I know the left tackle is coming across to help me. If a [lead] block is missed, I can cut back and pick up that tackle. You kind of know where everybody is, so you work your way towards them, and beyond."

Until Garrison Hearst's ninety-six-yard run in 1998, McElhenny had the three longest runs from scrimmage in 49er history—eighty-nine, eighty-six and eighty-two yards.

Until John Taylor's ninety-five-yard punt return in 1988, McElhenny held the 49ers record with that ninety-four-yard punt return against the Bears in 1952.

After that '52 season, McElhenny was voted All-Pro, NFL Rookie of the Year, and Sport Magazine's NFL Player of the Year. Rarely has an NFL rookie had a more sensational beginning. And McElhenny's punt return in Chicago during a 49ers' 40-16 victory was enough to elevate a prince into a King.

"As I remember it," said McElhenny, "Frankie Albert, our quarter-back, came into the locker room with the game ball. He said to Perry, 'Joe, you're still The Jet. But McElhenny, you're the king of the half-backs.' Then he tossed me the game ball."

The nickname stuck, appropriately. McElhenny is modest, in no way a self-promoter. But, occasionally, he has had to ask himself as others have asked him if he, The King, really has only pretenders to his throne.

"Through the '50s," he said, "I was probably one of the three best open-field runners along with Red Grange and Jim Thorpe. Grange ran all over the field. Thorpe was my size. It's probably conceited of me to put myself in their class..."

Not so in the mind of Ernie Nevers, Stanford's fullback in the 1920s who was voted the greatest football player of the first fifty years of the twentieth century, and who holds the NFL single-game scoring record of forty points. Nevers played against Grange, and he was very much aware of Thorpe.

"There have been running backs as big and fast as McElhenny," Nevers said in a 1970 interview, "but I've never seen another big back who had the elusiveness and the agility of McElhenny. I believe he could break through where, perhaps, Thorpe and Grange couldn't. McElhenny would have been a sensation in any era. The only guy who has come close to his speed, balance and elusiveness in recent years is Gale Sayers."

Greatness requires challengers to be truly appreciated. McElhenny and Sayers were two of a kind in the open field. But not even the electrifying Sayers escaped from as many harrowing situations as The King.

After considerable effort, McElhenny finally came up with a valid explanation of what might separate him from other great halfbacks.

"I could run straight and make a right- or left-angle cut without slowing down," he said. "Not many backs can do that. Maybe Sayers. You plant your foot and go left or right. That's why I had lots of ankle sprains."

But only one knee operation, in January 1963, when he was thirty-four. He retired in 1964 as one of only three NFL players at the time, along with Jim Brown and Ollie Matson, to have gained 10,000 all-purpose yards.

From 1954 through 1956, The King was surrounded by a regal court in San Francisco: quarterback Y. A. Tittle and running backs Perry and John Henry Johnson. Nearly a half-century later, McElhenny discussed his famed teammates as an art lover would assess a famous painting.

"The first thing was that God was good to all of us as far as physiques," he said. "Joe looked like he had bowling balls in his biceps,

thighs and calves. And he had unbelievable quickness. He wasn't a cut-
ter, but he had power and speed. You didn't have to make solid blocks
because he would be thirty yards downfield before anyone saw him.

"John Henry was a rawboned, big ol' tough street fighter. He was
extremely strong and did a lot of spinning when he ran. He'd get in
trouble and fight his way free."

Since Perry, McElhenny, and Johnson were all track athletes, who
was the fastest of the three?

"Both Joe and John Henry could go eighty yards with a football,"
McElhenny replied. "When we'd do sprints after practice, Joe would
beat us in the 50, but at the end of the 100, it was me and John Henry."

McElhenny's memory, though, is challenged by 49er teammates,
who don't remember the three backs ever squaring off.

"Y. A.'s just a natural leader," McElhenny continued. "Maybe that
came because he's extremely competitive. We'd play hearts, and he'd
cheat to win. You have to know what's going on to be a quarterback.
Y. A. also was one accurate thrower. It would be hard to find on film a
wobble in any of his throws. He also was a tough runner, a tough guy.
He's an athlete."

McElhenny downplayed his contribution to the Million
Dollar Backfield.

"When we got [close] to the end zone, Joe Perry was the man,"
he said. "I wasn't a tough runner like Joe and John Henry. And I was a
lousy blocker, though I got better as I got older."

Unlike Perry and Johnson, McElhenny never rushed for 1,000 yards.

"Everyone is measured by statistics today," said McElhenny. "My
statistics weren't very much. But I guess it's the way I played. I guess I
made the game exciting."

So exciting, in fact, that McElhenny is given sole credit for pre-
serving pro football in San Francisco. The 49ers actually were up for
sale in 1952 when McElhenny hit town with his fan-pleasing style.

Former 49ers executive Lou Spadia called McElhenny a "franchise-saver." And justifiably. The 49ers were taken off the market after the 1952 season. Thus Kezar Stadium remained a castle fit for a King.

It's mind-boggling to think that one-half of football's most legendary backfield once strolled the same campus halls. Perry grew up in Watts, McElhenny eleven blocks from Watts in Los Angeles. Both attended Compton Junior College, though not together. Perry is twenty-three months older.

As a boy, McElhenny would jump a freight train and ride it ten blocks, then walk back home. This was in the 1930s when the city of Los Angeles wasn't that far removed from country life, and McElhenny was getting a feel on the train of what it was like to be moving free and wild.

One day, McElhenny learned what it was like to be moving scared. He and some buddies crossed a carrot patch. The farmer who owned the property took offense with these trespassers and fired a shotgun into the air to frighten them off. And did he ever succeed.

"We thought he was shooting at us," said McElhenny.

That's when McElhenny became Hurryin' Hugh.

Life had all kinds of surprises for McElhenny, some more confusing than others. There was a bridge not far from where he lived. At night, black men approached from one side of the bridge, white men from the other side. They'd meet in the middle, black against white, then match up and start fighting. There would be a series of bouts. It was the same atmosphere as an old-time club "smoker," only outdoors and racially motivated.

"I didn't understand it," McElhenny said. "I didn't know why they'd be that way."

That experience made him sensitive to racial issues he would encounter later on in the NFL.

McElhenny attended the 109th Street grade school, which was halfwhite, halfblack in enrollment. He never fought black kids, but he fought plenty of whites. On one such occasion, while wearing white corduroy pants, a popular fashion at the time, he and a kid brawled in a mud hole.

"When I got home," he said, "my mother told me if I ever came home like that again, she'd give me a whipping I'd never forget. That was a mistake, because then I began fighting all the time."

McElhenny showed defiance before two events changed his life. First, while playing football in a vacant lot, he stepped on the broken neck of a milk bottle, tearing all the tendons and nerves in his left foot. After the foot was repaired surgically, doctors told McElhenny's parents the foot might not grow naturally. The diagnosis proved wrong, even though McElhenny was on crutches for six months with his foot in a cast.

As a result of that injury, he flunked the fifth grade. But he also used the rehabilitation period to develop himself as an athlete in a rather strange manner.

"I could walk on crutches without using my feet," he said, "and I also played hopscotch and dodgeball on crutches."

That was the start of McElhenny's becoming an uncanny runner.

Then when he was twelve, McElhenny and his family, which included his six-year-old sister, Beverly, moved to an upscale neighborhood in Los Angeles. That relocation was made possible because Hugh McElhenny, Sr., now was earning a good living as the owner of a coin-machine company. He rented out pinball machines, jukeboxes, and pool tables.

"When we moved," said Hugh Jr., "my whole life turned into a storybook. A kid couldn't have a more perfect life."

McElhenny joined the Boy Scouts and remained a scout until he was eighteen. He not only attained the highest scouting honor of Eagle, but also earned two palms, or ten more merit badges, beyond the rank of Eagle. He learned how to play the trumpet. He's the first to admit he wasn't a young Harry James, but he became the bugler of his scout troop.

At Brett Harte Junior High, he met pretty Peggy Ogston. McElhenny's foot speed came in handy. At school dances, when it was boys' choice, he'd beat the other boys across the floor to ask Peggy to dance.

"He was a pest," Peggy recalled. "I wanted to dance with someone else but him. I guess I hurt his feelings."

Showing an athlete's resolve, McElhenny didn't give up easily. He and Peggy started dating at George Washington High School. That's when she saw a less-persistent, more-pleasant side of his personality.

"He was a very considerate, very caring person," she said. "He knew his place and didn't take advantage. We got along, off and on. We were both stubborn. We broke up a lot."

McElhenny initially showed athletic prowess in track and field. As a senior, he was virtually a one-man show. McElhenny and shot-putter Bob Cameron combined for four first places at the 1946 state meet, scoring twenty of their team's twenty-four points as George Washington won its only state track championship ever. McElhenny's time of fourteen seconds flat in the high hurdles tied the national inter-scholastic record.

His football career didn't begin, really, until his senior year, 1947. He missed his junior season after breaking a collarbone in the very first game. McElhenny's football coach, Bill Sloan, then taught him two fundamentals that turned him into a heavily recruited runner overnight.

"First, he said to drop my shoulder and lift up," McElhenny explained. "This way, you don't take the brunt of the hit, and the tackler can't get to my legs. After being hit, I might bounce a few steps, but I'll keep on running. Second, he showed me how to use the straightarm in order to get tacklers off balance. The coach said it was the same principle as diving. He told me to watch how divers do their twists and to notice how their bodies always followed the head. A straightarm has the same effect. I'd put a hand on a defender's head, not to jar him, but to push him. And his body would follow his head."

McElhenny developed a third clever tactic on his own: the gimpy leg. He'd drop the leg in front of a tackler, who then would lunge, only to have McElhenny lift the leg at the last possible second, making the tackler miss. Often badly. McElhenny was so adept at this technique, he avoided tacklers with the gimpy leg maneuver even on the downside of his career.

McElhenny didn't run sprints in track, but from his hurdle times, it was determined he was the equal of a 9.7-second dashman over 100 yards. He trained as a decathlete for the 1948 Olympic Games in London, England. He had beaten Bob Mathias of Tulare High School in California in several events during their prep career. Mathias, seventeen, would become the youngest Olympic decathlon gold medalist ever in '48 after McElhenny had been forced to stop training.

"Physical exhaustion," he explained. "At first, doctors thought it was the flu, but my body just broke down from months and months of training."

But even as a boy against men, he held his own. In the Coliseum Relays in Los Angeles, McElhenny, a high-school senior, was leading a veteran field in the 220-yard low hurdles by several strides when he hit the second to last hurdle and fell. He picked himself up and finished next to last.

"I believe the winner set a world record, so I would have been a world-record holder if I had stayed on my feet," said McElhenny. "I guess destiny wasn't with me. I did take third in the high hurdles in that meet, but I never ran track again after high school."

He received between forty and fifty football college scholarship offers from as far away as the University of Alabama and the United States Naval Academy in Maryland. Cameron, who was the quarterback on George Washington's football team, accepted an appointment to Annapolis. McElhenny would have joined him as a midshipman except for one hangup. He feared losing Peggy.

"I told him to go wherever he wanted to go," said Peggy, "but don't expect me to wait for him for four years. I was young."

McElhenny and Peggy were the most popular couple on campus in high school. He was chosen campus Knight, and she was picked as campus Lady. Peggy was student body president. McElhenny was the best athlete in school. He finally rejected Annapolis, from which Cameron emerged as an ensign and Navy pilot. Years later, he was killed returning from Vietnam when his plane exploded mysteriously.

A mid-year high school graduate, McElhenny accepted a grant in aid from the University of Southern California. But when USC was late in paying him for a campus gardening job that same spring, he quit school. About then, he and Peggy had another breakup. And so with the brand-new Dodge his father had bought him as a reward for being undefeated in the hurdles and long jump as a high-school senior, McElhenny and a friend, Al Debbas, took off to see the world.

They first drove to San Jose State to check out the campus, then moved on to Eureka, California, where they worked stacking timber. They traveled next to Portland, Oregon, washing dishes and picking strawberries. Then it was off to North Dakota, where they stacked hay on a ranch. Working their way across America would have taken them to New York, where they planned to catch a cattle ship to Europe for more fun and adventure. But after washing cars in Minnesota and baling hay in Indiana, homesickness set in, and they decided to head back to California.

"What that trip taught me," said McElhenny, "was that I didn't like hard labor, and I wanted to get an education."

But by the time he got home, it was too late to matriculate at a four-year school. So McElhenny enrolled at nearby Compton JC, where he was a football sensation that fall, scoring twenty-three touchdowns, twelve on runs of thirty yards or longer. McElhenny led Compton to a win over Duluth in the Junior Rose Bowl. But his most memorable game came against the University of Mexico in Mexico City, where he returned a punt 105 yards as Compton won, 26-21.

McElhenny now was ready to transfer to a four-year school. But not alone. He and Peggy had patched up their differences and were closer than ever. He proposed marriage, she accepted, and they were wed. The groom was nineteen and his bride eighteen when they headed off to the University of Washington. McElhenny had three years of athletic eligibility and a king's life awaiting him in Seattle.

The rumor is as long as McElhenny's gridiron accomplishments: He took a pay cut when he left college for the NFL. McElhenny doesn't dispute that notion. In fact, he gives it credence. His first 49ers contract was for $7,000. He easily topped that figure in Seattle, although his income was coupled with what Peggy made as part of the everyday work force. But they also were kissed by financial angels. Angels hidden in the shadows.

Peggy decided not to enroll at Washington and have to deal with her husband being a big man on campus. She was attractive and bright, and fully capable of earning her own way. So she chose to work full-time in office jobs at a jewelry store and later at the King County Medical Center.

"We bought a 1950 chartreuse Ford convertible," she said. "People thought the school bought it for us, but that was my money."

Nevertheless, if Peggy ever had difficulty making car payments, which wasn't the case, her husband certainly was in a good position to assist financially. McElhenny wasn't ever a starving student in Seattle. In 1949, his campus job paid him $65 monthly to deliver athletic department mail to a post office a mile away. He also earned money as a ticket-taker at a race track. And, all too briefly, he was paid $100 daily by Rainier Ale to visit neighborhood bars and buy patrons a Rainier. However, the patrons, upon recognizing the local football hero, insisted on buying him a cold one instead. Being in training, McElhenny refused when he could, but normally he was able to pocket the full $100.

In addition to this easy income, a $300 check arrived monthly at the McElhenny apartment, which they moved into after living three months in a Seattle hotel, all compliments of University of Washington boosters.

"I don't know where the check came from," McElhenny recalled. "Every month, it would have a new name on it. It was illegal to accept it, and I was investigated every year over what I was making. But they never caught me."

A big grin crossed his weathered face. Of course, those who investigated could only investigate what they knew about. And McElhenny never told them about the monthly check. If McElhenny were caught today receiving the same largesse, would he and the University of Washington be in deep trouble with a more-diligent, ever-watchful NCAA?

"Oh, sure," he replied. "Five years after I was out of school, they clamped down [on collegiate athletic violations] much harder. But it wasn't just me. I heard of this one NFL Hall of Famer who received a partnership in several gas stations to attend college."

However, McElhenny wasn't aware of any other college halfbacks besides himself who made $1,000 a month in the summertime working on a fishing boat in Alaska. Now a thousand bucks a month was more than some company executives were making a half-century ago, and likely more than some officials in the Washington athletic department were taking home. McElhenny was like his own little corporation in college.

In 1956, after McElhenny had played four seasons in the NFL, Pacific Coast Conference commissioner Victor O. Schmidt turned down inquiries to investigate The King's college income, which McElhenny estimated at $800 monthly, including his $75 per month college job plus Peggy's paychecks. The basis of Schmidt's decision was that McElhenny's eligibility had expired. In truth, Schmidt didn't want the headache. He said if he knew McElhenny had "a part-time off-campus job paying that much money...I certainly would have questioned it, and made a full and thorough inquiry into it."

Whatever McElhenny received monetarily at Washington, he figured he paid it back to the university by heightening interest in the Huskies' football program.

"They said [quarterback] Don Heinrich and I built the high-rise on one side of the stadium," he said.

McElhenny and Heinrich were All-America candidates at Washington at the same time, although injuries limited the number of games they actually played together. Heinrich set many national passing records, while McElhenny broke numerous school and conference rushing records, and eventually would be named the Huskies' Football Player of the Century.

McElhenny's first season for Washington was 1949. In his very first game, he returned the opening kickoff against Minnesota, and future 49er teammates Leo Nomellini and Gordy Soltau, ninety-six yards for a touchdown.

"The only run I ever remembered in college was against Minnesota," he said. "It was so simple. I caught the kickoff, faked a reverse to Roland Kirkby, and just ran down the sideline. It was a no-brainer. You'll see it on the game film. Nine Minnesota players were blocked and lying on the field."

Later in the game, McElhenny made a sharp cut and the arch of the foot that had stepped on the broken milk bottle during his childhood gave out.

"I basically lost two years of my football career, 1949 and 1955, because of that foot," he said. "There were no razzle-dazzle runs those two years."

Washington was 3-7 in McElhenny's sophomore year, largely because the Huskies had the second most generous defense in the conference.

Healthy again in 1950, McElhenny scored fourteen touchdowns to lead the conference. He rushed for 1,107 yards, including a conference-record 296 yards against rival Washington State, which still is the Washington record. With Heinrich leading the nation in passing in 1950, the Huskies built an 8-2 record and a No. 11 national ranking. Only a 14-7 loss to California kept them out of the Rose Bowl.

The Huskies were primed for a New Year's Day appearance in Pasadena the next season. But Heinrich separated a shoulder in practice and missed the entire season. More responsibility fell on McElhenny's shoulders, even placekicking, which he hadn't ever done before.

"I became the kicker because we didn't have one," he said. "Against Oregon, I kicked nine conversions and they went through all different ways."

But they went through, proving McElhenny was one of the best clutch players in the country. He scored all of Washington's points in a 20-20 tie with UCLA. He scored twenty-two points as the Huskies lost to Cal, 37-28. He set a PCC record with a 100-yard punt return against USC, which also remains a Washington record. If USC hadn't been so tardy paying its gardener a few years before, McElhenny and Frank Gifford would have been in the same backfield. Instead, McElhenny faked out Gifford on that 100-yard jaunt.

"Our longest punter was Des Koch. But I did the punting when we got to midfield because, supposedly, I was more accurate at getting the ball down in the corner," said Gifford. "Well, in this game, I got the ball down in the corner, all right. The King took it there, right on the goal line. He started to weave down the sideline. All of a sudden, there was only one man, me, between him and the goal line. He left me flat on my face and ran it 100 yards. It was like a run out of a cornball movie. Only it was for real."

McElhenny led the conference in rushing yards, 936, and points, 125, while setting a PCC career rushing record with 2,499 yards. No other Husky but McElhenny has a punt return, kickoff return, and scrimmage run all exceeding ninety yards. And his seventy-seven-yard touchdown reception against Illinois ranks among the longest in school history.

Without Heinrich, there was only so much McElhenny could do by himself in 1951. The Huskies fell to 3-6-1 even though they outscored their opponents, 273 to 218. Heinrich returned in 1952 for his last season. By that time, McElhenny was in the NFL. Their timing wasn't the best.

"If I had a good foot in '49, and I had Heinrich with me in '51..." McElhenny mused. "But, in the long run, it worked out good for me in Washington. My popularity there took Peggy and I back to Seattle [twenty years later] to try and get an NFL franchise for the city."

Following his senior season, McElhenny was selected to play with other college stars in the East-West Shrine Game in San Francisco. But he hardly practiced with his West teammates because he had to return to Seattle to accept an award as that city's man of the year in sports. Thus when he got back to San Francisco, he played roughly a minute in the Shrine game.

He also played in a local charity game in Bellingham, Washington, in which he carried three times and scored three touchdowns. Then it was off to two all-star games in Hawaii, where he scored two touchdowns in one game, and three more touchdowns in the second from distances of sixty, thirty-one and twenty yards. Quarterbacking the opposition in the second game was Albert, who then assumed the role of talent scout and phoned Buck Shaw, the 49ers head coach, who was about to leave for the NFL draft back east.

Albert pleaded with Shaw to draft McElhenny. Shaw asked Albert about McElhenny's character. McElhenny believes he knows what Shaw meant by that question.

"There was an incident at Washington in 1950," McElhenny said. "I was late to practice because I had a 2 o'clock class. A class that lasted forty-five minutes. And practice started across campus at 3 p.m. That meant I had to hurry to make it, but I still had to get dressed in my football gear. So I was going to be late for practice.

"Howie O'Dell, our coach, told the team to give me the silent treatment until I learned how to get practice on time. Heinrich whispered to me, 'We're not supposed to talk to you.' So I went off by myself to do calisthenics. This way, I wouldn't have to talk to anyone. O'Dell didn't like that one bit. The end result was I stopped going to that 2 o'clock class, which I then flunked. I had to go to summer school to be eligible for football."

Shaw asked Albert if McElhenny was as cocky and unmanageable as the 49ers' silver-haired gentleman coach had heard. Albert, who had served in the Navy with Bill Sloan, McElhenny's high school coach, assured Shaw just the opposite, that McElhenny was every inch a team player.

"Mac did come off as cock of the walk," said 49ers teammate Gordy Soltau. "But he was."

Kings should strut when they walk.

"Everyone made me the cock of the walk," McElhenny reflected. "Maybe, looking back, I was cocky. I'm naturally outward in my personality, maybe a little too much. But I'm not a braggart, and I have a tremendous amount of integrity. My word's my bond. You can ask Peg."

That didn't take much effort, since they've been married fifty years.

"I don't recall that Hughie was ever cocky, though he had kind of a cocky walk. [John] Travolta, right?" said Peggy. "So maybe it was the way he carried himself. But he was always outgoing and friendly. Sometimes too much. The other [49ers] players could always get him to do things that would get him into trouble. That really used to upset me."

Albert convinced Shaw finally to draft McElhenny, which then required cooperation from others. The 49ers had to wait nine picks to get McElhenny. It would be a guessing game, because the NFL was different in those days. Scouting was piecemeal, and communication among teams prior to the draft wasn't as candid as today. Back then, teams didn't know the players that other teams were considering drafting.

Fortunately, the eight teams drafting ahead of the 49ers in 1952 cooperated. The Rams, with a bonus pick, selected Vanderbilt quarterback Billy Wade. The New York Yankees then chose Cal linebacker Les Richter. The Chicago Cardinals took University of San Francisco fullback Ollie Matson. Gifford was taken next by the New York Giants. Kentucky quarterback Babe Parilli went to Green Bay, Maryland fullback Ed "Mighty Mo" Modzelewski to Pittsburgh, Baylor quarterback Larry Isbell to Washington, and Mississippi end Jim Dooley to the Chicago Bears.

The 49ers then selected McElhenny, who promptly was advised by Albert to ask for a rookie salary of $30,000, which was unheard-of at the time, even for a seasoned NFL veteran. Maybe that's what Albert figured McElhenny was making in Seattle. When McElhenny brought up that outrageous figure at lunch with 49ers executive Vic Morabito, the latter's mouth opened so wide, you could have stuck a football inside. Morabito then excused himself and left the restaurant, sticking McElhenny with the bill.

Two weeks later, when McElhenny received his contract in the mail, it was for $7,000. Without consulting Albert or challenging the offer, he signed quickly and mailed it back. In the final analysis, he wanted to play football. Peggy was pregnant with their first child, and the expectant father was ready to get on with his life, having been stung by what had just happened at Washington.

After playing in the football games in Hawaii, McElhenny returned to Seattle intent on completing the thirty-two units he needed for graduation on the quarter system. That's when the school informed McElhenny his scholarship had expired, and there would be no more funding. He was incensed. So the McElhennys packed up and left campus. The King never bothered to complete those thirty-two credits. Maybe he figured he didn't need a rug leading to his throne.

"You know," Brodie pointed out, "that story about Mac's taking a pay reduction after leaving college didn't enhance his reputation in the NFL. But he is the No. 1 dude as a guy. It's just his humility, his niceness. The best guy that was."

As a rookie, McElhenny didn't envision having much of a professional career.

"Peg's and my legitimate goal was to play three years and earn enough money to buy a car, a house, and furniture," he said. "I didn't know how good I was. I really didn't."

McElhenny participated in the College All-Star Game, then joined the 49ers. He was given jersey number 39. He had worn 32 in college, but that number was taken by the 49ers' Norm Standlee.

"I didn't have any choice," McElhenny said as far as choosing a uniform number. "In those days, you didn't demand."

Thirty-nine seemed an odd halfback's number for a No. 1 draft pick. And odd, too, for a future Hall of Fame baseball catcher. But McElhenny and Roy Campanella of the Brooklyn Dodgers made that number famous.

McElhenny sat out his first game as a 49er, an exhibition against the Washington Redskins. He continued to idle the following week against the Chicago Cardinals until late in the game when Albert came to his rescue.

"Frankie called time out and went to the sideline," McElhenny recalled. "He told Buck, 'Put in McElhenny.' Buck said, 'He doesn't know the plays.' Frankie replied, 'That's OK, send him in.' So I get in the huddle, and Frankie kneels on the dirt at Kezar Stadium and diagrams a play. I'm thinking, 'This is the pros?' Frankie said, 'Just swing out to the right and I'll pitch it to you.' And I went right down the sideline, forty-two yards for a touchdown."

If that wasn't an omen, then McElhenny's performance in the fourth regular-season game at Soldier Field certainly was a portent of what was ahead for the NFL in inventing game plans on how to contain No. 39.

"I broke a cardinal rule by fielding a punt inside my 10," McElhenny said.

His ninety-four-yard punt runback ignited the 49ers' first NFL victory over the big, bad Bears, following three losses, since San Francisco joined the league in 1950. Afterwards, Bears coach George Halas called McElhenny "a great ball player." Notre Dame backfield coach and former Bears quarterback Johnny Lujack, who watched the game that day, said, "McElhenny is the best running back I've seen in a long, long time."

Papa Bear had one other reaction about McElhenny.

"Halas said, 'This guy is unfair. The commissioner should make him play with a different team every week,'" Spadia recalled.

Almost instantly, McElhenny became the most feared runner in the NFL. As a rookie, he had touchdown runs of eighty-nine and eighty-two yards from scrimmage, both against the Dallas Texans, who moved to Baltimore after that season and were renamed the Colts.

One of those long runs against Dallas is there on the VCR. McElhenny uses a straightarm on a defensive back. Both hit the turf briefly, but because McElhenny has created distance with his arm, he is able to get up and break free for a touchdown.

It wasn't until 1954 that the NFL changed the rules on tackling. From then on, anyone knocked off his feet couldn't get up and continue running. The new rule didn't slow down McElhenny, who ran eighty-six yards for a touchdown against Green Bay in 1956.

"Hugh was a race car alongside a lot of Mack trucks," said Albert. "He had star quality. He wanted a good field to run on, good footballs, good equipment. He didn't want shoulder pads that pinched or hung the wrong way. He demanded what his ability commanded. Everyone appreciated Hugh, and he wore his acclaim well. He was cocky, but you liked his cockiness. He had a certain aura about him. The fans thought so much of him that when he grabbed the ball and got into the open field, everyone was on their feet. You knew that all hell was going to break loose."

"They would get on their feet even before Mac got to the line of scrimmage," said Brodie, correcting Albert.

McElhenny remains Albert's favorite runner over Jim Brown, Sayers, Payton, O. J. Simpson, Eric Dickerson, and other Hall of Fame greats.

"I've seen a lot of 'em." said Albert. "People who haven't seen McElhenny say, 'How could you compare him with these modern guys?' Well, maybe you can't compare him. The modern guys don't entertain me like Mac did. Mac was the most electrifying performer I've ever seen. I called him The King. And why not? You can't be any better."

Before each game, McElhenny had a ritual of rising off the ground and driving his shoulder pads into the wooden goal posts, which were placed on the goal line at the time.

"It reminded me of a bull charging the matador," said Albert.

Or, with McElhenny's grace, perhaps Secretariat running away from the field in the Belmont.

"Mac was like a thoroughbred racehorse," Spadia agreed. "You didn't want to sit next to him on the bus going to the stadium. He'd say, 'Why are we stopping?' The driver would reply, 'The light's red.' Mac always was nervous before a game. He was ready to run, like a racehorse. He'd tell the driver, 'Hurry up. Hurry up.'"

The thoroughbred got plenty of rest between races.

"When McElhenny started to come on as a runner," said Soltau, "he developed the same personality as Joe Perry about practice. It wasn't until Thursday that we could get both of them to practice fully."

McElhenny averaged a phenomenal seven yards a carry in 1952, even though he rushed for only 684 yards. Besides the ninety-four-yard punt return in Chicago, he rushed for 103 yards that day against the Bears. Against Dallas, he carried seven times for 170 yards, a phenomenal 24.3 yards per carry, He was excitement personified as a rookie, scoring ten touchdowns, three on receptions, including a seventy-seven yarder.

The next day after playing the Rams, Shaw was showing the game film to the players, when he stopped the camera at the precise moment McElhenny engaged two defenders on the sideline.

"Buck looked at McElhenny and said, 'Mac, you're a rookie. When you've made your yardage, get out of bounds. Don't get hit,'" Soltau remembered. "We were all snickering in the room because Buck had a forgetful memory. When he turned the projector back on, Mac ducked under the two guys and kept running."

McElhenny repeated as All-Pro in 1953. He also was voted the most popular 49er as the team improved from 7-5 to 9-3, narrowly missing the playoffs. Though McElhenny's total yardage running and catching dropped slightly from 1,051 yards to 977, he was as exciting as ever. He rushed for only 505 yards (4.5), but demonstrated ability as a big-time pass catcher.

"I never saw a receiver who could get up in the air like McElhenny," said *Baltimore Sun* columnist John Steadman. "It was like he was on a trampoline."

McElhenny's game-saving run down the sideline against the Rams in 1953 was pure magnificence, even from a loser's perspective.

"That was the most incredible run I've ever seen," said Rams coach Hampton Pool.

Buck Shaw played that run through without stopping the camera.

Just imagine what kind of year 1953 would have been for McElhenny if seven of his runs, all touchdowns and all beyond 50 yards, weren't nullified because of penalties, mostly clippings that resulted because McElhenny reversed his field so frequently.

"Mac was just a beautiful runner," said teammate and fellow Hall of Famer Nomellini. "He was *the* outside running back."

McElhenny seemed coated with stardust. In a 1953 game, he was knocked down in the end zone on a pass pattern. While he lay flat on his back, the pass was tipped into his arms for a touchdown.

That football season also is remembered for the greatest fight in 49ers history, against the Philadelphia Eagles in the opening game. Late in the third quarter, 49ers defensive end Charlie Powell and end Bobby Walston of the Eagles had a disagreement and started swinging at each other. Walston must have just contracted amnesia, because he was taking on a professional heavyweight boxer in Powell. Both benches emptied. Pete Pihos went straight for McElhenny, who began hitting the Eagles' All-Pro end with his helmet.

"It was a dirty football game," McElhenny said. "You'd be down and the Eagles would grab you by the crotch, twist your ankle, pull at your mouth, get a knee in your face. But you know who broke the fight up? It was the 49ers band. They put their instruments down and got into it."

Not every band member laid down his instrument. The Eagles were ducking haymakers, trombones, and tubas. The fight was a draw, but the 49ers won the game, 31–21.

"What fight?" Eagles star Chuck Bednarik, who played in that game, said years later. Well, Bednarik engaged in so many fights during his career, what was one more?

Philadelphia wasn't the only NFL team guilty of hitting below the belt in the 1950s. The Eagles simply were one of the best. Or worst.

"The Eagles and Bears were the worst," McElhenny said, "but the Chicago Cardinals and Baltimore Colts would do it, too."

The NFL's acknowledged dirtiest player at the time wasn't the biggest physical specimen. Bears defensive end Ed Sprinkle weighed only 200 pounds, but he had to watched at every moment because he was the nearest thing the league had to a hockey goon.

"Oh, yeah," McElhenny said in agreement with the goon analogy. "One time, I returned a punt and Sprinkle tackled me out of bounds. He's choking me while the official took the ball out of my hands."

Sprinkle wasn't any more mean-spirited than his coach.

"One year," said McElhenny, "I got knocked out of bounds and George Halas kicked me in the head."

By 1953, McElhenny had gained confidence that his career would extend beyond three years. That season also produced a racist incident in San Antonio which had a profound effect on him.

"I'm a very sentimental, emotional guy," he said. "People I care about, I get emotional about. We played an exhibition in San Antonio. Joe Perry practiced with us during the day, but he wasn't with us at night. I found out later Joe wasn't staying in the same hotel with us. He was staying in someone's home. I didn't understand that. I'm white and I never had to experience [racism]. I was never directly involved in a prejudicial thing. *HBO* interviewed me recently for a special they were doing on Joe. I told them about San Antonio. That experience brought me closer to Joe."

Tears welled up in McElhenny's eyes forty-seven years later as he retold the San Antonio story during an interview for this book in his Las Vegas-area home. Once again, he felt like the kid at the bridge, watching whites and blacks fighting without premeditation, and wondering why life has to be this way.

McElhenny's salary improved from $7,000 to $12,000 in 1953. Even with a raise, McElhenny, along with other 49er players, had to buttress their salaries with off-field jobs, during the season! Forty-Niner practice began at 9 a.m. at Menlo Junior College in Atherton, thirty miles south of San Francisco, and ended by noon. McElhenny then headed for his second job at Granny Goose Foods, maker of a popular brand of potato chips.

McElhenny was one of the best players in football, but here he was sweeping floors and straightening potato chip racks. He eventually was promoted to truck driver. He drove a Granny Goose truck around the Bay Area, opening new accounts. He made it back home by dinnertime.

Pro football was primitive at the time compared to nowadays. No extensive film study existed in the early 1950s. There weren't that many team meetings. Basically, you practiced and played. But how did a player hold another job during the season if he were injured? McElhenny chuckled, thinking immediately of an anecdote.

"I twisted my ankle," he said. "Bob Kleckner, our trainer, taped an aspirin to my ankle and said, 'You're OK.' I went to work at Granny Goose that way."

Against the Bears in 1954, McElhenny received his first serious injury as a pro. Something an aspirin couldn't cure. And one guess who was the cause.

"It was a sweep to the left," McElhenny said. "Sprinkle grabbed me. Then other Bears got there just as the whistle blew. They drove me into the turf, separating my shoulder."

The 49ers won the game, 24-14, improving to 4-0-1. But no less than eleven first-stringers were injured for San Francisco that day. McElhenny was done for the season after rushing for 515 yards in just five games and averaging a staggering 8.1 yards per carry. He was headed for his only 1,000-yard season when he was Sprinkled on the turf.

All that early momentum, gone. Against Detroit, McElhenny carried seven times for 126 yards, eighteen yards per rush, including a sixty-yard touchdown run during the 49ers' 37–31 victory. McElhenny might have caused his own demise against Chicago's "Monsters of the Midway." Two weeks before his shoulder injury, he carried ten times for 114 yards and two touchdowns against the Bears in a 49ers' 35–28 win. Tired of his theatrics at their expense, the Bears then got even.

Without The King, the 49ers split the remainder of their schedule to finish 7-4-1. Shaw was fired. One of his assistants, Norman "Red" Strader, took over.

"It wasn't fair what happened to Buck," said McElhenny. "We were winning, but Tony [Morabito] didn't think Buck would ever win a championship. It turned out to be a catastrophe. I couldn't see Red Strader as a head coach. I didn't have confidence in him. He was a military disciplinarian. It was a big change."

In time, McElhenny would have a litany of memorable runs at Kezar Stadium, although the turf itself wasn't an open-field runner's paradise.

"It wasn't the fastest field," McElhenny said. "When it rained, it was like running in peanut butter."

Chunky or creamy?

McElhenny's physical problems carried over into 1955. During a preseason game against Pittsburgh in the California state capital of Sacramento, McElhenny uncorked a beauty even a Hall of Famer could admire.

"I was a rookie with the Steelers," said Johnny Unitas. "I remember standing on the sideline and watching McElhenny take a screen pass from Tittle and running some fifty yards for a touchdown. But he must have run 150 yards to get the fifty. He crossed the field three times, stop, start, stop, start, and I don't think anyone touched him. I had heard of McElhenny before, but I just stood there amazed. It was one of the most thrilling things I saw Mac do. He was super. The only other guy I saw who was close to him in the open field was Lenny Moore."

McElhenny's sideline-to-sideline special in Sacramento ended up unhappily.

"When I stepped in the end zone, pain shot through my foot," he said. The milk-bottle foot.

McElhenny would be of little use to the 49ers that year as he accounted for only 530 yards of offense. The foot was shot regularly with Novocain, and he tried valiantly to play. It was equally painful for 49ers fans seeing the normally explosive McElhenny stopped for numerous short gains. In two games, he was held to minus yardage. His longest run that season was forty-four yards against Baltimore. He rushed for eighty-three yards that day, and eighty-three more the following week against Green Bay. Those were the high points of his season as the 49ers fell to 4-8. They did increase their consecutive home victories over the Colts to six.

"They were always tough for us," said Unitas. "We always played them the last two weeks of the season, and always on the West Coast because of the weather [in the East]. You had high schools using Kezar, so the ground wasn't very good. We had to keep more offense than they did, but we always had a good rivalry with the 49ers."

After the 49ers beat Baltimore, 10-7, in 1954 to end a five-game losing streak for San Francisco, Strader was canned. His biggest impact that year had been the implementation of a full-day work schedule, which meant the players had to give up their other in-season jobs. McElhenny had just signed a three-year contract with the 49ers for $18,000 a year, so he didn't take a big hit financially when he told Granny Goose that he could only peddle potato chips in the offseason.

Albert became the 49ers' third head coach in three years in 1956, a popular move with the players. Albert was a leprechaun masquerading as a coach. Hollywood found him so captivating, a movie was made of his life at Stanford. Albert played himself as the campus hero.

The public didn't know that Albert was a manic depressive given to severe mood swings. He dealt with his condition, at times, with alcohol. Thus he became a constant source of amusement and curiosity to his team. But he was up front with his players, and after Strader's dictatorial ways, the 49ers even tolerated Albert's sometimes biting sarcasm.

For McElhenny, 1956 was a season of rejuvenation. Dr. Daniel Levinthal of Beverly Hills had discovered the problem with his foot, a growth that was the circumference of a quarter. The growth was removed, and McElhenny had his finest year, rushing for 916 yards and eight touchdowns on 185 carries, all career highs.

"If you get the ball enough, it goes to show what you can do," he said. "Looking back at what I did, what would I have done if I had carried more?"

Of course, if he hadn't played in the same backfield with two other Hall of Fame runners, Joe Perry and John Henry Johnson, and if the 49ers hadn't also been pass-oriented, McElhenny would have been the featured back in San Francisco and, barring injuries, a one-man highlight show.

Nevertheless, McElhenny ran free again in 1956, seventy-five yards against the Giants, eighty-eight yards against the Rams, sixty-three and 101 yards against the Bears, 119 against Detroit, 140 and 132 against the Packers, and eighty-four against the Colts. He had long runs of eighty-six, fifty-four, fifty [twice], and forty-four yards.

The Mac attack was back!

Watching that eighty-six-yard burst against the Packers on a VCR, the viewer is struck by the size of McElhenny's hips. For some reason, they look larger than normal. The King believes it was the camera angle, because he hadn't gained weight that year.

"Show me someone fast who doesn't have big buttocks," he noted.

His run production was cut nearly in half the following year, down to 478 yards. It wasn't injuries this time, but a shift in philosophy.

"I was out on the flank more," McElhenny said. "The Alley-Oop was the story. R. C. Owens was the king. Everyone else had to sit on the sideline."

There was no indication at the start of the 1957 season that McElhenny would be anything less than spectacular. He rushed for 125 yards in the opener against the Cardinals, including a season-long sixty-one-yard run. He added 109 yards the next week against the Rams, and fifty-nine more in thirteen carries against the Bears.

"It's amazing that Mac could run the way he did," said Brodie. "Here was a 200-pound guy with size 8 1/2 feet. That's real tiny. And he had a three-inch arch. No wonder he had so many foot problems."

Things slowed down dramatically for McElhenny in '57 after his fast start. A seventy-five-yard effort against Detroit was his only good rushing day over the last nine games. In three of those games, he had one carry or none at all. The 49ers' record improved to 8-4 as Tittle and Owens invented a lob-pass mentality that caught the NFL off guard. McElhenny joined the fun, catching a career-high thirty-seven passes, including the most important reception of his thirteen seasons.

When Tittle went down late in the eleventh game of the season, rookie quarterback Brodie of Stanford left the comfort of the sideline and walked into the 49er huddle with, of all things, an amused look.

"A cameraman caught me smiling," he said. "But it was the irony of it all. I hadn't played all season, and now I'm playing in the biggest game against Baltimore. So I asked the guys in the huddle if anyone had anything. Goose [Billy Wilson] said he could run a turn-in at the goal line. I hit him in the shoulder. That's one incompletion.

"I asked Mac if he had anything. He said to throw the ball in the corner of the end zone, and he would catch it. I didn't know what he meant, but I threw it. He must have pushed Milt Davis ten feet to make the catch. Mac should have been thrown out of the game, but he got the touchdown."

Brodie's fourteen-yard scoring pass to McElhenny gave the 49ers a 17-13 victory. McElhenny had eight catches in the game for 165 yards, the longest covering forty-three yards. The last reception was the most critical.

"It was a pushoff between Hugh and Milt that could have gone either way," said Steadman, who covered the game. "Hugh told me years later that he got half a game ball afterwards. The trainer sliced the ball in half and gave half to McElhenny and half to Brodie."

Idled much of the season, McElhenny was at his open-field best two weeks later in the Western Division tiebreaker game with Detroit. He scored on a forty-seven yard pass and later broke off a seventy-one-yard run to set up a Gordy Soltau field goal that put the 49ers ahead, 27-7, in the third quarter.

"Matt Hazeltine, Y. A. Tittle, Joe Arenas, Billy Wilson and I were going to rent a villa in Puerto Vallarta with our wives and spend our championship money there," McElhenny said. "Instead, after the game, we went to a place called The Snake Pit and drank our sorrows."

Incredibly, the Lions roared back for a 31-27 victory as an unknown fullback named Tom "The Bomb" Tracy rumbled sixty-seven yards for a touchdown.

"Tom The Bomb never had a game before or after like he had in that second half," said McElhenny, still affected by the crushing defeat.

Joe Schmidt believes the game turned around when the Lions reached the point of desperation.

"The 49ers went to sleep a little bit in the third quarter," he said. "We were out of the game, so we had nothing to lose. We blitzed every down, got some turnovers, and got some scores. They got a little nervous. And they were a little conservative. I thought the 49ers were a great team, just a shade behind us."

McElhenny had 178 yards of offense that day. He looked as dangerous as ever, but the demoralizing loss drained all life out of the 49ers for the rest of the 1950s and throughout the 1960s.

Wayne Walker was a Lions rookie linebacker in 1958 when he had his first opportunity to tackle McElhenny, who pulled yet another vanishing act.

"He caught a swing pass, and I came up to stick him," said Walker, who would play fifteen years with the Lions. "He gave me not one limp leg, but two. I don't know how he did it, but his legs disappeared, and I went right under him."

But 1958 was the last year McElhenny was used regularly by the 49ers. He ran for 451 yards (4.0) and six touchdowns. His best days were seventy yards against the Eagles on eighteen carries, and 154 yards against the Packers on twenty-two attempts. He had two touchdown catches that season. As McElhenny's production slipped with his thirtieth birthday approaching, nothing had changed with the 49ers, who had enough offense to win and just enough defense to lose.

"We'd score points," said McElhenny, "but we couldn't score enough."

In 1958, assistant coach Howard "Red" Hickey became a bigger factor in the offense. When Albert stepped down after that 6-6 season, Hickey immediately became the leading candidate to replace him.

"A bunch of us went Christmas caroling," McElhenny said. "We stopped to sing in front of Hickey's house. We were invited in and told Hickey, 'We hope you're our next coach.' I felt I was one of Hickey's favorites. He knew I could do a lot of things, and that he could always count on me."

Hickey got the job, all right. And the following fall, McElhenny, supposedly the coach's pet, had eighteen carries over a twelve-game season. And The King was perfectly healthy.

Part of McElhenny's problem was that the 49ers were evolving from the Million Dollar Backfield into the All-Initial Backfield of Y. A. Tittle, J. D. Smith, C. R. Roberts, and R.C. Owens.

"The guys that came along, J. D. and C. R., it was a few years before they found their niche," Owens recalled. "We just revolved in. And you know who was the first substitute on the All-Initial Backfield? J.W. Lockett."

Owens remembered McElhenny losing some speed in the late 1950s. Otherwise, The King's instincts and reflexes were as sharp as ever.

"Mac just had that football ability," said Owens. "He could go forward or backwards. He could go sideways. He had every move a back could have."

But in 1959, the NFL's most dangerous back seven years earlier rushed for a total of sixty-seven yards. (3.7). The best pass-catching back of his era had twenty-two receptions for a combined offensive output of a paltry 397 yards. To his chagrin, McElhenny had misread Hickey. After caroling in front of Hickey's house, McElhenny now wanted to brain his new coach with a yule log.

"Red Hickey was a foul-mouthed guy," he said. "He loved to call everyone 'chicken shit.' Everything that he said, there was nothing uplifting. For us, it was like 'get the season over.' I just found him to be a terrible person."

Hickey had no trust in players thirty and older. Thirtysomethings McElhenny, Tittle, Perry, and Billy Wilson all would be gone in another year. McElhenny's main involvement in 1959 was leaving Granny Goose's management training program to launch his own grocery business. But when given the opportunity, he showed he still had the moves in football.

Wayne Walker, for one, still was impressed after McElhenny caught two touchdown passes against the Lions one Sunday, including a sixty-two-yarder from Tittle.

"With Gale Sayers, Barry Sanders, Jerry Rice," said Walker, "the secret to what they do is they can make their cuts without losing speed. That's not written about enough. Some guys make their cuts and slow down. Sayers, Sanders, and Rice keep right on going. McElhenny was like that. He could fly."

McElhenny saw slightly more action in 1960, mainly as a slotback. He carried ninety-five times for 347 yards (3.7), but failed to score a rushing touchdown for the first time as a 49er. His best games, as always, were against the Bears, 122 and seventy-one yards. He caught only fourteen passes, including a two-yard toss from Tittle for his only touchdown.

McElhenny's unhappiness with Hickey reached a zenith in the seventh game, a 24-0 defeat to Detroit. On third down and long yardage, McElhenny was thrown a pass in the flat with a Lion linebacker shadowing him. Even if he had caught the ball, McElhenny would have been tackled for a huge loss. So he let the pass fall incomplete, right in front of Hickey.

"Chicken shit," Hickey yelled.

Fed up with Hickey's insults, McElhenny flipped him off.

"That was the end of me [as a 49er]," he said. "Hickey didn't play me one down from scrimmage the last five games. All I did was return kicks. I asked Spadia to trade me. He said, 'Nonsense.'"

Actually, it's not quite true McElhenny had no carries the last five games. He had four. But in his final game as a 49er, December 18, 1960, against Baltimore, McElhenny had no carries or receptions.

"We were all an unhappy bunch of campers," he said. "Hickey really picked on Frank Morze, our center, calling him a big, fat slob every chance he got. Poor Morze was beaten up [emotionally] something terrible. Finally, the players wanted me to meet with management to air a list of grievances they had against Hickey.

"My immediate answer was, 'Why not the captains?' And the players said, 'Because they won't cut you, Mac. Hickey likes you.'"

Nothing was further from the truth. Peggy McElhenny still grimaces over the thought of her husband being talked into making such a self-destructive move. McElhenny went ahead and asked for a private meeting with Spadia, who agreed to the request. But when McElhenny showed up, who was there to meet him but Hickey.

"I told Lou about all the foul language Hickey used," said McElhenny. "Hickey denied everything, saying he never used language like that, and I had something against him because he wasn't playing me."

The private meeting went nowhere. It was clear to McElhenny that there would be no going back to the 49ers. He was ready for a change, and Hickey was more than willing to accommodate him.

Bert Rose, general manager of the Minnesota Vikings, called McElhenny in the winter of 1961 to say they had traded for him. But as a new Bay Area groceryman, McElhenny didn't want to be an absentee owner. So he phoned the brand-new Oakland Raiders of the American Football League to say he would sign with them for $30,000.

The Raiders' hands were tied. AFL rules precluded its eight teams from negotiating with NFL players unless they were free agents. The AFL would have fined the Raiders $5,000 for pursuing McElhenny.

When the Vikings offered him $25,000, it was more money than he had ever made playing football, even at the University of Washington. McElhenny had no choice but to accept. Now thirty-two, he reported to his new team with, of all things, blood poisoning in his right arm. It was from a freak injury caused when a metal sliver became lodged under his thumb nail.

After the condition cleared up, McElhenny showed Hickey and the 49ers up close and personal that he was far from over the hill with that mind-boggling thirty-two-yard run. After the game, a 49ers' 38-24 victory, he commented, "I don't remember seeing any purple jerseys. I saw only white [49er] jerseys."

The 49ers were awe-struck on the sideline after McElhenny's unbelievable run.

"We started applauding," Brodie said. "We didn't know what else to do."

It's nearly unheard of for a football team to applaud an opponent during a game, unless he is injured. McElhenny warranted such respect without being hurt. He accumulated 1,067 all-purpose yards in 1961, 580 coming on the ground for a 4.8 average, his highest average in five seasons. He had a forty-one-yard run, his longest in four years. He had six touchdowns. All was well.

"It was my best all-around season," he said.

McElhenny was voted the Vikings' team captain as well as their most valuable player. And he was named to his sixth Pro Bowl.

"I really liked Van Blocklin," he said. "A lot of people didn't, but he was good at explaining plays. He was tough, but fair, and he liked to tease. He called me 'Amos Alonzo [Stagg]' because I was the oldest back on the team. If he caught players out after curfew, he'd make them roll from one end zone to the other and back until he told them to stop. But that '61 season, I still could go the distance. And I still had it the next year, too."

That may be true, although McElhenny's workload decreased at age thirty-three. He went from 120 carries to fifty. He did average 4.0 yards a carry in 1962, but didn't have a touchdown for the first time in his career. The Vikings wanted to make top draft pick Tommy Mason their marquee runner. So after the '62 season, McElhenny was traded by Minnesota to the New York Giants, reuniting with Tittle.

McElhenny and Perry would be on the field together for the last time on November 17, 1963 in New York, when the 49ers met the Giants. Perry had one carry for seven yards, McElhenny six carries for fourteen yards and two punt returns for thirteen yards. The Giants won, 48–14.

With the Giants now a playoff team, McElhenny was a happy camper in the Big Apple. By that time, his legs were giving out from years of punishment. And his fledgling grocery business also had taken a pounding, He opened the first McElhenny Market in 1959 in Santa Clara, an hour's drive from San Francisco. He was so optimistic about the bagging groceries that he opened a second market the following year in nearby Pleasanton. However, he wasn't as cut out for the business field as he was for the open field.

"We did real good for two years," he said. "Then when I went back to Minnesota in 1961, I got a letter of foreclosure."

Investigating the situation, McElhenny discovered both of his partners had employed their brothers and sisters in the stores. The partners then told McElhenny they didn't want him in the store any more. Nice guys. When McElhenny asked for and was refused the keys to either store, he hired an attorney immediately. McElhenny was successful in ousting the partners, and both stores stayed open somehow.

"There wasn't a penny saved in either store," McElhenny said. "I wrote a check for $500 just to put money in the cash registers."

That brought only momentary relief. He was forced to declare bankruptcy.

"It felt very degrading," he said. "You get to keep your car and house, that's all. If that business had worked out, I would have retired from football. Now I had to keep playing."

McElhenny's predicament was compounded by his first knee surgery after the 1962 season. Thus when he played for the Giants in 1963, his knee filled up with fluid so often, it had to be drained on Mondays and Fridays.

McElhenny averaged 3.2 yards a carry in a limited backup role. There would be occasional flashes of the McElhenny of old, including one pass play against the Cleveland Browns. Tittle tossed him a ball in the flat. Suddenly the years peeled away and The King ruled again. He faked inside, then cut back to the outside as Browns defenders tried futilely to catch him. He dove into the end zone for the touchdown that helped the Giants win the NFL Eastern Conference title.

There were times, of course, when McElhenny asked himself why he couldn't have been a 49er for life. Otto Graham had played only for the Cleveland Browns, and Sammy Baugh for just the Washington Redskins. Surely McElhenny could have remained an aging role player in San Francisco. Then he reminded himself why it couldn't be that way: Hickey.

"Years later," McElhenny said, "I was at a function when I felt someone touch my shoulder. I turned around and it was Hickey. He had a big smile, and he offered his hand to shake. I walked away."

The 1963 and 1964 seasons wrapped up McElhenny's career. The broken-field runner now was broken down. But the $40,000 he made combined with the Giants and Detroit Lions brought financial relief after his bankruptcy.

"Mac made 300 [speaking] appearances in New York to pay off his supermarket debt," said Brodie. "He won't tell you that, because that's the kind of guy he is. Honorable. The quality of the game was better back then, and there were much-better citizens. Remember, the 49ers and their league [the AAFC] were started with guys who were involved with World War II. Some guys played football in the service, but some guys fought for their country. You don't see that kind of character in the game anymore."

"Twenty-one percent of the players who enter the NFL now are felons," added Unitas. "Unfortunately, that's the direction the game is heading."

It wasn't like that in the 1950s and 1960s, when football players stayed four years in college before entering the professional ranks. Hence, they were better taught about the game when turning pro. Though NFL players are faster overall these days, they aren't as fundamentally sound as the players in McElhenny's and Brodie's era. Brodie certainly can make that distinction: His son-in-law, NFL quarterback Chris Chandler, played four years at the University of Washington, where McElhenny is an alumnus.

McElhenny began the 1964 preseason with New York, where one play put his fading career in clear focus. It's all right there on the VCR. The King sweeps to his left, but is blocked off. He cuts back to his right, where there isn't running room either. So he reverses back to his left, giving a gimpy leg to a defender who swipes and misses. Even as an old man, McElhenny still could still make them look foolish. And once again, like days of old, McElhenny is running free down the sideline. Then he ages thirteen years in three steps. He slows down and almost stops in his tracks. It's as if the VCR suddenly has lost power. A defender who wouldn't have gotten within ten yards of McElhenny a decade earlier appears on camera and drags him down with absolutely no resistance.

"If I maintained the gas in my body, it was a touchdown," McElhenny recalled. "But I was tying up, and I just couldn't go anymore. I was puking as I was running. That run really was the end of my football career."

He was thirty-five when the Giants cut him. The Lions, in need of backfield depth, signed him as a fringe player.

"When he came to Detroit," said Walker, "I asked our coach, George Wilson, if I could room with him. He asked why, and I said, 'It's the closest I've ever been to him.' I got my wish, and we had a great year together. I'd sleep with him tomorrow."

Walker chuckled over the phone from Idaho, where he lives.

In his swan song, McElhenny averaged an embarrassing 2.2 yards per carry. His longest scrimmage run was fourteen yards, an NFL all-time low for him for one season. Ironically, his last football game was played against the 49ers in Detroit. He watched from the sideline as the Lions won, 24-7.

"He was great for us to have," Walker said. "He was great in the locker room, great in practice. He was a real good addition. I love the guy. He's one of my all-time favorites."

McElhenny recalled the difficulty in watching his free fall as an NFL legend. It reached the point where he no longer recognized himself.

"When the [Lions] guards started to sweep, I couldn't catch them," he said. "My legs went dead."

Thus The King abdicated his throne and joined the commoners. He went to work for Burns Security, which trained him for a management position and even built the McElhennys a home in Briarcliff Manor, New York. But the lure of the West Coast remained too strong. The McElhennys packed up and left New York. Hugh entered the advertising field. But traveling two weeks out of every month wasn't what he had in mind, so he resigned.

Then came what he thought was an ideal career opportunity: a chance to bring pro football to Seattle.

"Wayne Field of Minneapolis called out of the blue and asked, 'How would you like to own an NFL team in Seattle? You're Mr. Football there.'"

McElhenny was named executive vice president of the expansion organization. The proposed name of the team was the Seattle Kings, although not necessarily after The King himself. Seattle is located in King County.

The Kings' target date for NFL entry was 1974. But Field's group needed more financing, so McElhenny set up a meeting with the Nordstrom family, owners of the popular department store chain with Northwest roots.

"The Nordstroms asked Wayne if he would give up his 51 percent ownership. He said no," McElhenny said. "Three weeks later, I heard that the Nordstroms formed their own group. And it was the right group, filled with local heavies. The NFL really likes home ownership. So in 1974, they chose the Nordstrom group over us."

The new NFL franchise in Seattle, known as the Seahawks, joined the NFL in 1976. McElhenny was left with the memory of what almost was.

"We didn't get credit for it, but we generated local enthusiasm for pro football in Seattle," he said proudly. "We made it happen."

McElhenny said the opportunity was there at one point for him to join the Nordstrom NFL group. Since he was friendly with Lloyd Nordstrom, he was optimistic that he would be involved with the Seahawks. But when Lloyd died, that opportunity passed.

McElhenny then worked again in advertising before teaming up with a Washington fraternity brother in the thrift store business. Once again, an ugly partnership ensued for McElhenny, and he ended that friendship, too.

Finally, in 1981, he became a marketing director with Pepsi-Cola. This time, he found a positive working relationship that continued until his retirement in 1995, when he was left with a handsome pension.

In 1970, McElhenny was named to the Pro Football Hall of Fame in Canton, Ohio. He was enshrined along with Tom Fears, Jack Christiansen [who had replaced Hickey as 49ers head coach] and Pihos, McElhenny's old helmet-swinging adversary.

Knowing greatness when they see it, the Pro Football Writers Association's members, who vote on Hall of Fame candidates, elected McElhenny the first year he was eligible.

The King told the crowd in Canton he hadn't prepared a speech because he knew he would become emotional. Then he proceeded to become emotional anyway as he accepted this "greatest honor ever bestowed upon me" in the name of his parents, his wife, and his daughters.

"Statistics are hollow," Spadia, president of the 49ers, told the Canton audience that day in introducing McElhenny. "There are no statistics that can describe the beauty and artistry of McElhenny's running...He is the greatest runner of all times."

McElhenny was able to transfer his talents from the playing field to the broadcast booth. As a radio commentator on 49ers games, he proved as bold with his analyses as he had been with his running style.

In January of 1985, McElhenny received a singular honor. He was selected by NFL Commissioner Pete Rozelle to flip the coin for Super Bowl XIX at Stanford.

"I was kind of flabbergasted," McElhenny said. "Pete went to Compton JC before I got there, so maybe that had something to do with it. But that was one of the real highlights of my life. They treated me like a king."

After McElhenny was chosen for the coin flip, President Ronald Reagan decided to become part of the act since California was the state he governed for two terms before setting his sights on Washington, D.C. McElhenny remembers the exact script of that coin flip, which he enjoys reciting as he plays the roles of himself and the president. Reagan wasn't at the game, but was seen on a video screen by 84,059 fans.

"Good afternoon, Mr. President," said McElhenny, replaying the scene in his office at home. "Are you ready to toss the coin? Yes, Mr. McElhenny, we are ready. [The coin is flipped.] Thank you, Mr. President. Thank you, Mr. McElhenny."

Fourteen years later, McElhenny paused to digest that gesture of respect from the White House.

"Thank you, Mr. McElhenny," he repeated, smiling.

Well, even presidents bow before kings.

In October 1996, The King became sick. Very sick. McElhenny awakened in his Seattle home one day, and he couldn't move. Doctors diagnosed his condition as Guillain-Barré syndrome, a paralysis of the motor nerve system.

"I cried for two days thinking I would be paralyzed the rest of my life," he said. "It was a horrible experience. Even when I got out of bed, I wobbled as I walked. We went to Providence Hospital, and doctors thought they would have to fuse my back. I had been having trouble with my back for years.

"For ten days, I'm in intensive care, and I'm not moving. Only I don't know this, because I'm out cold. I was dreaming about frogs walking, things coming out of walls, and seeing myself seated upside down in a chair. When I came to, I wasn't in pain, but I couldn't move. Peggy told me, 'You'll be OK. It's reversible.' But the only thing I could turn was my head. I was scared."

That's when McElhenny learned Guillain-Barré was a virus, not a disease. Nevertheless, his weight dropped from 205 pounds to 145. He couldn't lift five pounds. It would be two months before he could comb his hair, and three months before he could get around with the aid of a walker. But the virus was, indeed, reversible. In a year, McElhenny had regained his lost weight, and he could function normally again.

"I'm doing fine," he said in September, 1999. "I don't have any paralysis, but I have numbness in my toes. And my thighs and buttocks feel weak. Being an athlete, the doctors told me, I progressed so much faster than anyone they had ever treated."

McElhenny's weight is at a trim 190 these days. Opening the door to his Henderson, Nevada home, he has the appearance of a twenty-two-year-old body with a seventy-year-old face. McElhenny still has a full head of hair, only it's gray. He also has upper dentures and partial lower dentures.

"But it's not from football," he said. "I see former players who are limping around. Pete Pihos has had a knee and hip replaced, and he needs another hip. Joe Perry has a new hip and knee. I came out pretty good. No, I came out real good."

Now if he would only cut back on cigarettes. There were numerous smoke breaks during the two days of interviews for this book. He couldn't make it through lunch at a local restaurant without excusing himself so he could light up in the entry way.

After his illness, why would he chain-smoke?

"I stopped for a long time," he said. "Then I started smoking again after my mother died. I can't break the habit."

Peggy gave him a look that said she didn't buy the mother explanation.

McElhenny was asked about his legacy as a football player.

"Strong legs," he replied. "I was gifted. Mom and dad gave me some good genes."

What about the following legacy that others discuss with reverent tones: McElhenny's reputation as the greatest broken-field runner ever?

"No," The King said flatly. "I don't think there's anyone who is the greatest. Nobody can say they're the best. Someone's always a little better, whether it's yesterday or tomorrow. You can't take away from Barry Sanders, Walter Payton and Gale Sayers. They were good at changing directions. As Deacon Jones and Joe Perry like to tell me, 'You weren't bad for a white boy.'"

He's Hugh the Humble. *Sports Illustrated's* Paul Zimmerman picked McElhenny as the third-down back on his All-Century Team. Dr. Z left off Sanders, Payton, and Sayers.

"I think of my favorite play in football, the throwback screen," Zimmerman explained. "With that play, it's minus eight or plus thirty. Only McElhenny never lost yardage. He was the ultimate broken-field runner. How many backs in the NFL today can make you miss? Charlie Garner [of the 49ers] can make you miss."

Who else? Such eminent NFL backs as Terrell Davis, Emmitt Smith, and Jamal Anderson possess speed, strength, and power. But they lack dazzling cutback skills. They're all scaled-down, faster Mike Alstotts.

"My memories of McElhenny are punt returns, kickoff returns, long runs," said *FOX-TV's* Pat Summerall, who used to tackle McElhenny in the NFL. "He's one of those players that when you look across the line of scrimmage, you better be sure you know where he is at all times. He was scary. The closest thing to him I've seen is Gale Sayers. I have this one picture of McElhenny running down the field and pointing out to his blockers which guys to block."

A super-talented back, and a timeless talent.

"I could see McElhenny today in a role like Marshall Faulk's, an every-down back coming out of the backfield, running and receiving." said Summerall. "You'd want him to have as many carries as possible. But you'd worry if McElhenny could hold up. Like most thorough-breds, they do get hurt."

Of NFL backs in the 1990s, only Sanders resembled McElhenny in terms of twisting defenders into human pretzels.

"Hugh is one of those rare guys," said Schmidt, "with sprinter speed, explosiveness, and a lot of football ingenuity."

Then how did Schmidt prepare himself to stop The King?

"With fear," he replied.

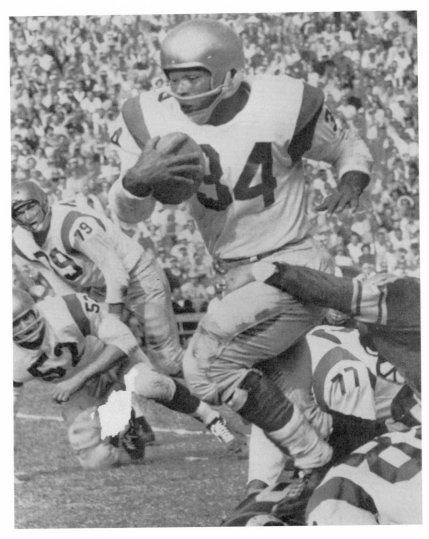

Perry breaks tackle on draw play for 31-yard gain against Rams.

John Thomas provides McElhenny clearing block against Philadelphia.

McElhenny and Perry enjoy a win with 49er executive Lou Spadia (seated between them).

McElhenny's separated shoulder in 1954 means hospital food.

Pete Costanza (left) helps Johnson sign 49ers contract with co-owner
Vic Morabito.

John Henry taking a Minnesota Viking along the the ride.

Upside-down landing for Tittle against the Rams after 8-yard gain.

Y. A. and Minnette on "The Ed Sullivan Show" during the Giant years.

Y. A. Tittle, Joe Perry, Hugh McElhenny, John Henry Johnson—teammates, friends, Hall of Famers—reunited in 2000.

JOHN HENRY JOHNSON
MISTER MEANER

Two of life's certainties: death and taxes. Well, add a third certainty: John Henry Johnson was the meanest football player who ever lived.

What qualifies John Henry as the No. 1 meanie? That's easy. Viciousness. Cunning. Malice. Revenge. Spite. Arrogance. Strength. Hate.

No other football bad guy has ever been so mean-spirited. No other gridiron goon has kept so many plastic surgeons working overtime.

John Henry had all the necessary ingredients of evilness. Away from football, he was as nice and cozy as a warm soft bed. But dress him in football gear, and he was a bed of nails. John Henry was born with a mean gene that spread throughout his body like Dr. Jekyll's laboratory potion, turning him into football's Mr. Hyde.

There is a ton of proof that John Henry was a monster in shoulder pads. No one football player ever injured more people or hit harder in the process. John Henry was Dick Butkus with an attitude, Eugene "Big Daddy" Lipscomb with an ingrown toenail, Hardy "The Hatchet Man" Brown with an impacted tooth, Doug Atkins with a migraine, Ed Sprinkle with his wallet stolen, Jack Tatum with a chip on his shoulder the size of Mt. Whitney.

John Henry had all that meanness, and more. He had enough vitriol inside him to take on an entire league. When John Henry was on the field, he had to be watched more closely than a Mafia family member. In fact, after one of his most destructive hits, the Mafia considered revenge.

John Henry's trail of victims can be found on National Football League medical insurance forms. Or on a Monday morning, standing before their bathroom mirrors and staring at their reworked faces after running into John Henry's forearm on a Sunday afternoon.

"I'd knock them down or knock them out," John Henry said, matter-of-factly, of his unrelenting, unforgiving, punishing style.

Being knocked out by John Henry was seen as a blessing. For he did far worse things to his numerous victims.

"He went out of his way to hurt people," said Bob St. Clair, a former teammate of Johnson's on the San Francisco 49ers.

"John Henry had a shoulder hunch, and he busted a lot of jaws," said Ernie Stautner, both a teammate and an adversary of Johnson's.

John Henry fractured opponents, and he also fractured manufacturing. With one blow.

"The people who played with John Henry liked him. But when he put on a costume, he was dangerous," said onetime Cleveland Browns defensive lineman Paul Wiggin. "When he was with the Steelers, we hit head on with our face masks. We both went backwards. John Henry got up and walked back to the huddle. I got up and went to the sideline. He had totally twisted my face mask. A full face mask, and he sprung it, which is almost impossible to do.

"Another time, when John Henry played for the Lions, he was blocking on the punt team. Ed 'Mighty Mo' Modzelewski was rushing the punter for us. He had two bars on his helmet, and John Henry split both those bars. Just sprung them. I remember Modzelewski on the plane going home. You wouldn't have recognized him. His nose was broken, his face was swollen. John Henry had deformed his face and, I believe, ended his season.

"Then there was the time John Henry hit me on the chin, causing blood. They sewed up my chin up at halftime, then John Henry hit me there again, only in a different spot, causing more blood. The trainer told me, 'The first time was John Henry's fault. The second time was your fault.'"

Johnson caught a blitzing Larry Wilson with such a wicked block that Wilson's teammates on the St. Louis Cardinals feared the little safety was dead. Wilson wondered the same thing.

"He damn near killed me," Wilson said. "It was one of those blows you don't forget over the course of time. I made it back the next series, but I found John Henry and held onto him while everyone else blitzed."

Holding onto John Henry was as difficult as trapping a hurricane inside a baby's blanket.

"He had a forearm," Wilson said, "and he got his butt under him so he could hit you with that forearm and lift you off the ground. He was one of those gifted people who had a built-in pop, no matter if he was blocking or running. He'd really coil up and sock you. He was mean."

Mister Mean. Better yet, Mister Meaner. That's closer to misdemeanor.

John Henry's brand of meanness was hard to emulate. Vincent Price had it on the silver screen, Jack Dempsey in a boxing ring, Bill Laimbeer on a basketball court, Ty Cobb on a baseball diamond.

However, no athlete in any sport broke more opponents' bones than John Henry. He re-arranged faces with a single thrust of the most ferocious forearm in football history. But he wasn't some paid assassin. John Henry was a genuine football hero, a hall of famer who has a long trail of impressive statistics to match his lengthy list of victims.

John Henry rushed for 1,000 yards twice. He played defense, he caught passes, he threw passes. He was the best blocking fullback of all time.

"He'd spring at you, like a Jack-in-the-box, and smack you in the face," said Joe Schmidt, another NFL great who played with and against Johnson. "He'd get pissed off at guys. He laid a lot of guys out pass-blocking. He was explosive."

John Henry listened to descriptions of his take-no-prisoners style. He offered an explanation, much like a mugger telling a victim that he's sorry.

"It was payback time," he said in 1999. "When I had a good day running the ball, they'd step on me as I got up. I'd tell them, 'You got one coming.' And when I'd get them back later, I'd say, 'Oh, man, I didn't know it was you.' Then they'd play the game the way it was supposed to be played."

And if they happened to forget, John Henry was there to remind them. And he was always fair about it, because he didn't delineate between scrubs and Hall of Famers such as Sam Huff.

"He crushed my face mask against my face," said Huff, the former New York Giants and Washington Redskins linebacker.

Huff got off luckier than Carl Taseff of the Baltimore Colts.

"John Henry hit Carl so hard, he broke his nose, and Carl damn near died," said Johnny Unitas, Taseff's teammate. "Carl was a hypochondriac anyway, but they kept sticking cotton in his nose. Every time they took out the cotton, the blood rushed out. So they had to stick in more cotton. It was a deliberate blow."

But that hit was a love tap compared to what John Henry did to Charley Trippi. Trippi, the Chicago Cardinals' Hall of Fame halfback, was playing safety against the 49ers during a 1956 exhibition in San Francisco. Trippi was trailing a scrimmage run, which was almost whistled dead when Trippi turned just in time to catch Johnson's full venom.

"John Henry tore his face up," recalled Joe Perry, who was a witness that day.

Johnson had a machete disguised as a forearm.

"It looked like someone had butchered a hog," recalled Pat Summerall, who was Trippi's teammate. "John Henry hit him under the eye socket, crushing his cheekbone, breaking his nose, and knocking out some teeth. We walked into the locker room at halftime. Blood was everywhere. Charley's face was a pulp. There was talk about getting even, and there were late shots by both teams in the second half. I was the Cardinal captain that day, and the officials called me and the 49er captain together. The officials told us they would take time off the clock [for every penalty because of a late hit]. Finally, they shortened the game by five minutes.

"Charley made some token appearances at defensive back that season, then he retired. I still see Charley, and he never looked the same after that hit. It changed his whole facial look."

Football judges throwing flags couldn't stop John Henry's violent nature. It was suggested on any number of occasions that a higher judge should throw the book at him.

"John Henry would have been banned from football if that [Trippi hit] happened today," said Lou Spadia, a 49ers executive on that bloody Sunday. "They may have put him in jail."

Or maybe six feet under. Trippi was Italian, you see. And after Johnson caved in his face, word circulated back to San Francisco that the Chicago Mafia was ready to pay its respects to Johnson.

"That's true," said Summerall. "I heard Charley say, 'I've got some guys who can even things.'"

But nothing came of it, fortunately for Johnson.

"I heard about that [rumor]," John Henry said in an October 1999 interview near Cleveland, where he lives. "But I ain't seen nobody looking strange at me all these years."

He broke into a grin, a wry grin with the slightest hint of evil at the corners.

There must be a statute of limitations on NFL mayhem that runs its course even with Mafia dons. Thus Johnson was free, from 1956 to 1966, to continue breaking up body parts. Johnson hit with everything he had, and with anything he could get his hands on. Three irate Los Angeles Rams charged him one day, seeking retribution. Johnson grabbed a sideline marker and began swinging wildly at his attackers. He made enough contact to keep all three at bay.

"I needed some help," explained John Henry, still defending himself against accusations of thuggery as he approached his seventieth birthday.

Johnson didn't need assistance normally. He fought his football battles alone, whether he initiated the violence or merely reacted in order to gain revenge. His roughhouse style invited many challengers, but few rematches. One time around with John Henry was enough for anybody.

Engaging him was like swimming in an ocean without shark repellent. John Henry's favorite blocking technique was to hunker down behind a big lineman, then spring at the last second, catching an unsuspecting defender below the jaw or, before full face masks, across the cheek.

That's how he surprised Wilson, who didn't see him hiding there until it was too late.

"I'd pop up like a snake," Johnson said, hunching his right shoulder for effect.

John Henry had the shoulder, the forearm, and the knee to bust up, bruise, and bloody. He had an entire football tool kit of malicious methods. Opponents had to guess instantly which one he would use.

"If I really wanted to get even, I'd use my head in their chest or gut," he said. "Or if I really got mad, I'd put a helmet on their knees."

Or a knee on their helmet. John Henry wore a knee brace that he utilized more to punish others than to protect his knee. But it wouldn't be wise even now to insinuate Johnson was a cheap-shot artist whose sole mission on Earth was to terminate football careers. Although in the autumn of his life, John Henry's hooded eyes instantly warn others that to invite this old-timer out into an alley wouldn't be the wisest decision.

"I was no dirty player," he insisted. "I was a player, a good player. I played both offense and defense in the pros. It was survival. That's a good word for it. To play football, you've got to have desire and love of the game. And then the physical attributes will come. But you've got to love contact."

Contact to Johnson was like an oasis to a wanderer in the Gobi desert. John Henry thirsted to hit. And he hungered for flesh to pound.

Contact was the very measure of his manhood. Finesse, to him, was for the fainthearted.

John Henry preferred to make a dent on the game of football, and on his fellow players' anatomies. Along the way, he evolved into one of the game's highest-echelon players. He was inducted into the Pro Football Hall of Fame in 1987. None of his fellow enshrinees who were there asked for protection.

"John Henry Johnson was 200 pounds of hate," wrote the late Jim Murray, the Pulitzer Prize-winning sports columnist of the *Los Angeles Times*, "with or without the football, from the time the kickoff was in the air 'til they pulled him off some hapless ball-carrier...John Henry made the German Army seem like the Salvation Army. He played football games against people as if he were trying to extract confessions from them. He went after complete strangers as if he had just caught them rifling through his pockets at the foot of his bed or passing notes to his wife."

Johnson showed no expression in 1999 as Murray's nineteen-year-old column was read to him. The old fullback shrugged.

"I can't think of anyone I hated," he said. "I wanted to play the best I could to win. I wanted guys to know they had played against one of the best. I wanted them to say, 'John Henry, he's going to hit you.'"

Schmidt noted that Johnson sometimes missed a block in his zeal to settle a score. Misses were OK with John Henry. The way he looked at things, there would be other opportunities for payback. And like a Royal Canadian Mountie, he would get his man eventually.

But let's not forget that Johnson was a natural athlete, and not just some helmeted hit man. At the overly ripe age of thirty-five, when running backs are either retired or getting by on past reputations, Johnson became the oldest NFL back to rush for 1,000 yards.

So John Henry had ways of punishing teams without resorting to violence. However, amassing all those rushing yards had to be dangerous, since opponents now had more opportunities to exact a piece of him for all the damage he had done to them.

Looking back, it can be said assuredly that they failed in their revenge motives. For one thing, John Henry's face isn't disfigured. And his body isn't stooped like Quasimodo's from someone trying to break his neck. John Henry was hostile, but he could move. The revenge-minded never caught up to him.

Thus John Henry has aged as gracefully as any fullback who ever played. Possibly because he was underused in his twenties, he grew stronger in his thirties. When he retired in 1966, his late charge had made him pro football's No. 4 all-time rusher (6,803 yards) behind Jim Brown, Perry, and Jim Taylor.

John Henry was, first and foremost, a football player. Hate was secondary to his passion for the game. He even loved to practice. If he ever needed extra motivation to suit up and play, he found it whenever his Pittsburgh Steelers played the Cleveland Browns and the formidable Jim Brown. On one such occasion, Johnson rushed for 200 yards and three touchdowns to lead a 23-7 Steeler victory.

His best games always came against the Browns—and Brown.

"It was true," said Johnson. "I had to outgain Jim Brown. I wanted to be the best [back] on the field. Pittsburgh and Cleveland were a natural rivalry. The Browns were always going to the playoffs. And so if we beat them, it made our season."

Brown is regarded universally as the greatest fullback of all time. But Johnson doesn't shrink from comparing himself with Brown.

"We had different styles," John Henry said. "I was more powerful and a better blocker."

Brown was, by all accounts, an inadequate blocker. He and Johnson were fine receivers. They were similar in speed and size.

Johnson was six one, 230, Brown six two, 228. Brown was shiftier, smoother, and sounder. Injuries plagued Johnson during his career, while Brown enjoyed better health, not to mention better offensive lines and more chances at carrying the football.

Before critics dismiss John Henry Johnson historically as a second-tier fullback, they should check out his highlight films. Then the critics will find, or rediscover, that he was, indeed, something truly special.

One film clip in particular shows John Henry's underrated running skills. Pinned in between some linebackers and defensive backs, he makes not one, but two amazing lateral cuts in quick succession. And it's merely an attempt to shake loose. John Henry succeeds in immobilizing the defenders, like statues, then he barrels ahead for a touchdown.

Ninety-eight percent of today's backs don't run that way. The trend now is to run straight ahead with speed and power. John Henry could do that as well, but he had swivel hips to match his brute strength.

Also on the video, John Henry leaps over tall piles for touchdowns. He was vaulting this way before the University of Southern California's Sam "Bam" Cunningham popularized the goal-line fullback high dive.

And there on film is John Henry making one-handed catches, throwing touchdown passes, bulling through tacklers, running away from tacklers, spinning out of tackles, and changing directions as he jukes and jerks his way free. He skips lightly across a snow-blanketed field as if maneuvering on cross-country skis. After he ends this run in the end zone, he casually flips the ball to an official. No big deal.

It's all there on tape, a remarkably skilled talent.

"John was a full football player," Pittsburgh Steelers owner Art Rooney said the day he presented Johnson for induction into the Pro Football Hall of Fame.

"John Henry went three ways—offense, defense, and to the death," Bobby Layne liked to say.

Layne and Johnson were teammates in Detroit and Pittsburgh, and still friends years later. But before those two teamed up, Johnson was with the San Francisco 49ers from 1954 to 1956.

Unlike Hugh McElhenny, Perry, and Y. A. Tittle, the three other members of the Million Dollar Backfield, John Henry spent the bulk of his professional career outside of San Francisco. Nevertheless, he had an immediate impact on the 49ers. As an NFL rookie in San Francisco in 1954, he ran for 681 yards (5.1) as the 49ers set an NFL team record by averaging 5.7 yards per rush.

Perry, McElhenny, and Johnson. Choose your poison. Their first game together was the 1954 season opener against Washington. Perry rushed twelve times for ninety yards and two touchdowns. McElhenny had nine carries for fifty-four yards. Johnson had only one attempt, but it was an eight-yard touchdown run.

The next week against the Rams, Perry rushed four times for forty-seven yards, McElhenny eleven for seventy-three, and Johnson nine for sixty. McElhenny had a twenty-eight yard touchdown burst, while Johnson scored from twenty-four yards.

The 49ers' ground attack was a three-headed monster. In the third game, against Green Bay, Perry had twenty-three attempts for 100 yards, McElhenny fifteen for ninety, and Johnson fourteen for seventy-nine. That's 269 yards among them. The three were even more lethal the next week against the Bears with 287 yards-Perry eleven rushes for 119, McElhenny ten for 114, Johnson thirteen for fifty-four.

The 49ers improved to 4-0-1 against Detroit as Perry carried thirteen times for fifty-one yards, McElhenny seven for 126, and Johnson eleven for eighty-three. That's 260 more yards, plus thirteen rushing touchdowns among them in five games.

The NFL hadn't ever experienced three running backs like that before, not on the same team, anyway. The 49ers began to look unstoppable on offense, especially with Tittle passing to Billy Wilson and Gordy Soltau.

One week later, it all came apart. McElhenny, the NFL's leading rusher up until that point, carried twelve times for fifty-eight yards against the Bears before separating his shoulder. He was done for the year. Perry had ten attempts for thirty-nine yards that day, while Johnson had eight tries for forty-nine yards, including a thirty-eight-yard touchdown run.

The 49ers' 31-27 defeat triggered a three-game losing streak. Only one of the three losses was a blowout, 48-7 at Detroit, before the 49ers recovered, winning three of their last four for a 7-4-1 record. It was a respectable finish without McElhenny.

"Mac was an excellent runner and receiver," Johnson said. "He was a good open-field runner. He had the moves. I can't think of anyone better. I miss watching Mac run. Joe was a serious, determined runner. He had good speed and power. Y. A. had good quarterback sense. He was a nice guy who got along with everyone."

Since Johnson was the new running back in town, he had to wait his turn in the huddle if he wanted to share the football.

"That could have been a problem," he said. "But Mac was no power runner, so that made a difference."

With McElhenny sidelined, Perry and Johnson presented a dangerous duo for the NFL in 1954. Against the Rams in the seventh game, Perry carried twelve times for 124 yards and a fifty-six-yard breakaway for a touchdown. Johnson had thirteen rushes for eighty-one yards and two touchdowns, including his most exciting run as a 49er, a thirty-seven-yard scoring burst in which he did a full 360 to avoid one tackler, and then dragged another defender the final five yards into the end zone.

"John Henry had different styles of running, slow motion or fast," said St. Clair. "Running was a rhythm for him. He was like a dancer."

While Perry had thirteen carries for eighty-six yards in the onesided loss in Detroit, Johnson was held in check with twenty yards in fourteen attempts. It was a different story the following week in

Pittsburgh when Johnson rushed seventeen times for 124 yards, highlighted by a twenty-four-yard touchdown run. Perry added 122 yards on twenty-one rushes.

The 49ers then blew out the Packers as Perry had twenty attempts for 137 yards, and Johnson two carries for thirty-two yards. In the season-ending game against Baltimore, Perry bulled for forty-two yards on eighteen carries, while Johnson had fifteen yards on only three carries.

With McElhenny gone, Perry and Johnson finished 1-2 in the NFL.

"We felt like we were pretty good moving the ball," Johnson said. "Billy could catch anything, and we had a good offensive line. The defense was only fair. We had a couple of good linemen in Leo [Nomellini] and Charlie Powell, and that was pretty much it."

John Henry had a nervous habit of speaking inaudibly. The words either came from deep down in his throat or from under his breath. Or sometimes he'd lump together a succession of words that produced a mumbling effect.

John Henry's 49er teammates still refer to him affectionately as Mumbles.

Johnson planned a much longer stay with the 49ers than three years because San Francisco was close to home. His teenage years were spent across San Francisco Bay in the towns of Pittsburg and Moraga.

A half-century after he played high school sports in Pittsburg, John Henry is considered the greatest all-around prep athlete ever produced on the east side of the bay.

John Henry's athletic career, interestingly, would take him from Pittsburg, California, to Pittsburgh, Pennsylvania. But, geographically, he is a child of the South. He was born November 24, 1929, in tiny, honest-to-goodness Waterproof, Louisiana.

"Good ol'Waterproof," he said. "It's a little town with one main street. There were no stoplights. Didn't need one. Only a wagon came through."

Along with John Henry's inherent meanness is a sly, mumbly sense of humor.

"Schools in Waterproof were segregated," he said on a more serious note. "I went to the black school until the sixth grade. We played the white kids in sports, but just in basketball and baseball. There was no football. I can't remember whites and blacks ever fighting, nothing like that. My mother was a cook for a white family, so I played with white kids."

Ella Johnson was John Henry's mother. She raised five children after her husband, a railroad porter, was killed when the train he worked on derailed. John Henry, the baby of the family, was three at the time.

"My mother was a self-taught piano player," he said. "There was this bar in Waterproof owned by a man named Louis Chester. The bar was segregated, whites in the front, blacks in the back. My mother played and sang in the colored bar for recreation. I did my homework at the bar waiting for her to finish. Sundays, she played and sang in the Baptist church."

What's life like in Waterproof these days?

"I haven't been back to Waterproof in a long time," said Johnson. "I thought it had fallen down by now. I hear, though, the old house still is sitting there on the corner."

When John Henry was thirteen, his mother decided he needed male guidance. So she sent him to California to live with his brother, Milford Simpson, and Milford's wife in Pittsburg, a blue-collar community. Milford had found work in a steel mill. He was ten years older than John Henry. They lived together in Columbia Park, a project housing development in Pittsburg, where blacks and whites co-existed.

"It was a pretty normal upbringing," John Henry said. "All the kids in Columbia Park were poor, Depression kids with holes in our pants.

That's when I started playing all sports. I was a natural athlete pretty quickly. Football was my favorite sport because I got to hit people."

During that time, America had emerged from the Depression and was heading into a world war. Blacks such as Milford Simpson emigrated from the South to Pittsburg and other East Bay towns looking for work in the early 1940s. A main source of employment was building the warships that engaged the Japanese in the Pacific.

Athletic as a teen, John Henry was far ahead of his peers. Every sport he participated in, he not only stood out, he set new standards. In basketball, he led Pittsburg to the Contra Costa County Athletic League championship. He was the county's top scorer two straight years. He set a single-game county basketball record with thirty-three points back in the late 1940s, when some prep teams didn't score thirty-three points over an entire game.

"I was a six-foot center who played inside a lot," he said. "I used my size and leaping ability to rebound and put the ball back in the basket. I was a good leaper, and I had a good hook shot from the free-throw line."

Johnson played one season of baseball at Pittsburg High, batting .550 as a first baseman and outfielder. He hit the long ball, showed a strong throwing arm, and demonstrated speed on the bases. Then, abruptly, he quit.

"There were no opportunities for blacks in baseball at the time," he explained.

Jackie Robinson was the only black playing major league baseball in the spring of 1948, when John Henry gave the national pastime a whirl. The Cleveland Indians brought up outfielder Larry Doby that same summer, making him the first black to play in the American League.

There were no blacks playing professional basketball in 1948. Football and track were the two most integrated sports in our country. Johnson excelled in both.

"Football was my best sport. I did track and field because it was track and field time," he said. "If something was going on that was competitive, I had to be involved."

John Henry broke records in the discus, shot put, and low hurdles in a sectional meet. He then won the California state discus championship with a record throw of 148 feet, eight inches. He trained for a while as a decathlete and entered the 1949 Amateur Athletic Union Decathlon Championships, competing against 1948 Olympic gold-medalist Bob Mathias. Johnson was a longshot, at best, but led Mathias after a few events. John Henry then injured an ankle and was forced to withdraw. He never competed again in a national AAU meet.

Track and field was Mathias's No. 1 sport. He played football as a diversion, although his 1951 kickoff return for a touchdown against USC put Stanford in the Rose Bowl. Conversely, track was a hobby for Johnson, who used the sport basically to stay in shape for football.

"The 1,500-meter run scared me to death," he said of the tenth and final decathlon event.

At Pittsburg High, Johnson was known as the "Mayor of Columbia Park" and the "Midnight Express" for his athletic exploits. One nickname was taken from the project where he lived, while the other nickname reflected his skin pigmentation.

The 1940s was a time of social stigmatizing. White sportswriters pinned racist nicknames on black athletes, and got away with it because they had white editors and publishers. Referring to Johnson as the "Midnight Express" was comparable to calling heavyweight boxing champion Joe Louis the "Brown Bomber." Johnson should be thankful he wasn't known as the "Pittsburg Pickaninny."

In football, he was a three-time all-league fullback, and a one-man show. He led Pittsburg to an unbeaten record in 1948, his senior year. On defense, he made 75 percent of the tackles. On offense, he was a touchdown machine, with at least one fifty-yard run per game.

One East Bay sportswriter tagged Johnson as a "combination of Bronko Nagurski and Red Grange." John Henry didn't mind the comparison, because it connoted an offensive player, although he hadn't ever seen Nagurski and Grange play.

"I enjoyed offense more," he said of his career. "Defense gave me a chance to get even. But on offense, you got a chance to score and run over guys."

Which was typical John Henry football: Bury 'em.

"If they're in the way, I'm in a position to roll over them," he said. "I liked to run straight ahead, because if you're going sideways, you're not making any yards, and tacklers have a better angle on you."

Johnson developed his "pop up like a snake" blocking technique in Pittsburg. His high school friends wondered how he came up with that terminology, knowing he was deathly afraid of snakes. He dealt with this fear in the summer while working for the United States Forest Service. Like Smokey the Bear, he prevented forest fires. Part of his job was cutting grass and establishing fire lines so that potential flames wouldn't spread. He walked the hills and mountains, searching for fire signs and also plants which killed pine trees.

Working all summer long in a remote area allowed Johnson to save money, except for occasional misfortunes while playing cards. All that walking worked his legs into shape for football, and sharpened his reflexes in order to avoid reptiles.

"I hate snakes, and there were rattlesnakes and water moccasins around where I worked," he said. "I did kill some rattlesnakes. I pinned them with a stick, and then killed them. I always had someone to help me."

During the school year, he worked for a jukebox company, thanks to his benefactor, Pete Costanza, a Pittsburg man whom everyone called "Cherry," and who liked the soft-spoken youngster from Waterproof. John Henry's job was to stack the latest, hottest records in jukeboxes in restaurants and bars around town. Costanza even bought him a car, a Dodge, so he could get around. To keep the car, Costanza told John Henry, he had to maintain good grades, which he did in high school and college.

"Pete Costanza took John Henry under his wing and became like a father to him," said Leona Johnson, John Henry's second wife. "Whenever we went to see this man, he'd cry every time we had to leave. He named his first son, John, after John Henry. Pete loved my husband. The whites in that town loved him, too.

"When John Henry went into the Pro Football Hall of Fame, a number of his white teammates from high school came all the way to Ohio for the ceremony. Pete Costanza and his wife, Dorothy, came, too. They were the most wonderful couple. Pete died in the 1990s. We miss him terribly."

Because of his competitive nature, Johnson played a variety of sports in high school. But he recognized that a scholarship was his best chance at a college education. And he received offers in football, basketball and track. Black colleges such as Grambling and Jackson State in the South contacted him, but he didn't want to go that far away from Pittsburg.

When St. Mary's College, an all-male integrated school in nearby Moraga, offered Johnson a football scholarship, he accepted. He knew the Gaels had a rich football tradition. They played a national schedule and had appeared in major bowl games. Only a few years before, in 1945, St. Mary's had a legitimate first-team All-America back in Herman Wedemeyer, known as "Squirmin' Herman." Years later, Wedemeyer achieved widespread fame again for his supporting role as a detective on the popular "Hawaii 5-0" television series.

"In the Wedemeyer era, they really cut it up," Johnson said of the Gaels. "He was a great football player. That was the place for me."

Johnson was the first black to play football at St. Mary's, and the second black to play a competitive sport on the picturesque campus that looked like an old California mission. Enrolling in 1949, Johnson played on the freshman football team. Unfortunately, Gaels football had taken a turn for the worse by the time he got there. Joe Verducci resigned as varsity coach after the Gaels went 3-6-1 that season.

Verducci could see an attitude change at St. Mary's, and so he got out. The school's administration had become increasingly apathetic towards big-time football. And St. Mary's faculty said, sarcastically, that the "SMC" painted on the hill overlooking the campus really stood for "Slip Madigan College."

Madigan coached football at St. Mary's for 20 years until the late 1930s. He is directly responsible for moving the college from the "Old Brickpile" building in downtown Oakland to the spacious Moraga Valley because of the football powerhouse he had built. His Gaels beat some of the best teams in the country while Madigan became a guest of the White House and Hollywood, and he even found a place on the team bench for Babe Ruth.

Madigan became bigger than the school. The administration didn't like playing butler in Slip's self-built castle, and eventually forced him to resign. It was downhill from there, and Gaels football was about to hit rock bottom when Verducci bailed out. He even took a pay cut to become head coach of less-prestigious San Francisco State College. His replacement at St. Mary's was Joe Ruetz, who later became Stanford's athletic director.

There was one marvelous moment left for the Gaels. On September 29, 1950, in San Francisco, sophomore John Henry Johnson gained national recognition when he took on eighth-ranked Georgia practically by himself. The Bulldogs, favored by four touchdowns, saw the Gaels as an easy mark on the schedule.

Imagine Georgia's astonishment when St. Mary's pulled off a 7-7 tie. John Henry made the tie possible. The Gaels put up two successful goal-line stands in the first half as Johnson made tackle after tackle. Then with the game still scoreless at halftime, Johnson returned the third-quarter kickoff ninety-one yards for a touchdown.

"That was the greatest game I ever saw John Henry play," said Paul Zimmerman of *Sports Illustrated*. "I was going to Stanford, and a bunch of us went up to see the game on a Friday night at Kezar Stadium. John Henry kept St. Mary's in the game. He was a mean, rough guy. He backed up the line with both fists. Whoever came through, he slaughtered them. He was the reason the game was a tie."

John Henry was the first black to play football against Georgia. After the game, teammates and fans carried him off the field, an unusual display of affection for a black athlete back then. These same fans then waited an hour for John Henry to re-appear from the locker room. He was greeted with more back-slapping and another chorus of cheers.

"He's a great football player," Georgia coach Wally Butts said, rather reluctantly, of Johnson.

"I don't remember that kickoff return. It passed me by," Johnson said nearly 40 years later. "I do remember it was a tough game. I played both ways so I could smack them."

The Bulldogs wanted a rematch the following year on their turf. Butts sought revenge. Ruetz agreed, but only if there was no objection to blacks playing "between the hedges" in Athens, Georgia. Butts told Ruetz he would think about it, although no one in Moraga expected the game to come off because it takes two teams to make a football game.

A week after the Georgia tie, John Henry encountered the first controversy over his rock-'em, sock-'em style. The Gaels visited Loyola University of Los Angeles, a game the home team won in a breeze, 48-0. As a harbinger of things to come in Johnson's career, spectators and the Los Angeles-area media accused him of playing overly aggressive. Translated: Dirty football. Ruetz defended his player, saying he had watched John Henry closely for four quarters, and didn't see him do "anything seriously offensive. Rough, yes. But football is a tight, hard game."

Ruetz pointed out that while Johnson was penalized for illegal use of the hands, he wasn't ejected. The problem, Ruetz added, was that

John Henry declined to wrap his arms around an opponent when tackling. Instead, he held his arms in a blocking position in order to stun the ball-carrier.

A half-century ago, coaches didn't teach tackling that way at any football level. John Henry was an innovator, though he didn't get the recognition that inventors normally receive.

"It's a trick the boy learned at high school," said Ruetz. "We're trying to break him of the habit. I told John Henry, 'You're a marked man.'"

And he would remain that way for the rest of his football career. But Ruetz's counsel left no lasting impression on John Henry. In boxing terms, he was a slugger, not a jabber. His style was attack, not counterattack. In fact, John Henry was told by boxing people that he had the skills and toughness to become a heavyweight champion if he would give up football.

If Johnson had pursued the "sweet science," pity the opposition. He would have been Mike Tyson, only more scientific and without quit. The way Johnson sized it up, though, he didn't need to box. He could get the same licks in playing football without gloves, and wearing protective headgear.

"They make you play tough in football, and I could hit them," he said. "I'd uncoil on people."

However, wrapping his arms around a ball-carrier wasn't John Henry's concept of football. Wrapping, he felt, should be saved for Christmas gifts.

St. Mary's next game after Loyola was against the University of San Francisco. The Dons had three future Pro Football Hall of Famers in end Gino Marchetti, fullback Ollie Matson, and St. Clair. USF blew out the overmatched Gaels, 33-7. Matson rushed for seventy-eight yards while Johnson was held to minus fourteen yards on the ground. As St. Mary's only threat, he was swarmed on by the Dons every time he touched the ball.

On defense, though, Johnson owned the field. San Francisco sportswriter Prescott Sullivan observed as much afterwards. While the local literati had declared Matson the winner of this battle between two "Negro" stars, Sullivan had a different perspective.

"There he was," Sullivan wrote, "the most dramatic figure on the field and, inexplicably for our dough, the star of the game. John Henry is the most vivid personality to grace a local gridiron in years. It begins with his name, a Paul Bunyanesque kind of moniker.

"Measured by football standards, Johnson isn't a big man, but he seems to be a giant out there in everything he does. You wonder how far he would have rambled had he the benefit of a bonafide college line, one, say, like that which provides Matson with racing room. Defensively [Johnson] was great. Once he threw a tackling block at USF's six-foot-seven-inch St. Clair, and all but knocked him out of the stadium. St. Mary's hasn't much of a team this year, but it has in Johnson a boy who is worth the price of admission by himself."

St. Clair hasn't forgotten that tackling block.

"I was playing end on offense," he said. "I remember catching a pass and running over one of their defensive backs. I'm heading for the goal line and I see another jersey coming. I lowered my shoulder, and I was really going to give it to him. And the guy went through my legs and flipped me five, six feet in the air. I landed upside down in the end zone, but I couldn't walk. My leg was numb. He had given me a charley horse. That was my first introduction to John Henry. Oh, was he tough. He tackled like hell. He loved to hit. And he had a mean streak."

Joe Rubay, a defensive tackle on that 1950 St. Mary's team, said Matson hit him hard in that game, but Johnson hit him harder in practice.

"I was trailing Ollie on a sweep when he reversed his field, and I hit him head on," said Rubay. "I thought I was hit by a truck. He almost knocked me out. But I thought John Henry was a better player. He was very powerful, bigger than Ollie, with these big, hammy thighs. He played with such reckless abandon. Ollie loped when he ran, but John Henry ran right into you.

"He was kind of a prima donna when he came to St. Mary's. If he didn't get through the line, he'd blame the linemen. Don't get me wrong, he was great. An outstanding player. I saw him a few years ago. He's a nice man."

After playing Georgia even, the Gaels finished 2-7-1 in 1950. Their season finale, against visiting Villanova, nearly was called off after three days of heavy rain pelted the Bay Area. It was decided at the very last minute to play. Only 200 tickets were sold, and maybe 150 people showed up to watch the Philadelphia school win, 13-7.

The game's gross receipts added up to $658. St. Mary's had to reach into its general fund to fulfill the $15,000 it had guaranteed Villanova. The handwriting was on the wall for St. Mary's. But not only the Gaels. The Bay Area's two other Catholic schools, Santa Clara and USF, also were getting ready to shut down high-profile football programs that were drowning in red ink, even though USF produced an undefeated team in 1951.

Johnson scored St. Mary's final touchdown as a major college power. In the rain and mud at Kezar, he slid across an indistinguishable goal line against Villanova following a short sweep to his right. St. Mary's dropped football after that game. Football would return to Moraga seventeen years later, but as a small-college program, the only football of its kind left in the San Francisco Bay Area. Santa Clara and USF gave the sport another scaled-down run themselves before pulling the plug for good.

"My dad used to take me to those games at Kezar Stadium involving USF, St. Mary's, and Santa Clara," said John Brodie. "And watching John Henry, it was a man against boys."

Brodie missed by one year playing with Johnson on the 49ers. But Brodie played against Johnson when he was a Lion and a Steeler. Brodie recognized that John Henry was as mean as a room of starving wildcats, yet he never showed an evil side.

"I know John Henry had a reputation, but in football back then, it was get 'em first," said Brodie. "And there was an ethic. John Henry never got anyone in the back."

Johnson was upset when the Gaels got out of the football business. Although he didn't have the same calibre of talent around him as Herman Wedemeyer, John Henry thrived those two years at St. Mary's. He enjoyed getting to nearby Orinda or Oakland to spend some of the hundred dollars he received monthly from alumni. But he had no interest in staying around St. Mary's to play intramural football. If he had, there wouldn't have been enough students to attend classes. He began looking into schools where he might transfer, schools that wouldn't be giving up football.

He settled on Arizona State University, for two reasons. He preferred a sunny climate. And some St. Mary's teammates already had transferred to the Tempe, Arizona, campus and recommended he join them. Arizona State then was a member of the Border Conference. During a 1952 game against Hardin-Simmons in Abilene, Texas, Johnson and his black teammates had to stay in a hotel separate from the white players.

"That made me mad," John Henry recalled, "so I took it out on the other team."

He scored three touchdowns, including a sixty-three-yard punt return, as Arizona State triumphed, 26-7, the Sun Devils' first series victory over Hardin-Simmons after eleven defeats.

In Arizona, Johnson became an all-around athlete once again. He went both ways in football. He made an impact on the Sun Devils basketball team. He excelled in track, hurling the discus more than 150 feet, tossing the javelin 200 feet, broad-jumping twenty-three feet, high-jumping six-three, putting the shot forty-seven feet, and sprinting 100 yards in 10.1 seconds.

Talk renewed about his becoming a decathlete. But his heart was too much into football. Besides, there was no money in track, and he had others to worry about under the same roof. He had married Barbara Flood, sister of baseball star Curt Flood. Johnson now was a father. He would have five children to feed before he was thirty. So money was a primary consideration by the time he graduated from Arizona State with a degree in physical education and social studies.

What were Johnson's professional prospects? Arizona State lacked the football reputation then it would acquire a decade later under Frank Kush. Under Clyde B. Smith, Johnson's football coach with the Sun Devils, ASU had a decent program, but wasn't yet a conveyor belt to the NFL. Smith was extremely positive about Johnson's potential.

"John Henry has the greatest all-around ability of any lad I've ever coached," he said. "He should be great as a pro. He's big enough at 200 pounds. He has cat-like reflexes. He's adaptable and can play equally well on offense and defense. I predict he'll be one of the most promising rookies in pro ball next year, especially if they play him at safety or defensive halfback."

Defense? What, no offense? John Henry had other ideas.

The Steelers selected Johnson in the second round of the 1953 draft, then offered him a $12,000 contract. But Calgary of the Canadian Football League offered him $15,000, which would buy more groceries for a growing family. Johnson took the Stampeders' money and headed north of the border.

Calgary's record was 3-12-1 in 1953. However, Johnson was named the CFL's Most Valuable Player after playing superb defense and offense.

"The people were so nice and friendly," he said of his Canadian experience. "They treated me royally. No racism. I loved Montreal and Toronto, my two favorite cities there. But I wasn't happy playing with three downs and a big soccer field."

So Johnson gave up Canadian sunsets after one year. He now was ready for the NFL. He found a booster in Frankie Albert, the onetime 49ers quarterback who had ended his career with Calgary in 1953.

"Johnson is as good as Hugh McElhenny and Joe Perry," Albert said. "He played sixty minutes of nearly every ball game, and was the main ball carrier. He also was outstanding on defense."

With Albert as his pitch man, and Pete Costanza lobbying on his behalf in conversations with 49ers owner Tony Morabito, Johnson was about to become a member of the most celebrated backfield of all time. The 49ers traded defensive back Ed Fullerton to Pittsburgh for the negotiating rights to Johnson and signed him for $20,000. Fullerton lasted one season with the Steelers, while Johnson blazed a Hall of Fame career over the next thirteen seasons.

His 49er debut came during the 1954 preseason. Johnson's number was called on almost every play early in the game by quarterback Y. A. Tittle, who wanted to check out the heralded new addition. After yet another carry, Johnson returned to the huddle exhausted. He confronted Tittle.

"Listen, ABC or XYZ or whatever your name is, give the ball to somebody else because I'm tired," Johnson said.

John Henry had a sense of humor. He could pop up like a snake, or he might pop up on Bob Hope.

With the forming of the Million Dollar Backfield, media in the San Francisco area wanted to know: Who was the fastest? Perry, McElhenny, and Johnson all had track backgrounds. A sprinter, a hurdler, a decathlete. A perfect match race.

So how did it turn out?

McElhenny said that for forty, fifty yards, Perry was the fastest. But after 100 yards, McElhenny contended, it was a tossup between himself and Johnson.

Gordy Soltau was their teammate those three years, and he doesn't remember one match race among the threesome.

"They never did sprint," said Soltau. "Buck Shaw never did hundreds. We did fifties. Those three guys never were in a heat. But on any given day, it would have been a dead heat."

John Henry's recollection?

"Don't know," he said. "We were all pretty fast."

Johnson would have three head coaches during his three seasons in San Francisco: Lawrence T. "Buck" Shaw, Norman "Red" Strader, and Albert. Shaw was fired after the 1954 season, even though his winning percentage was .638 (72-40-10). Team owner Tony Morabito felt Shaw was too lenient with the players.

"Buck was an excellent coach," said Johnson. "He was soft-spoken, but he had good control of the team. Guys liked him."

Strader, unlike Shaw, prohibited drinking and smoking. He became unpopular with the players almost immediately.

"Strader came in there like a dominator, a controller," said Johnson. "Some of our players had been in the NFL longer than he had. He wasn't as sociable as Buck. It was just the opposite atmosphere when Buck was the coach."

Albert had a totally different personality from Shaw and Strader. Albert was like the players' good buddy.

"Albert? He was OK, nothing special," said Johnson. "But we weren't scared anymore to breathe, laugh, or smile."

What makes a good coach, John Henry?

"Someone who can control the situation, but he's not dominant and he's open to suggestions," he replied. "And he won't bring in stuff that's way out of date, and no one's doing it."

Was Strader outdated?

"A little bit," Johnson answered.

Johnson's second season with the 49ers was diametrically opposed to his first. He had only nineteen carries, gaining sixty-nine yards (3.6) and scoring one touchdown. A shoulder injury was partly responsible as John Henry missed five games. Without Johnson and McElhenny at full strength, the 49ers fell to 4-8. Johnson carried eighteen times for fifty-six yards against the Rams in the opener. Then the shoulder took the starch out of his season.

Johnson blocked more than he ran in 1955. But injured or other-wise, he laid the leather to opponents. He still had one good shoulder. Against the Bears, Perry was about to be tackled by McNeil Moore when Johnson appeared out of nowhere and sent Moore flying with a thundering block, freeing Perry for a big gainer.

"I played with Nagurski in college [Minnesota]," 49ers line coach Phil Bengtson said in the locker room afterwards, "and I can assure you Bronko never threw a block that hard."

John Henry was inventive on the field during his time with the 49ers, either with the blocks he threw or the runs he made.

"Sometimes he'd make his own plays," said standout 49ers lineman Leo Nomellini. "He was good at creating."

There were times when Johnson seemed more like a combination of Perry and McElhenny than Grange and Nagurski. John Henry had the speed, he had the moves, and he had the power. But he had one thing The Jet and The King didn't have: ingrained nastiness. Which made Johnson appealing to the 49ers' defensive coaches. On goal-line stands, his fierce tackling staved off touchdowns. He also played linebacker and defensive back in normal defensive situations. He intercepted a pass against the Rams and returned it twenty-seven yards in 1955.

That season was Red Hickey's first as a 49er assistant coach. He was responsible for the offensive backs and ends, but he had problems almost immediately with Johnson.

"Hickey didn't like John Henry because he was lackadaisical," said Soltau. "He'd come to practice with his shoes untied. Or he'd go out in motion in the flat, slow down, and walk back to the huddle. He drove Hickey crazy.

"One time on a blocking play, John Henry slid off into the flat, and the defensive end clobbered Y. A., who said, 'John Henry, what were you doing?' And he replied, 'I was open.'

"John Henry had the best personality of all of us. He loved to laugh, he loved to play. We had Joe and Mac in the backfield, but John

Henry was such a good athlete, we tried to fit him in. It wasn't easy. Our huddle sometimes was a sewing bee. Joe wanted the ball all the time. John Henry wanted the ball. Mac was the only guy who wasn't a ballhawk. When he got tired, he'd go over and sit on the bench. Joe would stay until he died."

John Henry wanted to play offense, defense, and as much as he could. Hickey got his way, and Johnson played more defense than offense in 1955. Opponents were able to take advantage of his aggressiveness. The most obvious incident occurred against the Bears in 1954. Rookie receiver Harlon Hill from tiny Florence State Teachers College in Alabama burned the 49ers that day with seven catches for 214 yards and four touchdowns.

Hill's final touchdown was scored over Johnson, giving Chicago a 31–27 victory. The 49ers weren't the same team again that season after the demoralizing defeat.

"Buck put John Henry in for one play and he got beat," said Spadia. "He bit on a play-action, coming up to defend the run. Ed Brown's pass went right over his head."

Not only was John Henry's shoulder a deterrent, but one of his knees wasn't in the best shape either.

"He wore this big steel knee brace," said Spadia. "He wore it for years. You could hear him coming. It clanked."

Sometimes against opponents' heads.

"I don't say John Henry was mean," Spadia hedged. "He was tough. There wasn't ever an injured player who played more brilliantly."

Injured or otherwise, Johnson stepped up when others stepped back. The 49ers were getting humiliated one day. Tittle asked for volunteers to carry the ball. Everyone in the huddle kept his head down except John Henry.

"OK, XYZ," he mumbled. "Call my number. But, man, there's sure some hitting going on out there today."

Everyone in the huddle cracked up. It was the only laugh the 49ers enjoyed all afternoon.

"I remember John Henry coming out of Tony's office one day, and he was mumbling something as usual," said Spadia. "It took me a while to realize that what he was saying was, 'Chicken-shit raise. Chicken-shit raise.'"

In 1956, Johnson was healthier, but he carried only eighty times for 301 yards (3.8). He had regressed into a bit player. Perry and McElhenny remained the featured backs, while Johnson blocked for them. He broke off a fifty-four-yard run against Detroit, but otherwise wasn't ripping off big gainers with the frequency of two years earlier. The last game of the '56 season, against Baltimore, he carried once for three yards.

The 49ers improved slightly to 5-6-1, but there were constant stories in local newspapers about Johnson's marital difficulties and custody battles over his children. Leona Johnson, who wouldn't enter John Henry's life until a year later, believes his family problems as a 49er, well documented by the local media, served to punch him a one-way ticket out of San Francisco.

"They didn't want a scandal," Leona said of the 49ers. "That's why they traded John."

Another line of thinking was that Tony Morabito, Italian like Trippi, disapproved of John Henry's devastating block on the Cardinal star. So Morabito got rid of Johnson, even if it meant getting very little in return.

Spadia is the only 49er management type left from those days. He shed little light on what actually made Johnson an ex-49er.

"I wasn't privy back then," he said. "I was picking up jock straps and ordering buses."

That's not true. Spadia had become the 49er general manager in 1952. But 49er players from that era corroborated what Leona Johnson said: it wasn't the face-altering hit on Trippi, but Johnson's personal life, that brought about the trade.

Brodie picked up jocks and socks at 49er home games after playing for Stanford the day before. He remembered John Henry as one of the friendliest players on the team

"I worked in the equipment room," said Brodie. "When players came off the field, I'd put capes around them. That little Jimmy Cason never wanted one, But John Henry was smiling, ready to take one."

By 1957, Johnson was ready for a change. The 49ers had two losing seasons out of the three he spent with them. He had a losing year in Canada. He wanted more than anything to play on a winner—anywhere.

"I was happy to leave the 49ers and go to Detroit, which was a good offensive and defensive team," he said. "They had the best defensive backfield in the league."

The Lions traded one of those defensive backs, Bill Stits, and fullback Bill Bowman for Johnson. Stits played adequately for two seasons in San Francisco. Bowman didn't even make the team.

"Three great running backs," Nomellini reflected on Perry, McElhenny, and Johnson, and the memory of their breakup. "I don't want to pick one over the other, but they could have made any team in the league."

Soltau thought about the NFL's greatest backfield, preferring to remember how it all came together rather than how it disassembled.

"The outstanding point is happenstance and how those four guys wound up together," said Soltau. "Joe Perry came from the Coast Guard [Perry was in the Navy]. Y. A. Tittle came from the draft after the team he was on [in Baltimore] became defunct. Hugh McElhenny was a legitimate first-rounder. And Frankie dragged John Henry down from Canada.

"We probably would have won a couple of league titles if we had a defense. We were a high-scoring team. We got a lot of yards per carry. We had some damn good offensive linemen: Billy Johnson, Bruno Banducci, Bob St. Clair, who knocked guys' blocks off. And Joe, Hugh, and John Henry blocked well for one another. The most obvious thing about the Million Dollar Backfield to a teammate was that they had completely different personalities. But they came together beautifully.

The only problem was that they didn't get to play all that much together because of injuries."

Then when they finally were healthy as a foursome, Johnson was gone. And minus John Henry, the 49ers were down to the $750,000 Backfield.

Johnson made an immediate impact in Detroit. He was the Lions' leading rusher in 1957 with 621 yards (4.8), and five touchdowns. New city, same forearm.

"When John Henry was with the Lions," Summerall recalled, "the Giants played them in a preseason game. One of our coaches, I won't say who it was, wanted revenge for something John Henry had done to one of our safeties. So this coach told us before we went out to line up against Detroit's punt team to forget about the punt. He wanted ten guys to go after John Henry, who was blocking for Yale Lary.

"Then as an afterthought, the coach said, 'But, you know, he hits back.' John Henry saw us coming and ran out of bounds."

Johnson showed that two could play this revenge game. He knew how to hurt somebody, and how to avoid getting hurt. John Henry's feet were as quick as his forearm, his reflexes as sharp as his mind.

When Detroit defeated San Francisco, 31–27, in the division tiebreaker, Johnson had five carries for twenty yards. A week later, he rushed for forty-nine yards as the Lions destroyed Cleveland, 59–14, for the NFL championship. Getting out of San Francisco was, indeed, the best thing that could have happened to Johnson.

"Getting John Henry was one of the reasons we won the title in 1957," said Schmidt. "Before he came, we were mostly a passing team. Our running game kind of sputtered around. He gave us an extra dimension."

It would be Johnson's only pro championship. But his reputation as a team player, which wasn't ever really disputed in San Francisco, was cemented in the mind of Bobby Layne.

"John Henry loved to play football and all that meant," said Layne. "He loved to run, he loved to block, he loved to hit. And that dang fool even loved to practice. Maybe that love for the game is why I've always seen him as more than a football player. To me, he really stood for football and everything it meant."

The close relationship of Johnson, a black man from Louisiana, and Layne, a white good ol' boy from Texas, stood the test of time through two football towns over two decades, and then deep into their retirements. They shared a mutual and absolute respect. Johnson worried about Layne and his reckless disregard for his own health.

"That was my buddy," John Henry said. "Bobby was a competitor. Oh, man, one of the best. If you weren't blocking, and Bobby's running out of the pocket, he would yell at the coach, 'He's hurt, get him out of here.' Did they take the guy out? Oh, yeah.

"Bobby would go out and drink, sometimes by himself. He'd bother nobody. But he always was ready to play. He'd drink that Cutty and soda. He'd want me to go with him. I'd drink gin. I didn't drink like Bobby, but I'm glad I didn't drink Cutty or bourbon. The guys who did would go to practice and start sweating. The coach would smell it and make them run extra laps. They suffered. My gin saved me. You can't smell it."

Johnson got a wistful look.

"Every summer, years after we were done playing, Bobby would send for me," he said. "I'd go to his place for a week with other guys we played with. We'd eat, drink, talk, fish."

"One year," Leona interjected, "we were out of town. Bobby called and called and called. Finally we got back, and Bobby wanted to know where we were, and were we coming to his ranch. We made it. Bobby loved John Henry."

All that hard living finally caught up to Layne.

"Bobby died, and I've sure missed him," said John Henry. "His wife and daughter were special, too. I don't know why he drank like that. He sure was my good buddy."

Three years in San Francisco, three years in Detroit. Same story statistically either place. Johnson's production also slipped his last two years as a Lion. He rushed fifty-six times for 254 yards (4.5) and no touchdowns in 1958. He had eighty-two carries for 270 yards (3.3) and two touchdowns in 1959.

The Lions drafted fullback Nick Pietrosante of Notre Dame with their No. 1 pick in 1959. He was being groomed to replace Johnson.

For the first and only time in his career, Johnson endured the slings and arrows of unprofessionalism. His Lions coach, George Wilson, told the media that some of Johnson's teammates felt he was "dogging it." The coach wasn't accusing Johnson himself. Oh, no, it was the Lions players who were doing the blaming. John Henry wondered if they had another Johnson in mind. For he hadn't ever been anything but dedicated.

The truth was, in Motown, the Lions had gotten old as a team after winning the title. And Johnson had battled injuries for two seasons. So how could he give 100 percent if he was hurt?

"He's full of crap," Johnson said of Wilson's veiled remarks. "When I was on the football field, I played the game. I never dogged it on a football field. That wasn't my thing at all."

Wilson intimated Johnson was getting money from the Lions for value not returned. Unitas, in Baltimore, wasn't surprised to hear that mindset.

"John Henry was the type of guy you'd have to trade every two years or he'd loaf on you," said Unitas. "He'd be good the first year he was there, then he'd just hang in there."

Johnson certainly understands the value of money, having increased his value as his NFL career progressed. However, he was no paper Lion. He considered himself a dedicated professional, nothing less.

"If I was at a good situation, then I was traded to some place where I didn't want to go, I'd ask for more money," he said. "But even if I felt I wasn't getting the money I deserved, I played up to my potential. If I didn't, I'd have gotten killed. You ain't got time to be doggin' it."

Johnson then turned it around on Wilson.

"I don't remember anything special about him as a coach," he said. "Now Buddy Parker, my coach in Pittsburgh, I liked him. He was an excellent coach. With him, you were well prepared."

Once again, it was time for John Henry to leave town. He moved farther east into an ideal situation. For a low-round draft pick, Pittsburgh acquired him from Detroit. With the Steelers, the team that drafted him originally, Johnson was re-acquainted with his favorite player.

"My bodyguard," Layne exclaimed when he spotted Johnson in camp.

Layne had left Detroit to become Pittsburgh's quarterback. He might have been the only Steeler genuinely excited to see Johnson, who was thirty and already perceived as over the hill. Johnson made believers out of his critics very quickly.

"I hadn't had the great opportunity in my career to make a lot of yardage like a back should," he reflected. "Now I got a chance to run that ball."

Johnson rushed for 621 yards in 1960, the last year the NFL played a twelve-game schedule.

"John Henry was one of those guys," said Brodie, "who you had to hand the ball to early to get him some pep."

Johnson was full of pep in Pittsburgh. That '60 season, he broke off a career-long eighty-seven-yard touchdown romp against Philadelphia. Forty years later, it remains the Steelers' second longest run from scrimmage.

"Buddy Parker really believed in older players," said Dan Rooney, the Steelers' current president who, in 2000, entered the Pro Football Hall of Fame, joining his late father, Art. "John Henry was Buddy's type of player."

And if Johnson is busting jaws, it's better that he's on your side.

"John Henry was something else," said Stautner. "He could make it tough on you. He did the unexpected, and he did it fast. He could sprint out of tacklers' arms. He was great for us in Pittsburgh."

As a Steeler, Johnson became, at last, the man. As his carries mounted in Pittsburgh, so did his production: 787 yards in 1961, 1,141 in 1962, 773 in 1963, 1,048 in 1964. Johnson refused to slow down as he grew older. From age thirty-one to thirty-four, he carried the ball 200-plus times three out of four seasons. Amazingly, his workload increased after he left his twenties.

"My love of the game kept me going. So did my ambition to be the best," he said. "I was in good shape. I took care of myself. I was no big drinker, and I didn't get fat so I had to lose all that weight. I got the ball more, though I got no help in the offensive line."

Pittsburgh lacked a dominating line. Johnson countered that negative by getting heavier. He weighed 210 pounds when he joined the 49ers, but bulked up to a steel-hard 230 pounds during his years as a Steeler. He used the extra weight to knock off defenders who his blockers failed to clear out of the way.

"John Henry was an outstanding football player," said John Baker, who was his teammate in Pittsburgh for three seasons. "We were roommates for two years. He mumbled a lot. We called him 'Mumbo-Jumbo.' He liked the fast life, but he kept himself in tremendous shape. He was totally dedicated to his sport. He taught me a lot about the game. To me, he was similar to fullback Jim Taylor in Green Bay. They'd look for someone to hit."

Because he relished contact, Johnson refused to avoid collisions regardless of the odds against him or the number of bodies involved.

"He was pretty nasty on his pass blocking, and he was a helluva runner," said Wayne Walker, who was Johnson's teammate briefly in Detroit and lined up against him in Pittsburgh. "But he had a tendency to run to the sideline."

That certainly wasn't Johnson's reputation, at least not in the mind of former Cleveland Browns defensive lineman Bob Gain.

"John Henry would never go out of bounds," said Gain. "He just kept coming at you."

And since it was John Henry who was approaching, it helped to duck.

"He was a tough man," said Dick Nolan, onetime NFL defensive back for the New York Giants and Dallas Cowboys. "He didn't ask any favors from anyone. Jim Brown was a shuffler. John Henry was a high-stepper who could pull away from you. He had balance and more speed than you. And he was strong. You couldn't hurt him. But if you did, he wouldn't let you know it. Like I said, he was a good tough back."

Johnson, at thirty-five, rushed for 1,048 yards and seven touchdowns in 1964, which gave him twenty-six touchdowns on the ground in five seasons as a Steeler.

"It was kind of significant, the old man gained 1,000," he said proudly.

What is age to a steel-driving man? John Henry pounded for his pay. And he worked in Pittsburgh, where the steel mill once was a way of life.

"I was a tough man out there, rough and tough," he said. "I was happy to be a Steeler."

Johnson hit his peak later than most backs. But, as it happens to all premier runners, he fell off the summit. A knee injury in the second game of 1965, plus age, caught up to him. He carried only three times that season. Nevertheless, the Steelers wanted to re-sign him for 1966. But Johnson jumped to the Houston Oilers of the American Football League.

"It was the money," he said. "I thought it would be close to the end of my thing."

Art Rooney, the team's patriarch, tried to stop him.

"John, you're making a big mistake," Rooney told him. "You're a Steeler."

Money mattered more than sentimentality with Johnson. But even as an old man in Houston, he volunteered for goal-line defense.

So what does all that say about this man? A mercenary at heart? Yes. Malicious in his mind? Sometimes. But a football player in every sense of the phrase? You bet. That last description is the real John Henry Johnson.

Houston coach Wally Lemm was hoping to acquire the same Johnson he had attempted to contain when Lemm coached the St. Louis Cardinals prior to taking over the Oilers in 1966.

"I devoted just as much time to defensing him as I did Jimmy Brown," Lemm said after signing Johnson. "Brown was faster, but they had the same rare running balance. It took more than just a solid shot to tackle them."

Only Johnson was no longer the same player Lemm had defensed.

"John Henry's lost some of his speed," Lemm conceded shortly into training camp. "But he's still a fine football player."

Johnson gave the Oilers false hope early in the season when he broke three tackles and scored on a twenty-eight-yard run against the New York Jets. Only he wasn't in the best of shape. His body had begun to desert him. After seventy carries for 226 yards (3.2) and three touchdowns in 1966, Johnson called it quits at thirty-seven. Including his one year in Canada, Johnson had made it through fourteen seasons as a pro football running back.

Tributes came in bunches with his retirement.

"John Henry was one of the best ball carriers in the league." said Art Rooney. "He rushed for 1,000 yards twice on ordinary teams, and he was well into his thirties. He was the best blocker I ever saw. He could play anything."

"John Henry's like Jim Thorpe," said Parker. "When he's running, he's the best fullback in the business. That's because he's a great blocker, too. He does everything a fullback should do."

"John Henry said he always left the game on the field," said Los Angeles Rams running back Dick Bass. "And I used to tell him, 'Yeah, usually unconscious.'"

Well, Johnson's forte was teeth-rattling blocks.

"I knew I was a good blocker because I never got the back of my uniform dirty," John Henry said. "Sometimes I didn't get the front of it too dirty, neither."

If Johnson came along in today's NFL, Summerall envisions him as a standout on either offense or defense.

"I'd play him at strong safety so he could blitz a lot." said Summerall. "You could also play him at tight end or in the slot."

That would be to take advantage of John Henry's blocking, receiving, and running.

Murray Olderman, in his book The Running Backs, believes the greatest feat in football history was Johnson's surviving fourteen seasons as a pro back. Olderman overlooked Joe Perry, who survived sixteen years at running back, an unsurpassed period of longevity later equaled by Marcus Allen.

Maybe Olderman should have said the greatest feat was those NFL players who survived Johnson's hits.

Johnson's greatest achievement, the Pro Football Hall of Fame, didn't come until after he had been retired from the NFL for twenty-one years. During that long wait, he found happiness at home after a stormy first marriage. In 1957, his first year in Detroit, John Henry met Leona.

"I had also gotten away from a bad marriage," she recalled. "I had moved from Cleveland to Detroit the year before. John Henry and I met in a cocktail lounge at the Garfield Hotel. It had been pre-arranged, but I was deathly sick at the time. I was ugly, ugly, ugly. And I didn't want to meet football players. They're like sailors, a girl in every city.

"There were four of us at this table. It was set up that I would sit next to John. The whole time, our backs were to each other. When he left, he turned and pointed a finger in my face and said, 'And, you, I'll see you again.' A week later, I still was sick. John showed up where I was living. He was wearing a suit, shirt and tie. He sat there with me, watching TV. After that, I was supposed to find him a girlfriend. I took him to clubs, then he kissed me. I liked the kiss, and I liked the next one."

They wouldn't marry for seven more years, in 1964, after Johnson had scaled the summit of his NFL career.

"He was so quiet," Leona learned. "He wasn't an aggressive man. He's so patient and kindhearted. We both were parents when we met. He's so generous. Both of us have great sympathy for people who have troubles. John's my best friend. I'm his best friend. Forty-two years later, I'm still in love with my husband."

If not for football, Leona believes her husband would have become a career musician. Likely not a drummer, though, by the way he hits objects.

"We both like music," she said. "We're always going out to clubs in Cleveland to listen to jazz. I thought I was the romantic one. Last night at this club, they played our song, 'I Know This Is Love.' John requested it."

What would all those NFL players who've felt the sting of Johnson's vitriol say if they knew he was, down deep, a true romantic?

"I'm getting soft in my old age," he said.

They're two aging lovebirds, Leona and John Henry, nesting comfortably in Cleveland, her original home.

What does Leona love best about her husband's, er, softer side?

"The type of honesty and sincerity he has," she said.

And what does John Henry love most about his wife?

"She already knows she's been good-looking to me," he said. "And she's like my left arm."

The Johnsons' love for each other reached new bounds the day their son, John Henry Johnson, Jr., was born. Junior inherited senior's athletic ability by becoming a decathlete at UCLA.

Meanwhile, senior designed a game plan for himself after retiring as a player. But it was a game plan that didn't work.

"John wanted to go into coaching," said Leona.

Who would have been a better football teacher than John Henry, since he knew offense, defense, toughness, meanness, and loved everything about practice? He could've been, though it's a stretch, the first coach to be an offensive and defensive coordinator simultaneously.

"But there weren't many opportunities for blacks back then," Leona went on. "So John went into a deep depression."

His wife then discussed his medical problems while John Henry sat in a chair, his wide shoulders slumped, his big hands folded. He looked straight ahead, stoically.

"He didn't work for a year or two," she said. "Then a man named Frank Ryan [not the onetime NFL quarterback] decided it was time to hire some blacks to work for the Columbia Gas Company in Pittsburgh. John was qualified. I have some of his report cards from school, A's and B's. Columbia Gas asked him to memorize this certain book for a test. John passed the test with flying colors. Then they fired him anyway.

"They had no reason to fire him. But they really didn't want a black man there. They were expecting John to make a scene when he left. That isn't John's way. He packed up his things and walked out quietly. Then he went into depression again."

Johnson continued to sit without moving, not even shifting his eyes. What was he mulling over Leona's comments about his depression? Nothing about his posture gave him away.

"Then he got this job repossessing cable TV boxes if people didn't pay their bills," his wife continued. "His last job was for Allegheny County. He was in charge of three offices that helped out poor people. He stayed there for ten years, then retired in 1989."

John Henry's face remained blank.

"By then," said Leona, "he was seriously ill. He couldn't remember where his offices were. He'd get lost on the freeway. He couldn't find the grocery store. He got so he was afraid to leave the house. He couldn't remember what day he was getting paid. He even accused me of stealing. So that's when I decided we would both retire."

Leona had been a supermarket cashier, entering that profession at a time when few blacks, and even fewer black women, were grocery cashiers.

John Henry faced the biggest battle of his life. The same year he retired, he was diagnosed with Alzheimer's disease, the malady of the aged. With his memory loss and personality changes, what else could it be?

Leona wasn't convinced, though, telling doctors she doubted it was Alzheimer's. They didn't believe her, but she persisted. Then she insisted on more extensive research to determine the exact problem.

She pushed hard for the truth, she said, because she didn't want John Henry Johnson, Jr., to face the same situation when he grew old.

The Johnsons were among the first wave of blacks to enroll in the Alzheimer's research program at University Hospitals and Case Western Reserve University in Cleveland.

Leona discovered that most black families prefer to take care of a problem as serious as Alzheimer's on their own rather than seek medical services. She took the opposite approach for John Henry following a 1998 study at Columbia University, conducted by the National Institute of Aging, which said blacks have four times as much chance as whites of being diagnosed with Alzheimer's before the age of ninety.

"Three years ago," Leona reflected in 1999, "a doctor said that John wasn't smiling, he wasn't talking. He was almost like a zombie."

It took all of ten years before doctors agreed finally with Leona that her husband didn't have Alzheimer's. How that earlier prognosis changed had more to do with his medication than anything else.

Since John Henry had been tested every three years, and he wasn't getting any worse, unlike people with Alzheimer's, Leona felt the problem all along had been the medication prescribed for her husband. With a change of medication in 1999, his condition improved dramatically. Then it was determined that what John Henry really had was dementia pugilistica, a condition more commonly found among boxers.

"It's something boxers get from too many blows to the head," Leona said. "John had four concussions [from football] that we know about, but we don't know how many he really had."

As his wife talked, Johnson continued to stare at the wall in front of him. He wasn't concealing anything, though, with his prolonged silence. The truth is, he can't remember his first concussion or where it occurred.

That was so long ago, anyway, and his memory is losing a little more ground each day. A third person in the room asks Johnson how he thinks he is faring mentally right now.

"I feel fine," he said. "I don't feel anything is wrong up there."

Leona reacted patiently.

"He doesn't remember being here yesterday," she said of the Cleveland suburb of Brecksville, where interviews with the Johnsons for this book took place over two days. "I asked him this morning, and he didn't remember our having dinner with you last night.

"I lay out his clothes. I put toothpaste on his toothbrush. He doesn't know where his underwear drawer is. He drove us here because I don't drive. He can drive, but he doesn't know where to go. I tell him where to turn."

Leona pointed out her husband's long-term memory is fine. He can talk about his football career with fairly good recall. It's his short-term memory, she said, that is faulty.

So when the Johnsons visit a jazz club to hear their favorite romantic tunes, the next morning, John Henry often won't remember having been there.

Listen to rap, John Henry?

"Some of it," he said without getting specific.

Pop music?

"I like R. Kelly," he said of a popular male singer.

Leona looked at her husband with a curious expression.

"When did you start listening to R. Kelly?" she asked.

He smiled knowingly, without answering. He had been holding out on Leona. R. Kelly, huh? Maybe his short-term memory isn't so bad after all.

"John used to be an excellent dancer," she said.

That's long-term. It only takes the right romantic melody, and the Johnsons are young lovers again, moving easily together on the dance floor, just like forty-some years ago when they first met.

"A doctor told John, 'That lady over there is the reason you're in great shape today,'" said Leona, letting go of her self-modesty.

Leona supports her husband daily, hourly, by the minute. There is no way he can function normally without her.

But even in John Henry's altered state of mind, he is a source of support to Leona, too. He is her bodyguard, just as he was for Tittle and Layne. And don't anyone dare test John Henry's natural protective spirit. For that forearm of his looks as if it could still crack a skull if necessary.

Two years before his mental condition changed forever, John Henry Johnson was voted into the Pro Football Hall of Fame.

It had been hard for him, all those years of anticipating, especially when running backs who didn't have his numbers or reputation were elected to the hall by the Pro Football Writers of America. It wasn't just his rushing yardage, John Henry felt, that was being overlooked. He was a complete football player, someone who could hammer teams from either side of the line of scrimmage. How many other running backs of the last fifty years could make that statement?

"I believe I'm the reason he's in the Hall of Fame," said John Steadman, the respected columnist and pro football guru of the Baltimore Sun. "I was the strongest voice in the room when we voted. John Henry played with no face masks and no lace on his underwear. Maybe he took a couple of cheap shots, but he was tough, a helluva football player. And the 49ers, back when John Henry played for them, really captured my imagination. They excited you. What a team to watch."

Johnson's acceptance speech at Canton wasn't delivered with any bitterness generated from the prolonged snub. John Henry isn't a bitter man, regardless of how he played the game. His speech was, instead, a perfect blending of humor, respect for the game and its history, and also Johnson's hard-nosed approach to football.

"I haven't been this scared since I was chased by Bob Gain and Don Colo," he said, referring to two former Browns for the benefit of the Ohioans in attendance.

Johnson then thanked longtime sportswriter Chuck Heaton of the *Cleveland Plain-Dealer* for convincing Pro Football Writers Association members that he belonged as a veteran's committee candidate.

"Let's talk about football for a few minutes," said Johnson. "I'm proud to be picked as an old-timer, because it's the old-timers who made the game what it is today. Many of the old-timers deserve...all the help you can get [them]."

Johnson thanked his high school coaches, Tom Cureton and Tony Knap, plus friends and family members, before getting back to the old-timers theme.

"I learned from the old-timers, who taught me to play hurt," Johnson said. "Bobby Layne was one of the toughest competitors I ever played with. We played hard all the time. I didn't ask any questions, and I didn't give any.

"The 49ers backfield, I learned teamwork from those fellas. Old-timers were driven by pride and not dollar signs. They looked at fame as something to be earned by performance, and not press clippings."

Sharing the stage with Johnson were fellow inductees Larry Csonka, Mean Joe Greene, Len Dawson, and Don Maynard. Tough, grizzled old-timers themselves.

"I was confident someday I would be here," Johnson continued. "But, then, on the other hand, I thought I might be dead because it had taken so long."

Johnson's lighthearted touch gave the audience needed relief from the hot, sticky, summertime climate. They responded with appreciative laughter.

"I'm real proud I've earned your respect," Johnson went on. "I want to say that respect is all I ever wanted. And today, I feel I finally have that respect, and I want to tell you it makes me feel damn good."

Those were the final words of Johnson's speech. His common man's straightforwardness made a direct connection with the audience, which erupted in applause.

Right on, John Henry!

Respect is what everyone wants, regardless of whether he wears a chin strap in his chosen occupation. And when you get that respect, it surely does make you feel damn good.

John Henry Johnson had his admirers and his enemies, both of whom may have needed medical attention after one of his crunching blows. He didn't play favorites or fools. He treated them all the same way while he was re-arranging their smiles.

But he was a football player, not some hired felon. If you needed him on offense or defense, he would do both without questioning why. If you needed him to just block, no one ever blocked any harder. If you needed him as the featured back, he proved he was one of the greatest fullbacks who ever plunged into an entanglement of body mass and came out the other side.

John Henry was, as Art Rooney said, a full football player. But it was the man's mean streak that turned him into a legend.

"A lot of people feared the hell out of him," said Wilson, now an Arizona Cardinals executive. "I'll tell you this, we'd take him in a minute today. We'd let the rest of the backfield sit down, and we'd play John Henry by himself."

Well, if any NFL player could be a one-man backfield, it would be John Henry. Heck, he could walk into a cage filled with lions without a whip and chair, then walk back out without a scratch.

The biggest sigh of relief heard in the NFL over its eighty-year existence occurred the day John Henry took his face-altering forearm and left. The league's injury list was cut in half instantly.

Bloodied and bowed, Tittle began his exit from football with this devastating hit by John Baker.

Y. A. TITTLE
THE BALD EAGLE

It is the greatest football photograph ever taken. Its graphic nature depicts the game's raw violence better than words could ever explain. This photograph, the perfect shot, is truly football.

Y. A. Tittle is on his knees. His helmet is knocked off. His eyes are dazed. His hands hang limply against his thighs. His lips are parted as he sucks in air through the burning in his chest. Blood runs down his forehead and in front of his left ear in tiny red rivers.

Tittle's bald head is rimmed with gray. He looks old, older than usual, too old to endure such pain. The camera's lens has captured a quarterback in high-top shoes who has stayed one year too long, taken one hit too many.

Tittle's belly is flat, for a true warrior at any age wouldn't ever enter a battle unfit. Nevertheless, Tittle's helpless expression and his slumped posture are indisputable proof that the time has come for him to leave.

The gripping photo, taken by Morris Berman of the Pittsburgh *Post-Gazette,* makes it emphatically clear that athletes don't stay young forever. In Tittle's case, it isn't only that an athlete's career is over, but that something more important is passing from the game.

"I've been told," Tittle said of the dramatic picture, "that it depicts the end of an era. It's like the Byzantine period, the end of an innocent age. It was the end of the old-time athlete playing with his blood and guts. It was Custer's last stand, with an arrow in the back. The last mea–

sure of devotion, the last energy you gave to this old period that's now history. Television and the big time were starting in pro football in 1964. It was the end of an era with no agents. Then came the big television contracts, Joe Namath making $400,000, the leagues merging two years later..."

When Pittsburgh Steelers defensive lineman John Baker left Tittle in a heap on September 20, 1964, at Pitt Stadium, football was, indeed, changed forever. Tittle would retire after that season, and the image of the duty-bound, field-general quarterback, which Tittle personified, was replaced by a swagger never seen before in professional football.

Namath paraded in public with a fur coat, a Fu Manchu mustache, and a gaggle of gorgeous women. He owned a nightclub that was put off limits by the National Football League because of its questionable clientele. He guaranteed a Super Bowl victory. And, Holy Yelberton Abraham!, he wore white football shoes.

Tittle, in sharp contrast, wasn't a parrot trapped inside a peacock. He wasn't one to predict wins or seek the limelight, which seemed to find him anyway. His image was noble, decent, victorious. Caesar with a football.

"No one ever died harder than Tittle," said Paul Wiggin, the former Cleveland Browns defensive lineman. "That picture of him on his knees, blood running down his face, that's him! When you think of football: character, heart, personality. He was classic. If you asked me about competitors, it would be Tittle and Bobby Layne. Right up until the final second, they always thought they could win. And they never lost, they just ran out of time."

Football gods aren't made anymore, not gods with Southern drawls. The year before Baker knocked him off his pedestal, Tittle set an NFL record with thirty-six touchdown passes for the New York Giants. And he once threw seven touchdown passes in a single game. Tittle's coach, Allie Sherman, believed he had a mythological presence. A sun god, perhaps.

Y. A. T I T T L E   149

But like another mythological being, Icarus, Tittle finally flew too close to the sun and his seventeen-year pro career went up in flames.

"You can see it in the picture," Tittle said of Baker's punishing hit. "He caught me under both armpits, picked me up, put his helmet in my chest, and just gored me. The cartilage in the sternum was torn. It was the worst injury I ever had, and it affected me the entire season. Every time I moved, it hurt. I couldn't throw, and when I did, I got hit again. You can tape other parts of your body, but you can't tape the sternum."

Baker sees himself with Tittle in the photograph, even though Baker isn't visible. But without Baker, there is no photo, and no real understanding of just how battered and bloody football can leave a body, even the body of a mythological god.

"One thing it means," Baker said of Tittle's fallen image, "is I was doing my job. It's the job of a defensive lineman to hit the person who has the ball. Y. A. had the ball. It was my duty to take him out. I mean, make a tackle. If I didn't hit him, I'd have heard about it at practice the next Tuesday. They'd have said, 'What's wrong with you? Why didn't you hit him?'

"That picture also says to me football is a very rough sport. If you don't go in there with that idea, you might as well get the hell down the road."

If it wasn't John Baker, some other behemoth would have taken Tittle out. He was thirty-eight, and vulnerable. So The Bald Eagle left the game he once dominated because he couldn't function physically anymore. Thirty-eight is ancient for a quarterback, which John Elway, Joe Montana, Dan Marino, and Steve Young later discovered when they also exited football at that age.

"I could write a book about that photo," said Dianne Tittle de Laet, who actually did write a book about her famous father. "It's a man at the dead center of his life. He's an older man, and somewhat of a paradox. He is my father, and he's not my father. It's an image of victory and also defeat. There is all that I find violent, hideous, and detestable about football in that photo, and all that I find provocative and beautiful. It is a man trying to get his breath to go again, to go again, to go again..."

However, there is no place to go. That's the final paradox of the photograph. Tittle wants to go again, but he has come to the end. His daughter attempted to interpret the photo's meaning in her 1995 book, Giants & Heroes. Did she succeed?

"No, I did not," she said during an interview for this book in April 2000. "But I will always wonder about a man who's bowed from his passion. There are those of us who seek pleasure in life, and those of us who seek passion. And if you seek passion, you serve passion. And if you serve passion, you will be humbled by it, and you may be destroyed by it. Fortunately, my father was not destroyed by his passion."

Not at all. Broken sternum notwithstanding, Tittle left a football legacy behind him as one of a handful of quarterbacks to play in three decades. Now he's building a financial legacy. Tittle is the only member of the Million Dollar Backfield to become a multi-millionaire, profiting from an insurance business he prospered from after football.

But destroyed? Certainly not his passion for living. Tittle travels constantly with his wife, Minnette, seeing the world, still craving knowledge in his seventies. Destroyed? Not his passion for work. Now in his seventies, he puts in a full day's work and is a couple of years away yet from retiring.

The Bald Eagle still sits at the top of the mountain, where mythological gods belong. Passion is his purview.

But even gods fall prey to barroom trivia. Tittle is the only pro football quarterback who has been drafted No. 1 three times.

In 1948, after playing at Louisiana State University, he was taken in the first round by the Cleveland Browns of the All-America Football Conference, and in the first round by the Detroit Lions of the NFL.

Tittle signed with Cleveland, which had future Hall of Famer Otto Graham entrenched at quarterback. Fortunately for Tittle's career, he never played for the Browns. AAFC Commissioner Jonas J. "Scrappy" Ingram had unlimited power to balance play, and he awarded Tittle's contract to the less formidable Baltimore Colts.

These weren't the Baltimore Colts we think of normally, with Johnny Unitas, Raymond Berry and Lenny Moore. These were the earlier Colts of Lamar "Race Horse" Davis, Stormy Pfohl, and "Chuckin' Charley" O'Rourke. A different franchise entirely, and one with a much shorter shelf life.

After the four-year AAFC went out of business in 1949, the original Baltimore Colts, with Tittle as their quarterback, lasted one year in the NFL before folding. So Tittle's name was put into the draft hopper again in 1951. He was selected in the first round by the San Francisco 49ers. Thus he became a No. 1 pick three times within three years.

Tittle played ten seasons in San Francisco, where his greatest fame occurred in 1957 with an innovative forward pass called the "Alley-Oop" that he threw to an acrobatic leaper named R.C. Owens.

Another 49er offensive innovation, the "Shotgun," ended Tittle's stay in San Francisco. He was dealt to the Giants in the worst trade in 49ers history. For Tittle, though, it was identical to being paroled. He experienced his finest years in New York, where he evolved into this higher being the poets wanted to write about. Well, one poet. His daughter.

But as Y. A. Tittle learned, gods don't always triumph. The Giants lost three consecutive NFL championship games with Tittle as their quarterback. Then John Baker ended any chance of Tittle's ever winning a title.

So there are only individual accomplishments when Tittle looks back upon his career. He was voted AAFC Rookie of the Year in 1948. He was NFL Player of the Year in 1957, 1961, 1962, and 1963, if all official and unofficial postseason award bestowers are included. Tittle was named All-NFL in 1957, 1962, and 1963, And he played in six Pro Bowls.

However, his most distinctive form of recognition occurred at birth, when he was christened Yelberton Abraham Tittle, Jr. This is football's equivalent of a boy named Sue. Or worse. A boy named Peggy Sue.

"My father's family came from Devon, England," Tittle explained. "A town there is called Yelverton. My father was supposed to be Yelverton Abraham. But on the birth certificate, they put down Yelberton. My dad was called Abe, and I never liked Yelberton. I have brothers named Jack and Don, and a sister named Huline. My kids are Dianne, Mike, Pat, and John."

What, no Yelberton Abraham the Third? Imagine the phone ringing in the Tittle household, and the caller saying, "Is Yelberton there?" And the response is, "Yelberton Junior or Yelberton III?" And then the caller says, "You mean there are three Yelbertons?" This scenario would get old quickly.

"I've been called Y. A. ever since I can remember," said Tittle. "Except when I got married. The preacher got confused and said, 'Do you, Wayne, take this woman...'"

"Wayne" did exactly that. But Wayne Tittle? So mundane. Such a name would have only impeded greatness. Y. A. Tittle is a name that's nearly impossible to forget, along with the man behind the name. For he was one of the toughest quarterbacks and fiercest competitors ever to play the game.

"Y. A. was the kind of guy you never could count out," said Joe Schmidt, the Detroit Lions defensive captain who tried to outguess Tittle. "He looked like a schemer, setting you up for something. He had that little naked bootleg, and he was successful with it. As a defensive guy, you never knew it was coming."

That's because Tittle, who called his own plays, was brainy and tough.

"Y. A. was an excellent quarterback, hard to corral," said Ernie Stautner, who chased Tittle for the Pittsburgh Steelers. "He'd drop back to pass, and he'd be gone. He could move well. Or he'd hit a receiver who was covered. He had a sense of what to do. He won a lot of games."

An all-time quarterback must be able to throw the football accurately. Tittle not only threw accurately, but artistically.

"No man in the history of the game has ever picked up a football and delivered it with more beauty and fluidity than Y. A.," said John Steadman of the Baltimore Sun. "I've seen every T-formation quarterback, including Sammy Baugh and Sid Luckman, and I never saw anyone throw a ball more perfectly than Tittle. It was an effortless move."

As effortless as an eagle in flight. And Tittle was The Bald Eagle, experiencing hair loss by his junior year at LSU. Facing a chrome dome existence at such a young age gave Tittle an unmistakable air of authority while barely out of his teens. He looked old even when he was young.

Before he was old enough to vote, Tittle had this heroic aura about him, which made him perfect book material for his daughter.

"Everything I write about has to do with the heroic," said Tittle de Laet, author of children's stories and a book on the ancient Olympic Games. "I play my harp as part of a lecture performance about ancient heroes. The poetry I do is heroic poetry. Pindar wrote that victory is 'a moment of transcendence briefly making radiant an otherwise dark and brutal world.' My book on my father is a victory song, an attempt to praise a hero.

"I'm the artist in the family. Maybe in my family, there hadn't been one in a thousand years, and I came along to fill the slot. I think of my mother as an artist without an art. She has an artist's traits. She is an intuitive woman, as is my father."

Intuition is an important quality for a football wife, who is often left alone with her children, trying to create a normal life while her husband is off ruining his body and working towards a retirement of painful arthritis.

Minnette Tittle, Y. A.'s high-school sweetheart from Marshall, Texas, bore her husband four children, Dianne and three younger brothers.

"My mom is a hero," said Tittle de Laet. "A lot of wives of professional athletes are heroes. They kept the family together while their husbands weren't there. My father spent three months away playing football. And as soon as he left for training camp, the phony phone calls began. I can remember my mom's hands trembling on the phone as she listened to this man describing what we wore at the airport when we told our father good-bye. We were stalked. We had to move out of the house once. I remember being followed home by people in cars. I remember cars parked across the street from our house. People knew when our fathers were gone.

"This is in the context of many wonderful things. But my mother was heroic for a lot of reasons. She understood my father's passion, and she was not a potted palm. She was a player in that passion. She supported him, and she supported us. It's not easy to shine by reflected light. Everyone wanted to talk about the great man when you had an interesting story of your own. My mother is a multifaceted diamond of a human being. The diamond is her soul, the depth of her experience, and her understanding of people."

Because of her mother, Tittle de Laet became an artist, a poet, a harpist.

"When Dianne was seven years old," Minnette recalled, "instead of buying her books by Dr. Seuss, I bought her books on Greek and Roman mythology, because that's what I loved."

While Dianne read about Zeus and Circe, the football god took out the trash at home. The god's wife made sure of that, and also that the god was a father, and not some living, breathing trophy whose total contribution to his family was bringing home the paycheck and reading about himself in the daily newspaper.

"We had a close family," said Tittle de Laet. "My mother kept that in perspective. I didn't know my father was a football player until he was traded to New York. I thought he was an insurance man. Football was not a part of our home life, and we were living in a hurricane. It is said, 'Fame is being loved by a lot of anonymous people.' Well, you're hated by them as well. My mother was her own field general, and she was able to lead us through all that and give us the sense that there wasn't anything we couldn't handle as a family."

Fortunately, for purposes of child-rearing, Y. A. Tittle had the demeanor of an insurance man. With reason. He first sold insurance fifty years ago after joining the Colts. It was an offseason source of revenue. He continued to sell insurance, but he didn't sell himself as a superstar. And he didn't burden his family with who he was or what he did. He said little about either.

"My dad never brought the game home," said Tittle de Laet. "For all the violence out there on the football field, there never was any complaining by him. He really managed to worry about us. Dad is like a grandmother chicken. He worries about everything."

Tittle de Laet learned as a girl how much her father worried about his family. He used the same block-everything-out concentration as a parent that he demonstrated as a record-breaking, thrill-a-minute, come-from-behind Hall of Fame quarterback.

"My dad would ride it home, the value of a dollar," Tittle de Laet said. "I remember walking with him down Broadway in New York City, where people actually stopped to clap as he went by. My father was oblivious to this. He was chewing me out because I had spent my $20 savings on a flute."

Tittle trained himself to be oblivious to adulation, the blitz, and also to the difference of human color even though he was reared in a segregated town. Tittle is respected by blacks and whites alike. And the philosophy of treating all people fairly was something he passed down to his children.

"I was lucky to grow up in a color-blind world, for which I'll always be grateful to professional football," said Tittle de Laet. "This was a luxury to me, a person who became an activist in the 1960s. Looking back, we were an emotional family. My parents fought. They had their arguments. My mother said, 'We fight to keep warm.' But they gutted it out, and they survived something with their values intact."

Marshall, Texas, is located in the northeastern part of the state on the highway from Shreveport, Louisiana, to Dallas. Television journalist Bill Moyers grew up in Marshall. So did heavyweight boxing champion George Foreman, technically, although his roots actually are twelve miles away in Elysian Fields. Marshall is built on seven hills, just like Rome, Italy.

"Marshall is a perfect little town," said Tittle. "Pine timber, red clay hills, lots of lakes, different than what you would typically think of as Texas. It was called the 'Big Thicket Country.'"

The main office of the Texas-Pacific Railroad was located in Marshall during Tittle's childhood. There was plenty of cotton to pick and enough lumber to chop to provide sufficient work for the roughly 20,000 people who lived there.

Marshall was very open about its political feelings during Tittle's youth. Both the Confederate and American flags flew at the county courthouse. The courthouse square was a congregating point for kids, though the town was plainly divided. White kids went to Marshall High School, black kids to Pemberton High. The town was 54 percent black. The two schools weren't permitted to meet in athletic competition.

Nevertheless, Tittle maintained a close relationship with a black kid named W. L. Mitchell. They played marbles behind Snow White Cleaners. Many years later, after W. L. and Y. A. had grown up and gone their separate ways, they reunited in Marshall and resumed fishing together at Caddo Lake whenever Tittle was in town.

"Blacks and whites were pretty isolated in Marshall," Tittle said of his boyhood. "We had two black males, W. L. and a fellow named Taft, who worked on our property. They lived in a room behind the garage.

We also had a full-time maid, Eliza, who was black. I can't think of her last name either, but she lived in an apartment above the garage.

"When I started throwing the football, W. L. would come out in a field with me and set up a box so I could throw through it. Before I could drive, he drove me to football practice. Unfortunately, at my football games, there was no place for blacks to see the games. So he'd watch me by looking through the fence. W.L. was like a brother more or less. He worked in my father's cleaners and learned how to press clothes. He became head presser, and eventually bought the Ideal Cleaners from my dad.

"My dad then signed the note that helped W. L. buy two houses to rent next to the cleaners. When I went to college, W. L. moved to California and did well, I hear. He owned six pressing shops. When the 49ers played the Rams in Los Angeles, I'd get him tickets. We'd talk when I came through the tunnel at the L. A. Coliseum. That went on for five years. Then he retired and moved back to Marshall. I asked him why would he go back to a racist society like the South, when in free California you can do everything. He told me that Marshall was his home, and he felt more comfortable there."

Minnette Tittle understood W. L.'s thinking.

"Because there is a place in the South where you are what you are," she said. "The black and white relationship is not what you understand it to be when you're living in a California. There is so much closeness to blacks and whites in the South. Other people would call it racism, but in the South they call it a close, close friendship that lasts for a lifetime."

Three members of the Million Dollar Backfield were born in the South. Two of them are black. Even in the segregated 1950s, when Rosa Parks became a symbol for equality, friendships were formed among all three men.

"Joe Perry is one of my best friends," said Tittle. "There is no way Joe Perry wouldn't stand up and go to bat for me. And I would do the same for him. You can ask Joe."

Tittle's comment was relayed to Perry.

"I love Y.A." he said. "He has always been straightforward and honest with me. There's never been any doubt about Y.A. and his true feelings towards me. I know he's got my back."

Perry's comment was sent back to Tittle.

"All the black athletes in California," Tittle said, "were friends of all the Southern football players, black and white. Joe Perry was a friend of Jimmy Cason, Ray Collins, and myself. Joe Perry would have a party and all the white people there were Southerners."

When Y. A. Tittle built a house in Marshall in 1980, he made the acquaintance of H.L. Blocker, a black man. Whenever Tittle returned home, the two of them fished Caddo Lake until Blocker died in the early 1990s. If fish of all colors integrate, then why not fishermen?

Back in the 1940s, Abe Tittle supported a wife and four children as a rural postman and entrepreneur. Two other Tittle children lived short lives. Stafford died of pneumonia at twelve. Another boy was stillborn.

"Being a postman was a good job during the Depression, because it was a Civil Service job and you couldn't be fired," said Tittle. "My father opened a country store in Clayton, thirty miles south of Marshall, after he married my mother, Alma. After they moved to Marshall, he opened another store, which he kept open after he became a postman.

"He would go to work at 5 a.m. and finish his postal route around noon. Then he'd go to work at the store. Or he'd work at his other job, building property. Although it was the Depression, we weren't poor because my dad had property everywhere, eighteen to twenty buildings around Marshall."

The Tittles lived on ten acres, and fed themselves with meat from the cows, pigs, and chickens on their farm. Plus there were home-grown peaches, figs, cantaloupes, corn, peas, and beans for family consumption.

Sports came naturally to the Tittle boys. Jack, who was seven years older than Y. A., was an all-district football player in high school and later an all-conference single-wing blocking back at Tulane. Don, the youngest brother, would play football at North Texas State. But Y. A. was the family's athletic star. The signs were there from the time he entered elementary school.

"When I was in the first grade, I can remember playing the third grade in roughhouse football," he said. "We tackled, which amounted to getting them down the best way you could. We never played touch. All the way through grade school, we played against classes older than ours and beat them every time.

"I was obsessed by football. When I signed my name, it had a football symbol under it. I knew by the fifth grade I could throw better than anyone else. This was when Sammy Baugh was throwing passes at Texas Christian University. Slingin' Sammy was my idol."

Tittle was a varsity starter as a freshman, when he earned the Sullivan Funeral Home Award as the Marshall Mavericks' most valuable player. And not just because he had the nerves of a dead man in the pocket. Tittle's passing accomplishments became the talk of Marshall, and also proved a source of revenue for Tittle.

"You may not believe this," he said, "but I can get you a voucher from the president of the American Trial Lawyers, Scotty Baldwin, who was my high school teammate. Scotty will tell you I could stand on one side of the football field and hit a telephone pole on the other side of the field three out of four times. That's how I earned my dating money."

That's how Tittle dated a pretty drum majorette at Marshall High named Minnette DeLoach, who was Princess of the Fall on campus.

"Marshall was a town built on the spirit of athletics," said Tittle. "Texas always was a big football state. So if you were six feet tall and a pretty good football player, you had a lot of pretty girls. And Minnette was the prettiest."

Their relationship would be hot and cold from Marshall all the way through college. But as a high school senior, Y. A. signed Minnette's yearbook by asking her to marry him after college. Then he gave

Minnette, who was one class behind him, a bracelet with two hearts etched with their initials.

"I dropped my pencil on the floor when I was thirteen," Minnette said of her initial attraction to Y. A.. "He picked up my pencil, and I really liked his looks. He had long cheekbones, and I thought he was very handsome. We never really dated in our early years."

"I'm going to correct you, darlin'," Y. A. said to his wife of fifty-one years as they sat on a sofa in their spacious home in Atherton, a swank neighborhood south of San Francisco. "Back in those days in east Texas, in small towns, there would be put-togethers, junior high school dances where Minnette and I danced.

"But we dated others. I went with one girl, and Minnette went with fifty different boys. I really knew in my heart, though, that Minnette was my girl. We started dating seriously the last half of my senior year in high school."

With admiration, Minnette watched Y. A. as he strived to succeed. But she also saw the damage that came with his football zeal. In junior high, he broke his nose, ribs, and left arm. His knees took a beating at Marshall High. At LSU, he broke an ankle and his nose again, and he was knocked out twice.

In the pros, Tittle was knocked out three times, broke his back twice, fractured his cheekbone in three places, had elbow surgery and a collapsed lung, plus fractures of the ribs, a hand, a toe, and numerous pulled muscles.

No insurance salesman ever took a worse beating.

Tittle played four sports in high school: football, basketball, baseball, and track and field. He picked the roughest one for a career.

"Odus Mitchell, my high school football coach, came from Pampa, Texas, and put Marshall on the map," said Tittle. "He came to Marshall with big ideas. We had played mostly small schools like ourselves, but he convinced us we could beat bigger schools.

"So he scheduled Waco, which had won the state championship the year before. We traveled 210 miles by bus to Waco, when no one back home traveled much in those days. We spent the night in a hotel, which none of us, I believe, had ever done before. I know I hadn't.

"There were twenty-nine of us in uniform. Then Waco ran on the field with something like 120 players. We were star-struck. But Bobby Furrh ran sixty yards for a touchdown for us, and we thought we could win. I threw a six-yard touchdown pass to Bobby, and I ran twelve yards off a lateral for our last score. Little Marshall beat the Waco Tigers, 20-6. On the bus ride home, we couldn't believe we beat Waco."

Tittle passed for 189 yards in the major upset. The next day, the lead paragraph of the Waco *News-Tribune* game story written by Jinx Tucker started out: "Y. A. Tittle, a big 185-pound bruising, punting, passing back almost single-handedly defeated the Waco High Tigers here Friday night..."

Those same little Marshall Mavericks went on to win their first conference football championship in years on the long runs of Furrh and the passing of Tittle, who was a deep back in the single wing. But in a 13-6 victory over Longview, Tittle injured his left knee when landed on by Chubby Grigg, a 300-pounder who later played for the Cleveland Browns.

Tittle sat out Marshall's district-winning 21-0 victory over the Tyler Lions, whose center, Bill Johnson, later was Tittle's snapper in San Francisco. Tittle returned with a splint on his knee for the state playoff game against Lufkin. He was ineffective as the Mavericks lost, 30-6.

Tittle was named all-district and second-team all-state. He received honorable mention on the All-Southern team chosen from twelve states.

Marshall also won the district title in basketball as Tittle was chosen second-team all-district. He pitched and played shortstop in baseball. He competed in the weights and relay events on the district-winning track and field team.

"I was on the 440-yard relay team that won the district," he said. "I want people to know I wasn't that slow [in football]. I just had a long stride."

Mitchell knew he had something special in Tittle. The coach told the youngster that, first of all, he was more talented than his brother,

Jack Tittle, and that this talent could take him a long way. And Y. A. listened like a son.

"Your coach in east Texas was like a father," he recalled. "The last class in school every day was P.E., which turned into a long football or basketball practice, whichever sport was in season. So your coach would have you from 3 p.m. to 6 p.m. nine months of the year. He'd spend as much time with you as a father would."

World War II was winding down when Tittle graduated from Marshall High in the spring of 1944. He signed a pledge to attend LSU after watching several LSU–Tulane games involving brother Jack. But after giving his word to LSU, Tittle discovered people in Marshall were irate that he hadn't visited any Texas schools. So the day after graduation, he traveled to Austin to check out the University of Texas. He had no idea he was about to become involved in a major heist.

"They treated me like a king in Austin," Tittle said. "I had never been to a restaurant where you had to pay. We always ate at home. Then I was told that summer school at Texas was about to start in two weeks, and would I like to change my mind [about attending LSU]."

Tittle could hardly say no since he was already on campus. Texas's football coaches put him up in Miss Poole's boardinghouse. His roommate was none other than Bobby Layne from Highland Park High in Dallas. Layne was a mid-year prep graduate who had taken two quarters of college classes and played on Texas's baseball team by the time he met Tittle.

"Bobby already was a big man on campus," said Tittle. "He was seventeen going on fifty. I was seventeen going on thirteen. He liked his beer. Marshall is in Harrison County, which was a dry county. I had never even tasted beer. None of my friends drank. Bobby would come in at night and throw his money on the table. He had won $1,200 playing poker. I didn't even know how to play poker. He was talking about all the girls he was moving around with. I was still holding hands with my now wife. He was unbelievable.

"I was led to believe he was going to be the fullback and me the tailback in Texas's single wing. We were both mediocre runners, even though we'd run against each other in front of Miss Poole's boarding-house. But when we worked out in the afternoon, I don't care what anyone says, I could throw better than Bobby. But one of us wasn't going to play. He was first-team all-state and I was second-team all-state. You didn't have to be a genius to figure things out."

About that time, LSU assistant coaches Slick Martin and Red Swanson showed up on the Texas campus. They asked Tittle if he would change his mind a second time, since summer school was opening the same day in Baton Rouge as Austin. Feeling he wasn't going to play for Texas, Tittle didn't need much persuasion. He went back to Miss Poole's to pack his clothes.

Then Martin and Swanson insisted that Tittle phone Texas coach Dana X. Bible to tell him about his change of heart. And so Tittle stepped into a phone booth with the two LSU coaches watching him closely.

"I faked it," Tittle said. "I dialed a bunch of phony numbers, then kept nodding my head so they'd think I was really talking. I was scared to death of Bible, who was known as the Knute Rockne of the South. After I was done, they asked me what he had said. I told them that he didn't like it, but he understood. Then we took off.

"I know Bible and LSU's head coach, Bernie Moore, had a falling out over that incident. They had been teammates at Carson-Newman and were good friends. The two coaches who got me out of Austin loved to tell that story. They called it, 'The Big Lousiana Heist.'"

Tittle might have played second fiddle to Layne in Austin, but he was first violin in Baton Rouge. He was an instant starter, and instant star, for the LSU Tigers, and someone capable of last-second heroics.

"We were playing Texas A&M and losing, 6-0, coming down to the last minute and a half of play," Tittle said. "The coach [Martin] had a [devious] way of sending in plays during time-outs. He'd send out the water boy, and my bottle would have a different colored cap than the others. Inside the cap, the coaches would write 'Sweep 29' or whatever.

"So I looked under the cap this time and it said, 'Punt.' I thought to myself, 'Punt? Are they conceding the game?' But I felt I gotta do what the coach says. All the guys in the huddle went crazy when they heard me call the play, but we punted it out of bounds on their 2-yard line. With thirty-five seconds left, they ran off tackle and fumbled. We recovered on the 9. I hit Jimmy Cason with a touchdown pass in the last second, and we won, 7-6.

"What had happened during that time out was Slick forgot to take the cap off the bottle from the previous quarter when we punted. Coach Moore didn't know we were cheating. He wouldn't have allowed Slick to do this. Coach Moore told the press afterwards, 'I've been at this school ten years, and that was the smartest play I've ever seen. That young seventeen-year-old boy figured we had to get a break to win the game, since we hadn't penetrated their 20. So he had the guts to kick it down there and trust the fortunes. I sure am proud of him.'"

From heists to highlights, Tittle was becoming the stuff of legends in Baton Rouge. But as his fame grew, his hair didn't.

"I had a full head of brown hair in high school, with a little wave in front," he said. "When I went to LSU, the freshman class had to shave its heads. I had the ugliest head I had ever seen in my life. I looked like a skinned onion. I wore a purple-and-gold dog cap. I think it stunted my hair's growth, because it never really came back. I started going bald at nineteen."

Tittle was of military age as a freshman, but when he took a physical, he was rejected for wartime duty because of asthma, a condition that continued to bother him years later in pro football.

Tittle completed fourteen of seventeen passes for 242 yards against rival Tulane, including his first twelve completions in a row, in a 25-6 LSU victory. But the Tigers finished 2-5-1 his first year. And Tittle knows why.

He pointed out LSU was the only school in the South that wasn't assigned football players who were serving in the military during World War II. Such assignments were common practice at the time, since schools had a shortage of athletes during wartime.

The war had ended by Tittle's sophomore season, in 1945, when LSU unveiled the T-formation against Rice. The Owls had no idea how to defend the T, since they hadn't seen it before.

"We sent Cason in motion on the first play, and nobody went with him," said Tittle. "They thought he was running off the field. So the next time Cason did it, I hit him in the flat, and he ran for a touchdown."

LSU won the game, 42-0, as Cason scored three touchdowns in thirteen minutes. The Tigers also pounded Tulane, 33-0, en route to a 7-2 record. The Bayou Tigers were even better in 1946. LSU went 9-1 to earn a bid to the Cotton Bowl, where they battled Arkansas to a scoreless tie.

"We played in an ice storm," Tittle said. "We made nineteen first downs to one for Arkansas. Every championship game I got into, in college and the pros, the Good Lord looked down and said, 'There's that bald-headed guy again. Let's get the weather down on him.'"

LSU was 5-3-1 during Tittle's senior year, when he suffered through the most embarrassing moment of his football career.

Playing Ole Miss on Halloween night in Baton Rouge, Tittle intercepted a Charlie Conerly pass in LSU territory just as a Rebel reached out and snapped Tittle's belt buckle. In a comical scene, Tittle took off running for the Ole Miss goal line, holding the football with one hand, and holding up his pants with the other hand. Finally, his pants fell down after he made it to the Ole Miss 30.

"I went to stiff-arm somebody and my pants came down," he recalled. "I tripped and fell. We then missed a field goal and lost the game, 20-18. The story was that LSU lost the Sugar Bowl bid when Y. A. lost his pants."

"And 20,000 girls fainted," added Minnette, who wasn't among them that evening, for she was dating someone else at the time.

Contrary to a popular rumor, baseball star Alvin Dark, who would win World Series championships as a player and manager, wasn't ever a backfield teammate of Tittle's in college.

"I don't know how that got started," said Tittle. "He played at LSU in 1942, when I was in high school, then he went into the service. After the war, he attended Southwestern Louisiana in Lafayette."

Tittle was all-conference as a junior and senior during a golden era for college quarterbacks: Conerly at Ole Miss, Johnny Rauch and Charley Trippi at Georgia, Frank Broyles at Arkansas, Harry Gilmer at Alabama, Bob Chappuis at Michigan, Johnny Lujack at Notre Dame, and Layne at Texas.

Georgia, led by Trippi, was favored to stomp LSU and Tittle. Instead, the Tigers took it to the Bulldogs, 32-0. After the game, Moore walked off the field with his arm around Tittle, his star player.

"What did you think of Trippi today?" the coach asked. Tittle looked puzzled. "Which one was Trippi?" he said.

Tittle also beat Alabama and Gilmer, 32-31. Gilmer later played quarterback for the Washington Redskins. Tittle didn't care who he played against. He always believed he was the best quarterback on the field.

"Even when I felt I had to prove myself," he said, "I never felt that I wouldn't. I was confident, but I wasn't cocky. There's a big difference."

Tittle ended his time in Baton Rouge as LSU's career total offense leader with 2,619 yards. He passed for 2,517 yards and twenty-one touchdowns. He was voted the team's Most Valuable Player as a senior, and not only for his offense. He averaged fifty-four minutes, more than any other Tiger.

Tittle then sought to win the heart of his high-school sweetheart, even though the marriage proposal was witnessed by the entire country. Minnette had attended college at North Texas State and Arkansas. When *Sport Magazine* asked Tittle his plans after college football, he said he would finish school, ask his high-school sweetheart to marry him, then join the pros. Sport, the nation's top-selling sports magazine at the time, printed his response.

"I'm going with another boy who was my love," said Minnette. "His mother called me after the article came out. She was very unhappy. But you follow your destiny, and my destiny always was Y. A. He was the only person I could ever be married to. I didn't know it, but he knew it."

She smiled affectionately at her husband.

"In football, he always had a second receiver to throw to," she said. "I was your second receiver, Y. A."

Y. A. Tittle, the yearbook prophet of Marshall, Texas, grinned.

"At one time I thought I was going to coach football after college," he said. "I was majoring in physical education. Then the Cleveland Browns came to visit me after my senior season. They asked me if I would go up and see their [1947] championship game against the New York Yankees. I agreed, and sat on the Browns bench next to George Connor of Notre Dame. Cleveland put us up at the Waldorf Astoria, where I signed a one-year contract for $10,000 with a $2,000 bonus. The Browns told me that Graham would retire in another year, then I would take over."

Graham didn't retire until nine years later, following the 1956 season.

"I didn't know much about pro football," said Tittle. "My whole football education was Alabama, Tennessee, Texas, and Georgia. Pro football was something up there in Yankee land. So when a Detroit Lions scout called to tell me I was their No. 1 draft choice, I said, 'That can't be because I'm Cleveland's No. 1 draft choice, and I'm already signed.' The scout said, 'Well, son, there are two leagues.' I didn't know there were two leagues."

Tittle was all set to join the Browns when he was re-routed to Baltimore. The lowly Colts had started out as the Miami Seahawks in 1946 before moving to Baltimore the next year. Before Tittle ever set foot in Baltimore, he reported for training camp with the Colts in, of all places, the skier's paradise of Sun Valley, Idaho.

The scenery at Sun Valley was picture-postcard lovely, but it wasn't an ideal setting for football conditioning.

"We practiced on a rodeo field," said Tittle. "It was a horrible place to have a training camp because of the high altitude. There were a lot of pulled muscles. It was a nice place to be, though, with beautiful mountains and a lot of beautiful college girls working there in the summer. And I had just been married two weeks."

Tittle challenged Charley O'Rourke, known as Chuckin' Charley, for the starter's job. Tittle won that battle during the exhibition season. Over the next two years, he held off the threats of Adrian Burk, who would start for the Philadelphia Eagles, and George Blanda, who was cut by the Colts in 1950 on the first leg of a long, long Pro Football Hall of Fame journey.

"The way I won the job in 1948 was kind of funny," Tittle said. "I played only the last four minutes of an exhibition game against the Los Angeles Dons. Before I got in, I was popping off on the bench to my roommate, Windell Williams, an end from Rice. I told Windell, 'If [Coach Cecil] Isbell doesn't put us in the game, we're gonna lose.'

"So we get in and I hit Williams with three sideline passes. Then I threw my first long pass to Johnny North for a touchdown. Only it wasn't supposed to be to North. Race Horse Davis was supposed to catch it coming across the middle. But I was so nervous, I overthrew Davis by fourteen yards. I went down, the crowd is screaming, and I thought the Dons had intercepted and were running for a touchdown. And there's North waving the ball fifty-five yards away in the end zone. So Windell tells the press what I told him on the bench, and that's what came out in the papers. Anyway, that was the pass that made my career."

The Colts were blown out next by the 49ers, 42-14. But Tittle made things happen again in another fourth-quarter appearance. He played the last three quarters the following week against Cleveland as the Colts upset the Browns. That was the clincher. Isbell made Tittle the starter.

In Tittle's official AAFC debut, he absolutely sparkled, hitting on eleven of twenty passes for 346 yards and five touchdowns as Baltimore throttled the New York Yankees, 45-28. He set three AAFC records that day. Tittle went on to throw for 2,522 yards and 16 touchdowns in 1948, completing 55.7 percent of his passes with only nine interceptions. He led the Colts to a respectable 7-7 record before they were eliminated by Buffalo in the playoffs. Not a bad start for a rookie about to learn of his own obituary.

A rumor spread after the 1948 season that Tittle had been killed in a car wreck near Marshall. The Dallas bureau of the Associated Press, acting on a tip from an East Coast source, phoned the Marshall *News Messenger* to see if it knew anything about Tittle's death. Phone calls from the *News Messenger* were made to Tittle's relatives and to the Marshall police.

Shortly thereafter, Tittle walked into the *News Messenger's* office and said, "Here I am, alive and on my own two feet." As author Mark Twain said of his own rumored demise, reports of his death had been greatly exaggerated.

As for the Colts, they turned into the AAFC's walking dead. The optimism of 1948 turned to pessimism in 1949 as Baltimore fell to 1-11-1 with the league's worst defense. Tittle's touchdown–interception ratio dropped from 16-9 the year before to 14-18.

"Pro football was different in those days," said Steadman. "I was a young reporter covering the Colts in 1949. We went out to San Francisco and stayed at the old Hearst Ranch in Pleasanton, across the bay. The Colts played a touch football game one day in practice. It looked like fun, so I asked the coaches if I could play. And they let me. Can you imagine such a thing happening today?"

Entering the NFL in 1950, the Colts were overmatched, winning one game. Tittle threw eight touchdown passes in twelve games compared to nineteen interceptions. He hardly could be blamed, though. With the Colts behind early, and with Tittle playing catch-up constantly, defenses knew he wasn't going to run the football. Thus he became an easy target for interceptions.

"We got no help," he said. "The Browns, 49ers and Yankees picked up other players from the AAFC when they went into the NFL. We got nothing. Two teams scored seventy points on us. The only thing about being in Baltimore that helped me was Isbell. He was an alcoholic, unfortunately, but he loved me, and convinced me I was the best. His offense was throwing the ball or running a draw play. He was a great passer himself [teaming with legendary end Don Hutson in Green Bay], and he had a great influence on me."

By the time the Unitas-Berry-Moore Colts were formed, Tittle was well established throwing passes for the 49ers. Baltimore's second NFL opportunity came after the New York Yankees moved to Dallas in 1952. After one shaky season as the Dallas Texans, the franchise was bought by Carroll Rosenbloom and relocated to Baltimore.

"I was real happy to come to San Francisco, and I'll tell you why," Tittle said. "I played in the Shamrock Bowl, which was the AAFC all-stars against the champion Browns. We won the game, but the two other all-star quarterbacks were Frankie Albert of the 49ers and George Ratterman of the Buffalo Bills. So I had a chance to be side by side with them.

"Frankie was a great quarterback, the best T-formation quarterback I ever saw. Trickery was part of the T-formation, and Frankie was the master, the best that has ever been. He was a bootlegger, he was a great leader, he could make things happen. He had that cocky flair about him. He could throw the slant, and he could run. He was like Steve Young, running around and making things happen. But he wasn't in my league as far as being able to fling the ball. Neither was Ratterman."

Tittle was delighted when the 49ers drafted him. He informed the team that he wasn't coming west to sit on the bench, though that's where he stayed during the 1951 season as Albert got most of the playing time. Competition has strange twists. Tittle's presence didn't make

Albert a better passer, but watching Albert maneuver made Tittle a better runner.

"I learned the bootleg from Frank," he said. "I got three, four touchdowns a year doing that. I was bootlegging even in my last year [with the Giants in 1964]. Frankie taught me to be free, to make the game fun. I felt like I was back on the sandlots in Marshall, Texas.

"Frankie would go back to punt, and 20 percent of the time he'd run for a first down. Or he would punt on the dead run. He was a nut. He put tackle Leo Nomellini in at fullback on an extra point, and moved Joe Perry from fullback to tackle. These are two all-time greats, but Frank was off the cuff. He'd call 'Nomo 34.' Leo would score and everyone would cheer."

Albert opened the 1951 season by leading the 49ers to a 24-10 win over the Browns. Tittle saw action and completed all three pass attempts. A week later, Tittle received more action, hitting seven of eighteen for sixty-nine yards and his first touchdown pass, eleven yards to Verl Lillywhite.

In the fifth game, against a Los Angeles Rams team that would win the NFL title that season, Tittle was brilliant with three second-quarter touchdown passes, all to Gordy Soltau, as the 49ers romped, 44-17.

"Y. A. was a Southern boy with great confidence in his arm," said Soltau. "He thought there was nobody who could throw a football or run a club like he could. He loved to throw the football, the farther the better, the harder the better. But that's all he could do when he joined us, drop back and throw.

"Y. A. liked to berate his receivers. He'd tell us, kidding of course, that he could outrun us all. What made Y. A.'s running effective was that no one expected him to run. He was that slow, a big, heavy-legged guy. He was a natural at the quarterback position, but it took him a couple of years before the club was his."

That's because a quarterback controversy developed in San Francisco in the early 1950s, identical to the Montana-Young standoff in the early 1990s. Albert had the history, but Tittle had the arm. And coach Buck Shaw, realizing he had two star quarterbacks, played them both, with Albert receiving roughly 60 percent of the action.

But Albert, the little lefthander, knew he was in trouble in the season finale. With a playoff berth possibly at hand, Shaw went with Tittle, whose three-yard touchdown run off the bootleg gave the 49ers a 21-17 victory over Detroit. Had the Packers beaten the Rams that day, the 49ers would have had a piece of the division title. Green Bay lost, and San Francisco settled for second place behind Los Angeles.

However, the balance of power was shifting at quarterback for the 49ers. Shaw decided to use Albert and Tittle evenly the following season.

"There was pressure on Buck to play us both," said Tittle. "So he alternated us. One of us would play the first and third quarters, the other the second and fourth. The next game, it would be just the opposite. It seemed to work out fine, because if one of us wasn't on, the other might be hot. But it was a stupid idea, really. You can't alternate, because you're not given a chance to build any kind of momentum."

Shaw felt a strong sense of allegiance towards Albert, who had been the 49ers' only quarterback since the franchise was formed in 1946. But Tittle had the stronger arm, and everyone knew it, even Albert. Eventually, the charade had to stop. Shaw realized the same thing after learning the team's owner, Tony Morabito, preferred Tittle to Albert.

The 49ers won the first five games in 1952 with their lefty-righty quarterback plan, plus the addition of rookie running sensation Hugh McElhenny. Then Albert made a strategic mistake not befitting a veteran, and it turned the whole season around.

The 49ers held a 17-10 second-half lead over the Bears when Albert dropped back to punt deep in his territory. Ever the gambler, he thought he saw an opening and tried to run for a first down. He didn't make it, thereby giving the Bears an easy touchdown and the impetus to pull out a 20-17 victory. The 49ers finished the year 7-5, and that one play effectively finished Albert as a 49er quarterback.

The more action Tittle saw, the harder it was on Albert. One week it was Albert's turn to start, and Shaw opted for Tittle instead.

"Frank pouted that whole week in practice," Tittle said. "He was off by himself punting to little kids. He wasn't even a part of the team. It was a tough year for both of us. We didn't have much scouting in those days. So when I'd go into a game to replace Frank, I'd ask him, 'Is that an odd-man front?' And he'd make some smart-ass remark like 'Why don't you figure it out? You're trying to get my job.' Frank was a good guy, but he was resentful of me. It was hard for him to sit down. The next year, he played in Canada."

In 1953, Tittle had his best record (9–3) in San Francisco as a full-time starter, even though he broke his cheekbone when Detroit defensive back Jim David deliberately drove a knee into his unprotected face.

"David did it to me like he did it in a lot of ball games," said Tittle. "I bootlegged, I scored, and David, let's put it this way, with today's rules, he wouldn't be playing very long. The rules back then allowed the Detroit Lions to get away with a lot of things. Just like they allowed the Chicago Bears and our own linebacker, Hardy Brown, to get away with things like his shoulder block that crushed people."

The 49ers had beaten Philadelphia and the Rams before David shattered Tittle's cheekbone in three places in the third game, a 24–21 Detroit win. Tittle sat out the next week and his replacement, Jim Powers, led the 49ers to a 35-28 win over the Bears. Tittle tried to come back the following Sunday in a relief role against Detroit, but both his passes were intercepted as the Lions won, 14-10. A season sweep for Jim David.

"I had to wear a special face mask after my cheekbone was broken," said Tittle. "That didn't stop David from going after people, even teammates. We were on the same team at the Pro Bowl. Practicing one day in shorts with no pads on, Billy Wilson, my receiver with the 49ers, runs across the middle on a pattern. Davis decapitates his head.

"David had that temporary craziness that when the ball's in the air, it's his, and anybody in the way is going to get cut down. Even in practice! He was horrible. He should have been outlawed from football. Then he came out and coached with the 49ers when I was coaching there. He was a nice guy off the field."

Lou Spadia, the 49ers general manager at the time, stayed behind with Tittle in Detroit after David delivered a Goliath-like blow.

"We didn't take a team doctor with us on trips in those days," said Spadia. "We had to get the jaw set, Y. A. had a broken bone beneath the eye, so we went to a hospital. But we didn't know what kind of hospital we were in until a doctor said, 'Get him out of that abortion mill.' We finally found the right hospital. The day after the surgery, they put Y. A. on a nonpressurized plane. It was Capital Air Lines, and we flew so low, we could see the houses down below. Y. A. was a sick puppy, but the people in Detroit had done a wonderful job."

Remarkably, Tittle had twenty touchdown passes in 1953, his career best with the 49ers. He ranked third statistically among NFL quarterbacks.

"Y. A. wanted to throw the longest touchdown there ever was," said Leo Nomellini, the 49ers' two-way Hall of Fame lineman. "He liked to throw the long pass."

Statistics bear that out. Tittle isn't listed among the top twenty NFL quarterbacks in terms of lifetime attempts and completions. But in terms of career yardage, he ranks seventeenth with 33,070. And he's twelfth in touchdown passes with 242. That's impressive, considering he hasn't played since 1964.

Five years after Tittle retired, and before the passing game was aided by more lenient blocking rules and the technically advanced West Coast Offense, he ranked second among all-time quarterbacks behind Johnny Unitas.

Now neither is rated in the top twenty, which includes Neil O'Donnell, Chris Chandler and Steve Beuerlein. Here's proof that numbers are overrated. Tittle is ranked sixty-first all-time, just behind Gus Frerotte. Tony Banks is seventy-second, while Baugh is seventy-sixth, Terry Bradshaw eighty-second, Namath 105th, and Layne 106th.

Would anyone choose Frerotte and Banks over any of those last four Hall of Famers?

"I'd see Y. A. successful today no matter what," said Pat Summerall, a onetime Giants teammate of Tittle's. "I don't see any reason why he couldn't be a quarterback. He's the same size as Steve Young, he could really throw the ball, and nobody had more heart. I remember playing defensive end for the Cardinals and hitting Tittle in the back as hard as I could. He was all stretched out. It should have hurt him, but it didn't. It knocked the wind out of him. So the impression you had was this guy loved to play, that he was a tough, competitive guy."

Tittle was the competitor's competitor.

"Y. A. always thought he was the greatest boxer, runner, passer," Nomellini said. "He was a great athlete."

The greatest boxer?

"After a play, he'd come back fighting," Nomellini explained. "He didn't take bull from anybody."

In 1954, John Henry Johnson slid into the backfield with McElhenny, Perry, and Tittle.

"That was our best 49er team," said Tittle. "We won all seven exhibition games, and our first five games. Then we lost Mac [with a separated shoulder], and that hurt us a lot offensively. But we also lost most of our defensive unit. We couldn't stop anybody."

After their impressive start, the 49ers limped to the finish line with a 7-4-1 record. Tittle passed for only nine touchdowns in spite of 295 pass attempts, his high as a 49er. He matched his touchdowns with interceptions. Perhaps he was too concerned with trying to keep all three of his talented backs happy. Since Tittle called all the plays, that was his responsibility and his headache.

"It wasn't an easy job," he said. "Today, you've got two backs. And in some cases, one back, like Emmitt Smith in Dallas. I had three backs to please. They all wanted to carry the ball, and they all pouted a little bit if they didn't get the ball. Joe was the workhorse. Thirty carries a game was not uncommon for Joe. But that was almost half the running attack.

"McElhenny didn't have quite the stamina of the others. It might have been his running style, with the high knee action. He worked everything in his body when he ran the ball. John Henry was the best athlete of the three. If he had been a boxer, he'd have been heavyweight champion of the world. He could run as fast as the rest of them if he wanted to. He could dog it a little bit. You'd have to light a fire under him."

Sometimes, Johnson played a game different from his Million Dollar mates, a game straight out of the John Henry playbook.

"One time, I went back to pass," Tittle said, "and John Henry was supposed to be in the flat. I turned to throw it, and he wasn't there. He was over the middle. Afterwards, I said, 'Dammit, John Henry, where were you?' And he said, 'AYZ or XYZ, whatever your damn name is, I was open over the middle.' And I said, 'You're supposed to be in the flat.' And he said, 'I didn't like it out there. They're paying you a lot more money than they're paying me. You should be able to find me any place.'

"John Henry was a punishing runner. He'd take that knee brace of his and punish linebackers. And he'd call them every name in the book. I'd tell him, 'Will you shut up? They're going to take it out on me.' But that was John Henry. There will never be another one like him personality-wise. He was mean, and he was tough, and he was fun to play with. He didn't care what they did to him, and he didn't care what he did to them."

Tittle had three sensitive egos to deal with in the celebrated backfield.

"Joe, Mac, and John Henry had prima donna tendencies," Tittle noted. "I had to be thinking all the time how many carries each of them had, although Joe wanted to carry the ball every down.

"McElhenny was, unqualified, worth the price of admission. He was the most beautiful broken-field runner I ever saw. He'd make some instinctive move and he was gone. One guy said, 'I tried to tackle him three times on one play, and missed him all three times.' Mac had the grace. He strutted like a prince. You could feel his presence. The King.

"Joe had the quickest start in football. With our running game, they had to pop through the line. Everything was quick, so you had to explode through the hole. And Joe, put this down, cheated 90 percent of the time. He'd get off before the count was completed. But he was so quick, the officials figured he was right and they were wrong. So they gave up [dealing] on it.

"With those three, we knew we had the best offense in football," said Tittle. "But there's offense and there's defense."

Even with Perry, McElhenny, and Johnson to please, Tittle became the first 49er to grace the cover of *Sports Illustrated*. That was on November 22, 1954, the first year the magazine was published, at a cost of twenty-five cents per issue, or $3.75 below what it costs in 2000.

Under the Morabito ownership flag, there wasn't unlimited spending by 49ers management in acquiring player talent, as there would be years later when Eddie DeBartolo owned the team. In the days before salary caps, DeBartolo spent money, sometimes recklessly, to pick up players who would plug roster holes during the 49ers' playoff runs.

In the early 1950s, there wasn't rampant player movement within the NFL, because there was no free agency. When you signed with a team, you were that team's property until you were traded or released. If you held out for more money and didn't get it, your only other choices were to retire or go play in Canada.

Tony Morabito, who owned the team from its inception, was a lumberman who lacked the personal wealth of the DeBartolos. Morabito was reluctant even to raise ticket prices. Relenting to pressure from other NFL owners after the 49ers joined the league in 1950, he finally raised midfield tickets from $3.60 to $3.75, reserved seats from $2.40 to $3, and general admission prices from $1.80 to $2.

After those increases, the 49ers still had the NFL's cheapest tickets. Therefore, it's easy to understand why the 49ers had a Million Dollar Backfield in name only.

San Francisco was Quarterback City. The 49ers wanted one capable quarterback in charge, and one capable backup ready at all times. That's why they had no less than four No. 1 quarterback draft picks in the 1950s: Tittle in '51, Bernie Faloney of Maryland in '54 [he went to Canada], Earl Morrall of Michigan State in '56, and John Brodie of Stanford in '57.

This accent on offense hardly benefitted the 49ers' playoff ambitions, because their defense was undermanned and overwhelmed. But it sure made for exciting Sundays. The 49ers scored forty or more points six times in their first five years in the NFL, and thirty or more points thirteen times. Conversely, the 49ers defense yielded thirty to fifty points ten times during this same period.

"Buck Shaw told me after he went to the Philadelphia Eagles [in 1958], 'I got a football team. If I had a pitcher, I'd have something.'" Tittle said. "Then he got Norm Van Brocklin from the Rams and won a championship [in 1960]."

Shaw had a championship defense, though, in the City of Brotherly Love in defeating Vince Lombardi and Green Bay, 17-13, for the '60 NFL title.

"Buck wasn't a hands-on guy during a game," Tittle continued. "He was a great teacher and a great motivator. But when the game started, he lost himself. He needed a leader on the field. He believed a pitcher was a leader."

Shaw had just such a pitcher in Tittle until 1954 when Shaw was relieved of his coaching duties. The 49ers struggled under Red Strader in 1955. Tittle struggled as well with accuracy. He threw five interceptions in his first game, a 23-14 setback to the Rams. He didn't have an interception-free game the rest of the season. He finished with a career-high twenty-eight interceptions compared to seventeen touchdown passes.

Not having McElhenny and Johnson healthy affected Tittle's performance. But he was partly responsible for the 49ers' 4-8 record that cost

Strader his job. Tittle then found himself under Albert once again, although in more harmonious working conditions. Albert was the new coach.

"Frank became one of my best friends," said Tittle. "He'd tell people, 'Here's the guy who sent me up to Canada.' It's tough for anybody when there's direct competition. It was tough for Brodie and myself. I wasn't a nice guy when I wanted to play. When Brodie was in the game, I sat there with my fingers crossed. If he threw two [interceptions] in a row, then I could get in there and win the ball game. I just wasn't a good sport when I wasn't playing. I didn't want to lose the game no matter who the quarterback was, but I didn't want to see my competitor be the hero either."

Tittle had another so-so season in 1956. He passed for seven touchdowns the entire season, and was picked off twelve times. And he played in every game but one. The rookie Morrall was used in close games. The 49ers had to win their last three games to finish 5-6-1. That's when Tittle finally came to life, throwing five touchdown passes.

Tittle now was thirty. He needed a comeback season desperately. And what followed was his most productive year in San Francisco, although there was no early indication that anything special was about to happen as the 49ers dropped the season opener to the lowly Chicago Cardinals, 20-10, at Kezar Stadium.

Preseason optimism had taken a beating in Fogville. Something or somebody would have to turn around the 49ers fast because their always tough rivals, the Rams, were next up. One week later, a 49ers receiver and a cartoon strip caveman would have something in common. The same name and the same fame.

The Rams led, 20-16, late in the fourth quarter when Tittle drove the Niners to the visitors' 11. The Bald Eagle then arched a looping pass towards the corner of the end zone to an unknown rookie from the College of Idaho. Owens easily outjumped defensive back Jesse Castete to pluck the football out of the autumn air. The 49ers won, 23-20.

The "Alley-Oop" pass had been invented.

"R.C. was a college basketball player, so it was like going up for a rebound for him," Tittle said. "After the game, he told me, 'I can do that every time.' So we decided to work on it in practice. We called it 'flanker right, Alley-Oop.' It became a long, high ball thrown short. The defender doesn't want you to get past him, so I'd throw it short and R.C. would come back for the ball."

The Alley-Oop emerged as the theme of the 1957 season not only for the 49ers, but the NFL. The origin of the pass dated back to Owens's high school days in Santa Monica under creative Jim Sutherland, later the head coach at Washington State.

"It was the same play at Santa Monica High, though not designated in the last second of the game," said Owens. "Eddie Cole, who was the Torrance High coach, then took Sutherland's pro-set offense with him to the College of Idaho along with eight Santa Monica players, including myself. We took the Northwest by storm. *Sports Illustrated* wrote about us."

Owens was a basketball star as well in college. The 49ers drafted him in the fourteenth round in 1956, but he didn't join them until 1957 after playing with an AAU basketball team. Against the Cardinals in an exhibition game in Seattle, he made his first Alley-Oop catch along the sideline. It didn't cause immediate attention. The 49ers didn't rush to put it in the playbook.

After losing to the Cardinals to start the season, Tittle and Brodie were running Rams' plays in practice on 49ers' defense day.

"Y. A. and John were throwing short passes," said Owens. "Red Hickey, who was our offensive coach, told them, 'Throw the ball down the field to give the defense a picture [of the Rams offense].' So they threw some long passes, and I caught a couple in the air against double coverage. Someone said, 'Let's put that in for the Rams.' Somebody else said, 'Yeah, but what do we call it?' It was one of three guys, either Hickey, Tittle, or Albert, who said, 'Let's call it Alley-Oop.'"

After thumping the Rams, the 49ers traveled to Chicago, where the Bears held a 17-14 lead with four minutes remaining. Tittle marched the 49ers into scoring position again, this time to the 7-yard line. He then looked for Owens in the end zone. But Owens had been driven to the turf by a defender. So Tittle smartly delivered a low pass that Owens caught on his knees for the winning touchdown with twenty-seven seconds left.

Two weeks later, San Francisco beat the Bears again by the identical 21-17 score. Tittle scored on a short run and hit Wilson with the winning eleven-yard touchdown pass as the 49ers battled back from tragic news: team owner Tony Morabito had died at halftime from a heart condition.

"That was the battle cry unsaid... 'C'mon, let's win this one for Tony,'" Tittle recalled. "It gave us that extra little adrenaline. You play a football game, and there is no such thing as playing at 100 percent or even 90 percent. If you played to your maximum ability, which is 85 percent, you'll probably be a champion."

Nobody plays at 100 percent?

"If you played 100 percent every game, you'd win," said Tittle. "But you don't. When you get to the goal line, you can't make any yards at all. Or on third down and a yard, it's hard to make two yards. Because [defenses] come up with that extra something. Their tails are up high, and they're tigers out there. That's why there are great players, and other players who don't reach their maximum because they can't hit it all the time. To play at 85 percent of your capacity, you'd win most games. It takes a spark to give you that extra effort to turn a ball game around."

Morabito's untimely death provided that extra spark.

Detroit came to town the following Sunday with John Henry Johnson, who carried nine times for forty-seven yards and a touchdown as the Lions carried a 31-28 lead into the final minute of play.

Tittle was magical that year. He marched the 49ers past midfield, then lofted a forty-one-yard pass into the end zone for Owens with eleven seconds left. The human pogo stick went up over two defenders to snatch the football and a 35–31 victory.

"The Alley-Oop wasn't ever a play that was stopped," said Owens. "It just became harder to make. Guys would cut me down, knock me out of bounds, try to keep me from getting downfield. It became tough duty, but I kept my wits, and I improvised. To make it work, you had to have a line that could block, and a quarterback who could get you the ball. Y. A. believed in you, and he believed in himself. He gave me confidence. Around him, you felt really good and blessed. That's why he got the nickname 'Colonel Slick.' He was the colonel out there."

Or the general, although Tittle wasn't worried about rank as much as rankings. The 49ers' record was 5-1 after beating the Lions. But, true to form, nothing came easy for them in the 1950s. They promptly lost their next three games, all on the road, to Los Angeles, Detroit, and Baltimore.

Still traveling a week later, the 49ers beat the Giants, 27–17. Tittle threw a touchdown pass to Wilson. Tittle also made some clutch runs to preserve the lead and deny New York the Eastern Division title. With two games left, the 49ers were 6-4. By beating Baltimore and Green Bay, both games in San Francisco, the Niners would share the Western Conference title.

"Y. A. was a competitor. He wanted to hang in there," said Unitas. "His idea of football was to throw it. He didn't care about running the ball. He was an aggressive guy who just loved the game, loved to play, like we all did back then. You ran, you blocked, you did everything."

Baltimore led the 49ers, 13–10, with two minutes left. Tittle finally got untracked with a twenty-eight-yard pass to McElhenny at the 14-yard line. On the next play, Baltimore's defensive line collapsed on Tittle. He pulled some leg muscles and had to leave the game. Enter the rookie Brodie, who calmly found McElhenny in the end zone for a dramatic 17–13 victory.

Tittle still had weak underpinnings before kickoff of the Packers game. So Brodie started. Green Bay led 20-10 in the second half, when Tittle entered and gamely rallied the 49ers to a 27-20 win and a share of the title.

The winner of the 49ers-Lions tiebreaker in San Francisco would face Cleveland for the NFL championship. Tittle was on fire early. He threw a thirty-four-yard Alley-Oop to Owens to give the 49ers a 7-0 lead. Tittle struck for two more touchdowns, hitting McElhenny for forty-seven yards and Wilson for twelve. Soltau's twenty-five-yard field goal put San Francisco ahead, 24-7, at halftime.

McElhenny kept the pressure on early in the second half with a seventy-one-yard run to the 9-yard line. The 49ers could do no better than a field goal, but their 27-7 lead indicated things were in hand.

Maybe the 49ers just weren't frontrunners after coming from behind so often during that storybook season. Whatever the reason, a twenty-point margin wasn't adequate. Three Tittle interceptions and two lost fumbles by the 49ers led to a Lion comeback that was more amazing than anything the 49ers had concocted all year. Detroit won, 31-27, and left town laughing.

If the success of the Alley-Oop wasn't incentive enough to earn Tittle the NFL's Player of the Year award, his 63.1 completion percentage also led the league. But honors didn't guarantee job security. When the 1958 season opened, Brodie had replaced Tittle as the starter based on their preseason performances. And some chutzpa used by Brodie.

"Red Hickey was giving a speech to 6,000 fans in Moraga that summer," Brodie said. "When Hickey was done, and we were getting ready to practice, Hickey said, 'Y. A., you warm?' And Y. A. said, 'I haven't thrown a ball. I've been sitting here listening to you.' Hickey turned to me. 'Brodie, you warm?' I said, 'I'm always warm.'

"I screwed Y. A. to get in. I saw an opening. And so I got most of the work in the exhibition games. Tittle was the best leader, the best quarterback. I think I became a pretty damn good one. But if they had played Tittle, it would have been the best thing for everyone.

"I'm competitive, and I'd have tried to play. But the 49ers should have let Tittle play two, three more years, then I would have taken over. Y. A. might have been the toughest guy I've ever seen. You had to kill him to beat him. But the 49ers decided to make it a battle between us. That's how they did it in San Francisco."

Albert, not Hickey, made the official switch to Brodie. Tittle now understood fully what Albert felt in 1951 when Tittle was the new fast draw in town, ready to take down the aging gunslinger. Brodie didn't disappoint his head coach in the opener, rallying the 49ers from a 20-7 third-quarter deficit against Pittsburgh to a 23-20 victory. Tittle was one for five, with two interceptions, in a cameo role.

Tittle, now the aging gunslinger, quickened his hand after that, and Brodie receded into the shadows following three interceptions in a 33-3 defeat to Los Angeles. Tittle was back in charge, but he couldn't recreate his MVP effort. Before long, Tittle and Brodie were sharing playing time, just as Albert and Tittle had seven years earlier.

And, once again, Albert was ready to bolt. He resigned after a 6-6 season. The 49ers were looking for their fourth head coach in five years.

"I held John off until the Shotgun," Tittle said of Brodie.

Not exactly. The two had comparable results that season, Tittle 120 of 208 passes for 1,467 yards, Brodie 103 of 172 for 1,224 yards. Tittle had nine touchdown passes and fifteen interceptions, Brodie six touchdown tosses and twelve interceptions. But only Tittle was picked off five times in one game.

The Alley-Oop worked in 1958 and beyond, no matter who was throwing, Tittle or Brodie. However, the end result with the Alley-Oop after its spectacular beginning was more first downs than touchdowns.

"What are you going to do on third-and-nineteen," asked Tittle, "throw a sideline pass and get twelve? With the Alley-Oop, you got a chance [for a first down], one out of three."

Tittle was the quarterback in charge for much of 1959 under his new head coach, Hickey. But Hickey was waiting to unleash the Shotgun, a short-passing offense similar to the single wing in its formation. And neither Tittle nor Brodie was a nifty runner, a Shotgun prerequisite.

Tittle also turned thirty-four in 1960, one more reason why the 49ers felt their future was with Brodie, who was ten years younger. Tittle made the transition easier for Hickey by injuring his groin against the Bears in week six.

Hickey unveiled the Shotgun on November 27, 1960 in Baltimore against the surprised Colts. The 49ers won, 30-22. They took four of their last five games to wind up 7-5. Tittle was still bothered by the groin, but there was no assurance he would have been playing much even if he were completely healthy.

Hickey was committed totally to the Shotgun, and Tittle was a T-formation passer. Hickey then drafted Billy Kilmer, a pass-run single-wing threat from UCLA who was perfectly suited for the new offense.

Tittle felt alone as he reported to training camp at St. Mary's College in 1961. Perry and McElhenny were gone. Wilson now was a coach. And Tittle was the odd man out at quarterback.

Hickey had pegged Brodie, Kilmer, and Bobby Waters as an alternating Shotgun triumvirate. And Tittle was trying to conceal the fact that his groin injury hadn't healed in the off-season.

For the first time, the thought of retirement crossed Tittle's mind. But until he decided what to do, he began a game of possum in summer camp.

"I was ashamed to tell the coaches and trainers I was still hurt ten months later," he said. "So I'd go into the toilet at St. Mary's, close the door, and tape myself. I'd flush the toilet, so no one could hear me taping. I'd flush some more, and keep taping. I'd spend twenty minutes in the toilet. I kept this up for three weeks. After practice, I'd go back inside the toilet stall, close the door, and start flushing again while I ripped the tape off. You can't tape the sternum, and you can't tape the groin either. Every time I moved, it hurt. I could throw, but I couldn't move."

Tittle continued this deception until the 49ers traded him to New York for guard Lou Cordileone, the Giants' No. 1 draft pick from Clemson. Even though Tittle now was someone else's property, and a better team at that, he was unsure of his next move. For he was damaged goods, and the Giants didn't know it. He decided to honor the trade and take his chances, although his Ole Miss rival, Conerly, was entrenched as the Giants quarterback.

"When I showed up and worked out," said Tittle, "Pat Summerall, who was the team's placekicker, paid me the greatest compliment. He said when I threw the football, it was like 'a cannon ball whistling through the air.' But I was in shorts. I didn't know what I was going to do in a game because I was still doing the taping-in-the-toilet thing."

The Giants actually had made the deal for Tittle before their preseason opener against the 49ers in Portland, Oregon, although Tittle was unaware of any transaction during the game.

"Brodie played the first half using the Shotgun, and the Giants just killed him," Tittle recalled. "I played the second half using the T-formation, and expected to get the same treatment. But there was no pressure. Andy Robustelli hit me one time, then picked me up and brushed me off. Sam Huff was always a mean S.O.B., and he took it easy. I just picked them apart, and we almost pulled out the game, losing 21-20.

"I thought I had buried the Shotgun forever, put John Brodie back on the bench, and I would have my job with the 49ers for the final three, four years of my career. I'm heading for the locker room afterwards, and Huff grabbed me. He said the Giants had traded for me, and the coach [Allie Sherman] had told the players before the game that if anyone hurt me, it would cost him $1,000."

Brodie was now the No. 1 quarterback in San Francisco. Or actually No. 1a, since Hickey needed three alternating quarterbacks to run the Shotgun. Brodie was happy to see Tittle leave. But Brodie also was envious.

"He got the best deal," Brodie said. "I wish they had let me go to New York."

In New York, divine intervention interceded on Tittle's behalf with, of all things, yet another injury. The Giants' second exhibition was against the Rams. Tittle was told by Sherman that he would start the second half.

"I wasn't even familiar with the Giants center [Ray Wietecha]," said Tittle. "He snapped the ball against the Rams, it hit me on the wrist, and the ball pops loose. I fall on it and Jack Pardee of the Rams hits me in the back with his knee. I go back to the huddle, and I can't speak. Pardee had broken three transverse processes in my back, making it hard for me to talk. I had played one play for the Giants, they had traded their first draft choice for a thirty-five-year-old bald-headed guy, and now I'm out five weeks."

But the five weeks off was a miracle tonic. Twice-daily whirlpool treatment not only healed Tittle's back, it cured his groin. Tittle could stop the toilet-taping and now seriously challenge Conerly for the quarterback's job. Chuckin' Charleys seemed to be easy pickin's for The Bald Eagle.

Conerly opened the year against the visiting Cardinals, starting their second season in St. Louis. The Cards put a 21-10 hurting on the Giants. New York then traveled to Pittsburgh. Conerly started again and was trailing in the second half. Tittle replaced him and hit ten of twelve passes for 143 yards. The Giants surged back for a 17-14 triumph.

Sherman continued with Conerly as his starter the third week of the season against Washington. That's when Tittle caught the break he was seeking.

"Del Shofner, our receiver, runs the wrong pass route," Tittle recalled. "Charlie throws the ball where Del was supposed to be, and a Washington player picked it off and returned it for a touchdown. Allie Sherman looked at me and said, 'You're in.' Charlie did nothing wrong. He was a perfect Southern gentleman, a really nice guy. But he blew his cork after hearing he was pulled. He threw his helmet and kicked it. I had a big day, we won the game [24-21], and I got the starting job."

Tittle was 8-2-1 in his eleven starts. He passed for more yards (2,272) than at any time since his first season in Baltimore thirteen years earlier. And his touchdown-interception ratio (17-12) also was his best since 1948. The Giants' one tie in 1961 occurred against Cleveland, 7-7, in the final regular-season game. Jim Murray once wrote a tie is like kissing your sister. But that tie remains the highlight kiss of Tittle's career.

"I didn't play one of my best games," he said, "but I can remember the feeling I had in the huddle as the New York fans counted down the seconds on our winning the Eastern Conference championship. I had played pro football since 1948, and this was my first championship. That was my greatest moment in football."

For Cordileone, 1961 was the worst memory of a short, undistinguished NFL career. He bombed with the 49ers, who didn't even bring him back in 1962. He wound up playing for the Saints in New Orleans, where he had more success as the owner of a French Quarter bar called The Huddle.

"When I was traded to the Giants," said Tittle, "Cordileone was quoted as saying, 'Just him for me?' He later had a helmet in his bar which said, 'Traded for Y. A. Tittle.'"

When Tittle got to New York, he recognized right away what he had been missing all those frustrating years in San Francisco: defense.

"I didn't have to start on my 20-yard line all the time," he said. "The Giants defense frequently would get the offense the ball in good position, so we didn't have to go that far to score."

However, the Giants were cliquish, something Tittle never encountered on the 49ers.

"The Giants were like two teams, the offensive team and the defensive team," he said. "The offensive and defensive players didn't like each other. When we stayed at the Concourse Plaza Hotel, the offense and defense stayed on separate floors and had their own parties. The defense thought the offense got all the stats and the big money, while the defense did all the work. Then I came over from San Francisco, and Del Shofner and Joe Walton came from Los Angeles and Washington. We started scoring more points, and that brought the team closer together."

Tittle helped heal the breach on the Giants. He and Shofner were the first offensive players invited to the defensive players' parties.

The Giants played the Packers for the 1961 NFL championship in Green Bay. More nasty weather for the bald-headed guy.

"It was sixty degrees when we got there," Tittle said, "and the next day we could hardly stand up because of the bitter cold. We weren't as good as the Packers, though."

Green Bay won in a rout, 37-0, for its first NFL title under Lombardi, who was a Giants assistant coach before taking over the Packers in 1959. Kyle Rote of the Giants dropped two Tittle touchdown passes in the first half, then complained of freezing hands afterwards. Paul Hornung, on leave from the Army, scored nineteen points for the Pack.

Dick Nolan was a Giants defensive back when Tittle joined the team.

"What made Y. A. special was he was such a competitor," said Nolan. "We had this rookie running back [Bobby Gaiters] who ran out of bounds against the Steelers. Y. A. ran all the way after him and said, 'You dumb-ass rookie, don't you ever do that again. You take it as far as you can.' The rookie looked at him and said, 'Yeh, but that was Big Daddy Lipscomb.' Y. A. wouldn't back off. He told the kid, 'I don't care if it was gargantuan, you take it as far as you can, even if it's one or two yards.'

"That's the kind of guy Y. A. was. Tough, all-out. He made some big plays for us. He was a sidearm thrower, but he'd get the ball there pretty darn well. He came to the Giants the same time as Shofner. Together, they were quite a team."

Gaiters didn't realize Eugene "Big Daddy" Lipscomb once chased Tittle off the field. Tittle smartly held onto the ball with one hand and Big Daddy's face mask with the other hand.

"I bootlegged to the right," Tittle recalled, "and Big Daddy chased me out of bounds. I jumped over our bench, and I was scared to death to let go of his mask. He said, 'When you turn loose, I'm going to kill you.' Then they penalized him fifteen yards because he followed me to the bench. He was only following his head because I was guiding it."

Tittle had a tremendous receiver in San Francisco in Billy Wilson. Del Shofner was Wilson with speed. Shofner was unbelievable in 1961 and 1962 with a combined 121 receptions for twenty-three touchdowns while averaging nineteen yards per catch. Shofner's star then descended, and he faded out of New York.

The Giants were 12-2 in 1962. Tittle's thirty-three touchdown passes that year included an NFL-record-tying seven against Washington on October 28, when he completed twenty-nine of thirty-nine passes for 505 yards. He threw six more touchdown strikes against Dallas on December 16.

Tittle's favorite targets that year, including receptions and touchdowns, were Shofner (53, 12), running back Alex Webster (47, 4), Frank Gifford (39, 7) and Walton (33, 9). Gifford had returned after a year's retirement, but as a receiver, not a halfback, after suffering a severe concussion in a collision with Philadelphia Eagles linebacker Chuck Bednarik in 1960.

Tittle won a number of postseason awards in 1962, but he wasn't a unanimous pick as league MVP. Giants defensive end Andy Robustelli was named the NFL's top player by one voting organization.

"Tittle was outstanding, one of the top three, four quarterbacks I've seen," said Bednarik. "He stood in the pocket pretty good. That took some courage to hold the ball that long until he found a receiver open."

Waiting for the Giants once again at the end of the season was Green Bay. Only the Giants got to play the Packers this time at Yankee Stadium.

"We were even with them that year," Tittle said. "But a storm came through New York, with a strong wind. Don Chandler punted the ball one time for us, and the ball wound up three yards behind him."

The Packers received three field goals from Jerry Kramer and a seven-yard touchdown run from Jim Taylor to beat New York, 16-7.

The Giants' only touchdown came when Erich Barnes blocked a Max McGee punt, and rookie Jim Collier fell on the ball in the end zone.

The Giants rebounded even stronger in 1963. Tittle, now thirty-seven, had a career year. The 11-3 Giants scored a staggering 448 points, or thirty-two per game, for what still is a franchise record.

About that time, a young singer from New York, Barbra Streisand, told the media she was a cross between Sophia Loren and Y. A. Tittle. What could she possibly have meant?

"We met Barbra one night over cocktails, and she looks like Y. A.," Minnette explained. "Her cheekbones and eyes..."

"She has squinty eyes like me," said Y. A.

The Giants' 1963 NFL championship-game opponent would be the Chicago Bears at Wrigley Field, George "Papa Bear" Halas's lair.

"We had beaten the Bears during the season," said Tittle, confusing 1963 with 1962. "But here came another blizzard."

The Giants failed once again to win the league crown. Arctic conditions greeted both teams. Tittle wrenched his knee in the second quarter when hit accidentally by linebacker Larry Morris. Tittle continued on gamely, but threw five interceptions.

"It was my left knee, so it was my planting leg," Tittle said. "He fell into me...rolled into the knee. It was a partial tear. But we were playing on a frozen field and wearing tennis shoes. So it's hard to stand up on a frozen field anyway, and now I have one leg..."

The Giants' only score came on Tittle's fourteen-yard pass to Gifford in the opening quarter. Shofner dropped another certain touchdown pass. The Giants led at the half, 10-7. But a second quarterback sneak for a touchdown by Billy Wade, set up by a Tittle interception, gave the Bears a narrow 14-10 victory.

"The last two interceptions, I was just throwing it up for grabs," said Tittle. "No sense taking another loss [in yardage] since I couldn't run."

Tittle could have limped off the field at halftime and not come back, and nobody would have criticized him. He was badly injured. But he returned to try and win the game, because he was the team's leader, and he wasn't going to let a partial tear, or any degree of tear, stop him.

"When I was a child," said Tittle de Laet, "people talked about my father as a hero. This is a word I grew up with. And the little girl wanted to know what a hero is, and why they are heroes. Is it because they try and win? Or is it because they try in the face of odds, and they're going to keep on trying? My book on my father was an attempt to give some meaning to that question, and to answer that for myself.

"My book had to do with that 1963 NFL championship game, in which my father lost, in which he was injured, and also because he went at it again and again and again. My father considers it the worst day of his life, and it was one of the worst days of my life. On one of his interceptions, I remember leaping from my seat inside the stadium for the ball."

A momentary flight of fancy from a daughter trying anything she could to save her father from yet another mouthful of bitter pudding.

"I chose that championship game for my book," she said, "not to honor a victory in my father's life, but a defeat, and what it means to be a human being. That Bears game was the end of my father's career. He played another year, but it was over.

"When he was blindsided in Chicago, it was a famous photo at the time taken by Robert Riger, who hand-delivered it to me years later at the San Francisco Airport so I could have it for my book. Then I drove Robert Riger to a 49ers practice at Candlestick Park. That's when he told me Lombardi really didn't say, 'Winning isn't everything. It's the only thing.' He said he was there when Lombardi said it. It was the imagination of the writer who was there that went wild. Robert Riger told me what Lombardi really said was, 'Winning isn't everything. Wanting to win is.' That photo [in Chicago] was about my father wanting to win.

"It has been a lifelong search for me, trying to find out what a hero is. I still want to know why are they heroes."

Because those who aren't need them.

Following 1963, the Giants ran out of heroes, and couldn't find capable replacements. The franchise wouldn't have another winning record for seven years. They wouldn't return to the playoffs for eighteen years. They plummeted into oblivion with a 2-10-2 record in 1964 after Sherman dismantled the team in an attempt to show he could win even without Jim Lee Howell's players, whom Sherman inherited in 1961.

The Eagles thrashed the Giants, 38-7, in the '64 opener, and it deteriorated from there. Baker bludgeoned Tittle one week later.

"It was a completely legitimate hit," said Baker. "I had a clean shot and I took it. That's football all the way. But what made it worse for Y. A., he threw the ball up after I hit him. Chuck Hinton intercepted it and ran it in for a touchdown. I still feel real good about what happened.

"That photo won a No. 1 prize that year. The next year, when I was introduced before a Steelers-Giants games in Yankee Stadium, I got one of the loudest boos you ever heard. Those fans at Yankee Stadium could really get on you. If I had a microphone, I'd have told them I was doing my job."

Berman's photograph took first place in the National Headliners' competition for 1964 without having appeared in the *Post-Gazette*.

"I covered the Steelers every Sunday for the paper because I liked sports," said Berman, now ninety and retired in Sun City, Arizona. "It was one of those games where it was three yards, four yards a play. So I started watching Tittle. Just then, Baker hit him. The *Post-Gazette* didn't use that picture because the editor said Tittle was all alone. The editor used three, four other photos showing Tittle being sacked and carried off the field.

"The Associated Press took about the same picture, but Tittle's head is up in their photo. His head is down in mine, and his expression is different. I entered my photo in a competition even though I didn't have a [required newspaper] clipping. My editor never said a word to me after I took first. I won a number of contests with that photo, but do you know that it never appeared in the *Post-Gazette* until thirty-five years later, in 1999, when *Sports Illustrated* published it as one of the photos of the century?

"It was the photo that got me the most attention. But I was an Army combat photographer during World War II, and I got Mussolini's mistress hanging from her ankles in disgrace in Milan. They had to tie her dress around her legs to keep it from coming down. That was a more dramatic photo [than Tittle's].

"I've met Tittle only once, when he was scouting for the Giants in Pittsburgh. He gave me a few minutes in the booth. He has used that photo a lot, I know, which is like stealing. Through [a mutual friend], I set him some [extra] photos. I never even got a thank you. Maybe he never got them."

Though Tittle tried to play through the pain at thirty-eight, he threw only ten touchdown passes as opposed to twenty-two interceptions in 1964.

"I could have played longer," he said. "I still had a good arm. How could I have thrown thirty-six touchdown passes, the most that had ever been thrown, and seven months later I was finished? I didn't booze a lot and I didn't have any ailments. I just couldn't come back from this injury. I couldn't move in the pocket, so I had a lousy 1964 season. The sternum was OK by the end of the season. But with all the criticism of the Giants' era ending, it really was the end of an era."

And the end of a Pro Football Hall of Fame career, too. Tittle retired, wondering who would replace him as Giants quarterback. For he had a different backup all four seasons in New York, from Conerly to Ralph Guglielmi to Glynn Griffing to Gary Wood. Tittle still gets a kick thinking about Guglielmi, the onetime red-hot prospect from Notre Dame.

"In 1963, I had success as a thirty-seven-year-old quarterback," said Tittle, "while an All-American quarterback like Ralph Guglielmi couldn't dance. We used to laugh about Ralph. Good guy, smart, handsome, could really throw the ball. He could hear the music, he knew the notes, but he couldn't dance."

Guglielmi was gone after the 1963 season. Tittle was replaced at starter in 1965 by his former backup in San Francisco, Earl Morrall, who then was succeeded by Fran Tarkenton, Norm Snead, and Craig Morton. None of the four produced a breakout year, unless the Giants' 9-5 record behind Tarkenton in 1970 counts as something significant. That season occurred, by the way, on Tittle's watch as a Giants assistant coach from 1969 to 1973.

How did the 49ers do the four years Tittle played in New York, building a 35-18-2 record? The 49ers were almost exactly the opposite: 19-36-1, shooting themselves in the foot with the Shotgun.

The 49ers fared much better, 27-25-4, with Tittle as an assistant coach from 1965 through 1968. He worked with the quarterbacks, including Brodie, his onetime competitor. Brodie, in his book *Open Field,* described a scene in which he and Tittle, player and coach, began fighting in a meeting room.

"I've had three fights in my life, and two have been with Tittle," said Brodie. "They weren't long, and nobody was hurt. One was in a meeting room, the other out on the practice field. He and I were close. He stuck up for me. But one time he said something about a play I had run in front of others in the room. And then he said it again and again and again. I was a smart aleck, and I told him, 'That's enough.' That started it. I won't talk about the other time we fought, but Y. A. and I are good friends. When I'm in town, I'll drop by his office."

Soltau believes Tittle might have created a distance between himself and Brodie through a controlling personality.

"Part of the problem between John and Y. A.," Soltau speculated, "might have been from when they played together. Y. A. was so possessive of the quarterback job that he took every snap. Y. A. also wasn't very happy as a 49er coach. Part of it was his fault. He wasn't a full-time coach because of his business interests. He didn't attend every practice or every meeting."

Tittle said he doesn't recall fighting with Brodie, but he acknowledged a difference in his and Brodie's personalities.

"He's one to do things leisurely, because it comes naturally to him," said Tittle. "I believed in the Vince Lombardi theory that if you run a play ten times in practice instead of six times, you'll run it better. Coaching Brodie was more difficult because he was off the cuff. I overcoached at times. I drive people sort of nuts. I'm just sort of that way. When I played, if we won last week, I wanted to sit in the same seat on the team bus, even if the head coach was sitting there. Or the owner."

In the late 1960s, the movie *Number One* was released with Charlton Heston playing an aging quarterback. Heston said he based his character on Tittle.

"I'll never forget the expression on Tittle's face," Heston explained, "in a picture taken of him on the sidelines in the final game he played with the New York Giants in 1964. It showed the classic face of a battered and bruised old pro dejectedly viewing his team going down to defeat."

When informed at the time the movie was made that he was Heston's quarterbacking role model, Tittle quipped: "I just hope he plays quarterback like he drove that chariot in *Ben Hur.*"

Tittle remained superstitious to the core after being hired by Webster, his former New York teammate who was the Giants' new head coach. Tittle changed seats often on the Giants' team bus, because the team had only two winning seasons out of five under Webster.

When Webster was fired in 1973, Tittle decided to give full attention to his flourishing insurance business on the Peninsula south of San Francisco, a business that began with Tittle knocking on doors in east Texas as a much younger man.

"I was trying to make a few extra bucks," he said, looking back. "Then in 1954, my wife was playing bridge with some ladies, one of whom had a husband who was a casualty broker looking for a partner. So I bought half of his agency before buying out his interest. Jack Jones then came in with me and we became Tittle and Jones. Then I bought his interest out."

The sign on the door in Palo Alto now says, "Y. A. Tittle & Associates."

"I'm selling property casualty insurance," said Tittle. "We're a brokerage firm...a $20 million agency. I'm working now to get my youngest son, John, set up in business. I have two more sons, Pat and Mike. One sells insurance, the other manages real estate. Two more years and I'll retire."

Tittle turned seventy-four in October 2000. He's considerably younger in the photos on the walls of his office, although it's hard to tell how much, because he hasn't aged in thirty years.

There's the famous photo of the Baker hit. Tittle said he holds no animosity towards Baker. In fact, Tittle helped Baker with his re-election campaign as sheriff of Wake County in North Carolina.

"He was the first black man to be elected in the county since Reconstruction," said Tittle. "He put my [bloodied] picture on telephone poles and ran on the theme, 'If you don't obey the law, this is what Big John is going to do to you.' I was told he was doing a good job, so I went and made a little speech for him to kick off his campaign. And he won in a landslide."

Baker played twelve years in the NFL. In 2000, he was serving in his twenty-second year as sheriff of Wake County. He represents the city of Raleigh and 600,000 in the county.

"There's no animosity between Y. A. and me," he said. "The only animosity is that I'm a Democrat and he's a Republican."

There's another photo on Tittle's office wall of a familiar-looking 49ers executive assistant: "To Y. A. The Greatest. R. C. 'Alley-Oop' Owens."

There's also a photo of Tittle and a 49ers quarterback of more recent prominence: "To Y. A. I think you can still do it. Joe Montana."

And, finally, there's a photo of a Hollywood director: "To a real champion. With the deepest respect. Oliver Stone."

Stone released his football movie, *Any Given Sunday,* in 1999 to mixed reviews. Stone turned up the volume on the tackling scenes, but the movie was believable until a third-string quarterback appears on the screen reading a newspaper on the bench during the game.

Oliver, Oliver, Oliver. No first-string quarterback would do such a dumb thing in real life. Though the script for *Any Given Sunday* was a joint effort by a former NFL player, Jamie Williams, and an NFL writer, Richard Weiner of *USA Today,* reality somehow got lost in the transition from the laptop computer to the movie set.

"Oliver Stone's normal tone of movie, and he told me this, is that he isn't saying things are true, like in JFK, but he wants you to think they might be," said Tittle, who played a pro football coach in Stone's movie. "He didn't want you to think that everything [about pro football] was Sunday school, God, and apple pie. So he showed sex scenes a little bit, and a little bit of the cussings. I didn't want it to be embarrassing. It wasn't. It was a little bit loud. Some locker room scenes were strong. It was pretty true."

In the movie, Tittle wore a sport coat, tie, and fedora. Any resemblance to a famous football coach from Texas who died in early 2000 was entirely accurate.

"I was dressed up as Tom Landry," said Tittle. "I didn't do anything [on the screen] but tip my hat and say, 'Send out the blitz team.' My grandchildren wanted me to make the movie. They said I was chicken if I didn't do it. I'm a little bit protective about having a bad image. I was worried the movie would cast a bad reflection about gambling and that kind of thing. And I don't want to do anything that would cast a shadow over the National Football League."

The Bald Eagle, speaking like an American symbol.

"I don't want to be the guy who says the game was better in my day," Tittle continued. "Unitas said how ungrateful the players are today compared to our guys. He said players from our time were better. I didn't believe that at all. Ball players are better today. They're bigger and stronger, and there are more coaches. There are too many substitutions, but the players are better. But you won't get Johnny Unitas to admit that."

Dianne Tittle de Laet remembers Unitas, whom *Sports Illustrated*'s Paul Zimmerman selected along with Montana as the quarterbacks on his All-Century Team, informing her father that he was thinking of asking the Baltimore Colts for a $14,000 contract.

"Don't press your luck," Tittle advised Unitas.

Unitas and Tittle were the premier NFL quarterbacks at the time. If Unitas was asking $14,000, maybe the Million Dollar Backfield really was the $80,000 Backfield. Or even less. The four 49ers aren't exactly sure, or about to admit to one another, what they made as teammates.

Regardless, they were four priceless football players. No 49er prospector in California's Mother Lode ever hit a bigger gold strike.

INDEX ★

A

AAFC, 19, 22–23, 43, 85, 150–51
Albert, Frankie, 3, 4, 19, 20, 23, 24, 27–30, 35–37, 53, 65–70, 75–76, 78, 124–26, 170–73, 179, 184
Allen, Marcus, 2, 138
Alley-Oop pass, 151, 180–84
All-Initial Backfield, 79
Ameche, Alan, 38
Anderson, Jamal, 91
Arenas, Joe, 78
Arizona State University, 123–24

B

Baker, Charles "Doc," 17
Baker, John, 135, 146, 148, 149, 151, 193, 197
Baltimore Colts, 39–41, 72, 151, 167–70
Banducci, Bruno, 4, 130
Banks, Tony, 174
Barnes, Erich, 191

Bass, Dick, 137
Baugh, Sammy, 84, 153, 159, 174
Beals, Alyn, 20
Beasley, Fred, 45
Bednarik, Chuck, 26, 50–51, 72, 190
Berman, Morris, 147, 193–94
Beuerlein, Steve, 174
Bible, Dana X., 163
Black players, early, 1, 17–18, 21. See also Racism
Blanda, George, 168
Bowman, Bill, 130
Bradley, Harold, 18
Bradshaw, Terry, 174
Breuil, Jim, 19
Brink, Larry, 2
Brodie, John, 38, 48, 67, 69, 77, 78, 82, 85, 122, 130, 134, 178–86, 195–96
Brown, Ed, 128
Brown, Hardy, 173

Brown, Jim, 26, 32, 38, 40, 54, 108–9, 136, 137
Brown, Paul, 22, 23–24
Broyles, Frank, 166
Burk, Adrian, 168
Butts, Wally, 119

C

Calgary Stampeders, 124
Cameron, Bob, 58, 59, 60
Campanella, Roy, 68
Cason, Jim, 46, 130, 158, 164, 165
Castete, Jesse, 179
Chandler, Chris, 85, 174
Chandler, Don, 190
Chappius, Bob, 166
Chicago Bears, 5, 72
Chicago Cardinals, 72
Christiansen, Jack, 27, 42, 88
Clark, Greg, 45
Cleveland Browns, 22–24, 108, 150–51, 167
Cole, Eddie, 180
Collier, Blanton, 22
Collier, Jim, 191

Collins, Ray, 46, 158
Colo, Don, 143
Compton Junior College,
    14, 56, 60, 88
Conerly, Charlie, 165,
    166, 186, 187, 194
Connor, George,
    26–27, 167
Cordileone, Lou, 186, 188
Costanza, Pete, 96,
    116–17, 125
Csonka, Larry, 144
Cunningham, Sam
    "Bam," 109

D

Dark, Alvin, 166
David, Jim, 173–74
Davis, Milt, 77–78
Davis, Terrell, 91
Dawson, Len, 144
DeBartolo, Eddie, 177
Debbas, Al, 60
Detroit Lions, 27, 84, 86,
    110, 130–34, 167
Doby, Larry, 114
Dooley, Jim, 66
Dorsett, Tony, 51

E

Elway, John, 149
Eshmont, Len, 20, 21
Ewbank, Weeb, 40–41

F

Faloney, Bernie, 178
Faulk, Marshall, 91
Fears, Tom, 88
Field, Wayne, 87
Follis, Charles, 17

Frerotte, Gus, 174–75
Fullerton, Ed, 125
Furrh, Bobby, 161

G

Gain, Bob, 135, 143
Gaiters, Bobby, 189
Garcia, Jeff, 28, 44, 45
Garner, Charlie, 44,
    48, 91
Gifford, Frank, 64, 66,
    190, 191
Gillom, Horace, 21
Gilmer, Harry, 166
Graham, Otto, 22, 23, 84,
    151, 167
Grange, Red, 18, 53–54
Greene, Mean Joe, 144
Griffing, Glynn, 194
Grigg, Chubby, 161
Groza, Lou, 23
Guglielmi, Ralph, 194–95
Gustafson, Bert, 25–26

H

Halas, George "Papa
    Bear," 17, 68, 72, 191
Hazeltine, Matt, 78
Hearst, Garrison, 53
Heaton, Chuck, 144
Heinrich, Don, 62–63,
    64, 65
Heston, Charlton, 196
Hickey, Howard "Red,"
    38–42, 79–81, 84, 128,
    180, 183, 185
Hill, Calvin, 51
Hill, Harlon, 128

Hill, Jerry, 41
Hinton, Chuck, 193
Hornung, Paul, 189
Houston Oilers, 136–37
Howell, Jim Lee, 193
Huff, Sam, 104, 186
Huston, Don, 170

I

Ingram, Jonas J.
    "Scrappy," 151
Isbell, Cecil, 168, 170
Isbell, Larry, 66

J

Jeffries, Jim, 18
Johnson, Barbara
    Flood, 123
Johnson, Billy, 44, 130, 161
Johnson, Ella, 113
Johnson, Jack, 18
Johnson, John Henry
    early childhood, 112–14
    high school, 112,
        114–17
    college, 117–24
    rookie year in CFL
        (1953), 124
    signs with 49ers, 125
    rookie year in NFL
        (1954), 30, 32,
        110–12, 128, 175
    1955 season, 126–28
    1956 season, 36, 129
    acquired by Lions, 130
    1957 season, 131, 181
    1958 season, 132–33
    1959 season, 133
    acquired by Steelers, 134
    1960 season, 134

1961 season, 134
1962 season, 134
1963 season, 134
1964 season, 134–35
1965 season, 135
acquired by Oilers, 136
1966 season, 136–37
retires from football,
    108, 137
career statistics, 108
after playing days,
    138–45
inducted into Pro
    Football Hall of Fame,
    107, 109, 117, 138,
    143–44
today, 141–43
nicknames, 112,
    115, 135
photos, 96, 97, 100
playing style of,
    101–7, 176
skills of, 55, 107–12
Johnson, John Henry, Jr.,
    139, 141
Johnson, Leona, 117, 129,
    132, 138–43
Jones, Deacon, 90

K

Kemp, T. Ray, 18
Kilmer, Billy, 185
Kirkby, Roland, 63
Kleckner, Bob, 73
Koch, Des, 64
Kramer, Jerry, 190
Kush, Frank, 124

L

LaBrucherie, Bert, 14
Landry, Tom, 198
Lane, Dick "Night
    Train," 34
Lary, Yale, 27, 131
Lavagetto, Cookie, 25
Lavelli, Dante, 23
Layne, Bobby, 46, 109–10,
    131–32, 144, 148,
    162–63, 166, 174
Lee, Fletcher, 11
Leiser, Bill, 28
Lemm, Wally, 136–37
Levens, Dorsey, 42
Lillywhite, Verl, 5, 20,
    21, 171
Lipscomb, Eugene "Big
    Daddy," 189
Lockett, J. W., 79
Lombardi, Vince, 42, 178,
    189, 192
Los Angeles Rams, 1, 16
Louisiana State
    University, 150, 153,
    160, 162, 163–66
Luckman, Sid, 153
Lujack, Johnny, 68, 166

M

Madigan, Slip, 118
Marchetti, Gino, 120
Marino, Dan, 149
Marshall, George
    Preston, 17
Marshall, Rube, 18
Martin, Slick, 163, 164
Mason, Tommy, 83
Mathias, Bob, 59, 115

Matson, Ollie, 54, 66,
    120, 121
Maynard, Don, 144
McDonald, Henry, 17
McElhenny, Beverly, 57
McElhenny, Hugh
    early childhood, 56–58
    high school, 58–60
    college, 56, 59, 60–65
    drafted by 49ers, 65–67
    rookie year (1952),
        28–29, 48, 49, 53,
        55–56, 67–70
    1953 season, 70–73
    1954 season, 30, 32,
        73–74, 110–11
    1955 season, 63, 74–75
    1956 season, 36, 62, 69,
        75–76, 129
    1957 season, 76–78
    1958 season, 78–79
    1959 season, 79–80
    1960 season, 80–81
    acquired by Vikings, 82
    1961 season, 82–83
    1962 season, 83
    acquired by Giants, 83
    1963 season, 83–84
    signed by Lions, 86
    1964 season, 84, 85–86
    retires from football, 54
    career statistics, 53
    after playing days,
        86–90
    inducted into Pro
        Football Hall of
        Fame, 88
    today, 51, 90–91

nickname, 28–29, 53
photos, 93, 94, 95, 100
running style of,
48–52, 54, 176
McElhenny, Hugh, Sr., 57
McElhenny, Peggy
Ogston, 58, 59–61, 62,
64, 66, 67, 81, 90
McGee, Max, 191
Mike, Bob, 21
Minnesota Vikings, 48, 82
Mitchell, Odus, 160–62
Mitchell, W. L., 156–57
Modzelewski, Ed, 66, 102
Montana, Joe, 149, 171,
198, 199
Moore, Bernie, 163,
164, 166
Moore, Lenny, 40, 74
Morabito, Josephine, 7
Morabito, Tony, 7, 16–17,
19, 22, 30–36, 74, 125,
126, 129, 172, 177, 181
Morabito, Vic, 7, 37, 39,
41, 67, 96
Morrall, Earl, 178,
179, 195
Morris, Larry, 191
Morton, Craig, 195
Morze, Frank, 81
Motley, Marion, 21, 23
Murray, Jim, 107

N

Namath, Joe, 148, 174
Neale, Earle "Greasy,"
27–28
Nevers, Ernie, 18, 54
New York Giants, 84, 85,
151, 186–95

Nolan, Dick, 37, 42,
135, 189
Nomellini, Leo "The
Lion," 36, 48, 63, 71,
112, 130, 171, 174, 175
Nordstrom, Lloyd, 87
Norris, Chips, 46
North, Johnny, 168

O

O'Dell, Howie, 65
O'Donnell, Neil, 174
Olderman, Murray, 138
O'Rourke, Charley, 168
Owens, R. C., 37, 76–80,
151, 179–82, 197
Owens, Terrell, 45

P

Pardee, Jack, 187
Parilli, Babe, 66
Parker, Buddy, 133, 134
Parseghian, Ara, 21–22
Patton, Mel, 16
Payton, Walter, 52, 90–91
Perry, Barbara, 19, 25
Perry, Donna, 9, 24,
34–35
Perry, Jewel Brown, 9,
14, 24
Perry, Joe
early childhood, 9,
10–11
high school, 11–14
college, 14
military service, 8,
9–10, 14–16
joins 49ers, 16–17, 19

rookie year (1948),
20–22, 40
1949 season, 22–23
1950 season, 26, 27–28
1951 baseball season,
24–25
1951 football season, 29
1952 season, 29–30
1953 season, 30, 32
1954 season, 30–32,
110–12
Joe Perry Day (Aug. 28,
1955), 33
1955 season, 35
1956 season, 36, 129
1957 season, 36–37
1958 season, 37–38
1959 season, 38–39, 80
1960 season, 39
acquired by Colts, 39
1961 season, 39–40
1962 season, 40
rejoins 49ers, 41
1963 season, 41–42, 83
retires from football, 42
career statistics, 32,
43–44
after playing days,
42–43
today, 43–46
nicknames, 20, 28–29, 53
photos, 92, 94, 100
racism and, 1–10,
11–12, 18, 21, 42–43,
46, 72
running style of, 26–27,
54–55, 175–76, 177
Y. A. Tittle and, 2, 21,
46, 157–58

Perry, Karen, 25
Perry, Laurah, 9, 11
Perry, Louella, 11, 12
Philadelphia Eagles,
    71–72
Piccolo, Brian, 5
Pietrosante, Nick, 133
Pihos, Pete, 71, 88, 90
Pirro, Rocco, 3
Pittsburgh Steelers, 41,
    108, 110, 124, 134–36
Pollard, Fritz, 17–18
Pool, Hampton, 71
Powell, Charlie, 71, 112
Powers, Jim, 173

R

Racism, 1–12, 17–18, 21,
    42–43, 46, 56–57,
    72–73, 115, 156–57
Ratterman, George,
    24, 170
Rauch, Johnny, 166
Reagan, Ronald, 88–89
Rice, Grantland, 18
Rice, Jerry, 44, 80
Richter, Les, 66
Riger, Robert, 192
Roberts, C. R., 79
Robeson, Paul, 18
Robinson, Frank, 1
Robinson, Jackie, 1, 2, 5,
    6, 7, 19, 114
Robustelli, Andy, 186, 190
Rooney, Art, 41, 109, 134,
    136, 137, 145
Rooney, Dan, 134
Rose, Bert, 82
Rosenbloom, Carroll, 170
Rote, Kyle, 189

Rozelle, Pete, 88
Rubay, Joe, 121
Ruetz, Joe, 118, 119–20
Russell, Bill, 1

S

Sanders, Barry, 32, 44, 48,
    50, 80, 90–91
Sayers, Gale, 5, 50, 54, 80,
    90–91
Schmidt, Joe, 51, 78, 91,
    103, 107, 152
Schmidt, Victor O., 62
Seattle Seahawks, 87
Seifert, George, 45
Shaughnessy, Clark, 4
Shaw, Lawrence T.
    "Buck," 20–21, 29–31,
    33, 65, 68, 70, 71, 74,
    125, 126, 172, 173, 178
Sherman, Allie, 148, 186,
    187, 193
Shofner, Del, 187, 189,
    190, 191
Shotgun, 185, 186, 195
Shula, Don, 41
Simpson, Milford,
    113, 114
Slater, Duke, 18
Sloan, Bill, 58, 65
Smith, Clyde B., 124
Smith, Emmitt, 32, 51,
    91, 175
Smith, Gideon, 17
Smith, J. D., 38, 39, 79
Snead, Norm, 195

Soltau, Gordy, 28, 30, 31,
    63, 66, 70, 78, 110,
    125, 130, 171, 195
Spadia, Lou, 7, 17, 56, 68,
    70, 81, 88, 94, 105,
    128, 129, 174
Sprinkle, Ed, 2, 72, 73
St. Clair, Bob, 8, 31, 50,
    102, 111, 120, 121, 130
St. Mary's College,
    117–23
Standlee, Norm, 4–5, 20,
    21, 22, 29, 67
Stanford University, 4
Stautner, Ernie, 51, 102,
    134, 152
Steadman, John, 39–40,
    71, 78, 143, 153, 169
Stits, Bill, 130
Stone, Oliver, 198
Strader, Norman "Red,"
    33, 35, 74, 75, 126, 178
Streisand, Barbra, 191
Strode, Woody, 1, 14
Strzykalski, Johnny, 3–4,
    20, 21, 29, 40
Sullivan, Ed, 99
Sullivan, Prescott, 120–21
Summerall, Pat, 42, 91,
    104, 105, 131, 137,
    175, 186
Sutherland, Jim, 180
Swanson, Red, 163

T

Tarkenton, Fran, 48, 195
Taseff, Carl, 104
Taylor, Jim, 135, 190
Taylor, John, 53, 108

Thomas, Duane, 51
Thomas, Joe, 39
Thomas, John, 93
Thorpe, Jim, 18, 53–54
Tittle, Don, 159
Tittle, Jack, 158, 162
Tittle, Minnette, 99, 150,
    153–55, 157, 159–60,
    166–67, 191
Tittle, Y. A.
  early childhood, 152,
    156–59
  high school, 159–62
  college, 153, 160,
    162–66
  acquired by Colts,
    151, 167
  1948 season, 22, 167–69
  1949 season, 169
  1950 season, 169–70
  drafted by 49ers, 28,
    170, 178
  1951 season, 170–72
  1952 season, 172–73
  1953 season, 173–74
  1954 season, 30, 32,
    110, 125, 175–77
  1955 season, 178–79
  1956 season, 179
  1957 season, 77, 78,
    151, 179–83
  1958 season, 183–84
  1959 season, 79, 80, 185
  1960 season, 80, 185
  acquired by Giants,
    151, 186
  1961 season, 186–90
  1962 season, 190–91
  1963 season, 83, 84,
    191–92, 195
  1964 season, 147–50,
    171, 193–94
  retires from football, 194
  career statistics, 174
  after playing days, 150,
    195–97
  today, 150, 197–99
  Joe Perry and, 2, 21, 46,
    157–58
  nickname, 153
  photos, 98, 99, 100, 146
  playing style of, 55,
    152–53
Tittle de Laet, Dianne,
    149–50, 153–56,
    192, 199
Towler, Dan, 6
Tracy, Tom, 37, 78
Trippi, Charley, 104–5,
    129, 166

U
UCLA, 14
Unitas, Johnny, 40, 74,
    75, 85, 104, 133, 174,
    182, 199
University of Texas,
    162–63
University of Washington,
    61–64, 67, 85
USC, 60

V
Van Brocklin, Norm, 49,
    83, 178
Verducci, Joe, 118

W
Wade, Billy, 66, 191
Waldorf, Pappy, 15
Walker, Wayne, 78–79, 80,
    86, 135
Walston, Bobby, 71
Walton, Joe, 189, 190
Washington, Dinah, 34
Washington, Kenny, 1, 14
Washington Redskins, 17
Waters, Bobby, 185
Webster, Alex, 190, 196
Wedemeyer, Herman,
    117, 123
Weiner, Richard, 198
Wietecha, Ray, 187
Wiggin, Paul, 50,
    102, 148
Williams, Jamie, 198
Williams, Windell, 168
Willis, Bill, 21, 23
Wilson, Billy, 28, 29, 31,
    77, 78, 80, 110, 173,
    181, 185, 190
Wilson, George, 133, 145
Wilson, Larry, 103, 106
Wood, Gary, 194
Woudenberg, John, 16
Wright, Elmo, 44

Y
Young, Buddy, 21, 27
Young, Steve, 149, 170,
    171, 175
Younger, Tank, 6

Z
Zimmerman, Paul, 3, 91,
    119, 199

ABOUT THE AUTHOR

Dave Newhouse has been a leading sportswriter for the *Oakland Tribune* for thirty-five years. He has been a columnist since 1979, finishing three times in the top ten of the nationally prestigious Associated Press Sports Editors competition. He is also the author of *Jim Otto: The Pain of Glory, The Jim Plunkett Story, Heismen,* and *Rose Bowl Football Since 1902* (co-authored with Herb Michelson). A father of two grown sons, he lives with his wife, Patsy, in Oakland, California.